Isherwood in Transit

ISHERWOOD IN TRANSIT

JAMES J. BERG AND
CHRIS FREEMAN, EDITORS

Foreword by Christopher Bram

University of Minnesota Press
Minneapolis
London

This book and the conference from which it arises received financial support from the Christopher Isherwood Foundation. The views expressed are those of the authors.

Photographs on pp. x and xvi: Christopher Isherwood, 1953, courtesy of Don Bachardy.

Excerpts from Christopher Isherwood's diary in chapter 5 by Christopher Isherwood; copyright 1936, 1937, and 1963 by Christopher Isherwood; reprinted by permission of The Wylie Agency LLC.

A version of chapter 6 was first published in *W. H. Auden in Context,* ed. Tony Sharpe (Cambridge: Cambridge University Press, 2013).

"A Conversation with Christopher Isherwood, 1979" was originally published as "Interview with Christopher Isherwood," *The Gramercy Review: A Journal of Contemporary Poetry and Fiction* 4, no. 1 (January 1980).

Published by the University of Minnesota Press
111 Third Avenue South, Suite 290
Minneapolis, MN 55401-2520
http://www.upress.umn.edu

The University of Minnesota is an equal-opportunity educator and employer.

Library of Congress Cataloging-in-Publication Data
Names: Berg, James J., editor. | Freeman, Chris, editor. | Bram, Christopher, foreword writer.
Title: Isherwood in transit / James J. Berg and Chris Freeman, editors ; foreword by Christopher Bram.
Description: Minneapolis : University of Minnesota Press, [2020] | Includes bibliographical references and index.
Identifiers: LCCN 2019054551 (print) | ISBN 978-1-5179-0909-3 (hc) | ISBN 978-1-5179-0910-9 (pb)
Subjects: LCSH: Isherwood, Christopher, 1904–1986—Criticism and interpretation. | Isherwood, Christopher, 1904–1986—Travel. | Homosexuality and literature—History—20th century. | Literature and society—History—20th century.
Classification: LCC PR6017.S5 Z743 2020 (print)| DDC 823/.912—dc23
LC record available at https://lccn.loc.gov/2019054551

To Tina Mascara and Guido Santi

Contents

Foreword

A Fan's Notes

I belong to the generation of gay men who discovered Christopher Isherwood through a movie musical. The movie, of course, was *Cabaret*, and there are many of us, the most notable being Armistead Maupin. For people who were just coming out and looking for stories about homosexuals who were neither evil nor pathetic, the 1972 Bob Fosse film was a revelation. The key scene came when Michael York and Liza Minnelli, as two kids in Weimar Berlin (and they really are kids), confront each other over their mutual friend, the Baron. "Screw Maximilian!" snarls York. "I do!" declares Minnelli. York smiles sheepishly and says, "So do I."

Home from college, I first saw the movie in Virginia Beach with my sister, Nancy. She was bummed that handsome Brian, the Michael York character, turned out to be a "fag." (Her word, not said meanly but factually. She didn't know about me yet.) But I was overjoyed. If someone like Brian—affable, human, bookish—could be queer, then maybe gay life wouldn't be so difficult after all. I promptly began to hunt down Isherwood books. But I didn't immediately find what I wanted.

Goodbye to Berlin, the source material, confused me when I read it and found nothing resembling the "Screw Maximilian" exchange. I already knew the Broadway musical. (I didn't know I was gay in high school, but I did know I loved musicals.) The stage show had been loosely based on the John van Druten 1951 play *I Am a Camera,* which was even more loosely based on Isherwood's stories. Herr Issyvoo became straighter in each version. (He also changed his name and became American instead of British.) But by the time a movie was made of the musical, screenwriter Jay Presson

Allen, with the encouragement of the producer, Cy Feuer, incorporated *some* of Isherwood's sexuality into the protagonist.

Ironically, Isherwood himself hated the movie, although not as much as he hated the stage musical. He later came around, but at the time he felt the movie presented Brian's homosexuality "as a kind of indecent but ridiculous weakness to be snickered at, like bed-wetting."[1]

I remember flipping through a friend's New Directions paperback of the stories, looking for sex scenes. There weren't any. Isherwood is the protagonist of these tales, but he carefully left his sexuality a mystery. He didn't lie about it, didn't make himself straight as the first adapters did. I recognized how beautifully written the stories were, sharp and well observed. But I was looking for sex scenes. I had been to bed with a couple of women at this point, but no men. I needed to feed my imagination with a literary rehearsal of the real thing.

The next book I read was *A Single Man*. There is no mystery about George's homosexuality, but the closest he comes to sex is a drunken skinny-dip with his student Kenny. That was more like it, yet too much like the clumsy encounters I had already had. Again, I recognized how smart and well crafted the book was. But I wanted sex. I would have been better off reading gay porn, but it was difficult to find in my Virginia college town, and I was too much a literary snob even to look. I told myself I would go back to Isherwood later, when I was older and wiser.

And I did, in 1976 with *Christopher and His Kind*. This was Isherwood's revised account of his Berlin years: he included his gay life. There was nothing pornographic, but I didn't need sex scenes anymore—I was finally having sex with men. I just needed to know what my future would be like. I had returned to Virginia after six months in Europe and moved in with my straight best friend (whom I was in love with). The public library was across the street. I found the Isherwood on the New Books shelf, checked it out, and wolfed it down in two days. It was so real, so direct, so necessary, like a glass of ice water on a hot day. Being gay was treated as an important piece of his life, but only slightly more important than writing or politics. He presented love and sex as plain facts of nature. I tried to get my best friend to read it—"Hey, it's the guy from *Cabaret*," I said—but he knew not to bite.

When Avon Books issued the memoir in mass-market paperback, they republished many of Isherwood's other titles, too, all illustrated with Don Bachardy's portraits of Isherwood on the covers. I explored further, liked some books, was disappointed by others, then moved on to new writers.

By the time Isherwood died in January 1986, I was living in New York with my boyfriend, Draper, writing a novel, and working in a bookstore. I cannot remember how I heard the news. But I was sad without feeling devastated. He had lived a full, rich life. I thought I was finished with him.

In 1993, now a published author, I began to research a new novel, *Father of Frankenstein*, about movie director James Whale. He had lived in Los Angeles at the same time as Isherwood, another displaced Englishman among the swimming pools and palm trees. I heard that the two men had actually met. Isherwood's diaries were not yet published, but my agents represented the estate. They had photocopies of the manuscript in boxes at the office. They let me take the box with the relevant dates home one weekend, after I promised not to quote from it. The loose pages turned out to be not the diary but a rough memoir in which Isherwood had reconstructed his lost diaries, later published as *Lost Years: 1945–1951*. This was a copy of Isherwood's actual typescript, not yet edited by Katherine Bucknell. It was absolutely fascinating. I became Christopher Isherwood for a whole weekend. It was mostly sex and gossip, but high-class gossip—Greta Garbo, Igor Stravinsky, W. H. Auden, Benjamin Britten—and lots of real-life sex. I felt like a total innocent in comparison. Then it struck me that this was the least productive time of this highly productive writer's life. He had just left the Vedanta Center after deciding not to be a monk. He was with a new lover, Bill Caskey, which meant endless fights. He was going through draft after draft of *The World in the Evening*, unable to make the novel work. A period that is wild fun for the reader had been hell for him. (I found a single paragraph about his meeting with James Whale. The two Brits were brought together by a mutual gay friend, Curtis Harrington, who later became a film director—he inspired the character of the pesky fan, Edmund Kay, in my novel. Also present was Kenneth Anger, who showed them his movie *Fireworks*. Everyone got drunk on martinis, and many mean things were said.)

Continuing my research, I reread *Down There on a Visit*. Part of it is set in Los Angeles after the war, but I fell in love with the entire book. This might be my single favorite Isherwood title. A continuation of *Goodbye to Berlin* on a larger scale, it consists of four long short stories representing different periods of his life. Here too he left his sexuality a mystery—it was published in 1962 when homosexuality was still a forbidden topic. We cannot forget how hard it was, until well into the 1970s, for gay writers to write about being gay and still be taken seriously. One of the hardest things about researching my project was the endless acid rain of contemptuous, sneering reviews for any book that dared to discuss homosexuality. But now readers of *Down There* can easily fill in what Isherwood left blank. My favorite section was the last, "Paul," based on Isherwood's friendship with the notorious beauty, Denny Fouts, the comic tale of two sybarites trying to achieve spiritual enlightenment by being "good." I liked it so much that Draper and I talked about turning it into a low-budget feature film. Nothing ever happened, but I still think it would make a terrific movie.

Ten years later, when I wrote a proposal for my literary history *Eminent Outlaws: The Gay Writers Who Changed America*, I did not include Isherwood. I am still shocked and bewildered by this fact. But I did not want to write an index-card style history and tried to keep it down to a half-dozen names. I think the real reason was that I knew his work too well; he was so much a part of the air I breathed that I took him for granted. All that changed once I started blocking out the book. When Gore Vidal went to Hollywood, I realized, Oh, here I can say a few words about Isherwood. And as soon as I started writing about him I couldn't stop. He became the hero of the book, for several reasons. First, his work holds up beautifully—I read or reread every one as I wrote. Second, he connects the pre- and post-Stonewall generations. Unlike Truman Capote and Tennessee Williams, who ignored the younger writers, Isherwood took them seriously and they liked him in return. Last but not least, he was the only figure of his generation to survive decades of antigay abuse and alcohol with both his sanity and writing abilities intact.

His survival fascinates me. Critics attacked him as viciously as they did Williams, Capote, and Vidal. And he sometimes indulged in alcohol as much as they did. But unlike them, he endured. I believe his strength came from two sources. One was his spiritual side, the aspect of himself that he explored and developed through Vedanta, the Hindu philosophy he studied for half of his life. I don't understand that school of knowledge myself, even after reading his detailed discussions in *My Guru and His Disciple* and *A Meeting by the River*. But his fascination with it showed a strong spiritual side that held him together, in much the same way his friend Auden used the Church of England for structure. (Recently, my friend Patrick Merla, an editor and lifelong reader of Isherwood, pointed out when we were talking that one of the appeals of Vedanta is that it presents worldly matters as transitory, fleeting, temporary—which makes life on earth more bearable.)

The other source of strength was his thirty-three years with Don

Bachardy. This was not always an easy relationship. It can be embarrassing to read the diaries with their endless accounts of arguments and anger, especially if you're in a long-term relationship. It is painfully recognizable. A married friend said that after reading the diaries, he was glad he didn't keep a diary himself or he'd have to burn it. But Isherwood never burned his pages, and Barchardy published them, making clear to the world how important they were to each other in bad times as well as good ones.

Isherwood endured not only as a person but as a writer. His sexuality gave him a solid rock to stand on, even at a time when he could not yet frankly describe his rock. He tried different subjects, even different voices, but in his best work he was artfully artless, writing deceptively clear, seemingly simple prose. It might be called mirror prose: the more the reader knows, the more the prose will give back. As a result Isherwood is one of those rare writers whose works grow wiser as the reader grows older. I've been reading him steadily since college and continue to find fresh meanings in his best books each time I return to them. *A Single Man*, in particular, became better and better, especially after I passed the age of its protagonist.

I have had a long, meandering, intimate history with Isherwood. I began by dancing around the man, not yet ready for him. His mirror prose is so deceptive that I often had to visit a book a second time before it made its full impact. Then I entered his world so deeply that he sometimes became invisible to me. I would actually forget his existence only to happily remember it again, like a close yet easy friend.

This is the third collection of essays on this fine writer compiled by James J. Berg and Chris Freeman. They continue to share new discoveries, make new connections. I am delighted to read whatever they find. Even my occasional disagreement with a contributor leads me to fresh ideas. The critics here all ask excellent questions. As the title *Isherwood in Transit* suggests, Christopher Isherwood is a rich, complex, changing figure replete with different meanings and shifting virtues. As we change, he changes with us. This timelessness is the mark of a true artist.

NOTE

1. Winston Leyland, "Christopher Isherwood Interview" [1973], in *Conversations with Christopher Isherwood,* ed. James J. Berg and Chris Freeman (Jackson: University Press of Mississippi, 2001), 103.

CHRIS FREEMAN AND JAMES J. BERG

Introduction
Christopher's Kind

THE WANDERING STOPPED

In his first "American" book, *Prater Violet* (1945), Christopher Isherwood is both author and main character. The short novel takes place in London in 1933–34, just when the young writer (in fiction and real life) has moved back from living a few years in Berlin. In the novel, he's been hired as a screenwriter to work with the eminent Austrian director Friedrich Bergmann, the fictional avatar of Berthold Viertel. Turbulent political themes throughout Europe haunt the process, which is amplified by the setting of the film, Vienna in 1914. At one point late in the story, Isherwood and Bergmann are interrupted at dinner by an English journalist, Patterson, who writes movie gossip. They get into an intense conversation about contemporary politics, the rise of Hitler and Mussolini, and the role of England and the English in this European crisis. Isherwood's first-person narrator engages in an extended moment of introspection after this difficult evening. Lamenting that he is "emotionally exhausted," he thinks:

> I no longer knew what I felt—only what I was supposed to feel. . . . The "I" that thought this . . . was divided, and hated its division.
>
> Perhaps I had traveled too much, left my heart in too many places. I knew what I was supposed to feel, what it was fashionable for my generation to feel. We cared about everything: fascism in Germany and Italy, the seizure of Manchuria, Indian nationalism, the Irish question, the workers, the Negroes, the Jews. We had spread our feelings over the

> whole world; and I knew that mine were spread very thin. I cared—oh,
> yes, I certainly cared—about the Austrian socialists. But did I care as
> much as I said I did, tried to imagine I did? No, not nearly as much. . . .
> What is the use of caring at all, if you aren't prepared to dedicate your
> life, to die? Well, perhaps it was some use. Very, very little. (104–5)

This passage reveals so much about Isherwood's state of mind—his state
of being—in this critical, transitional period in his life and career. "Perhaps
I had traveled too much, left my heart in too many places": in truth, this
sentiment describes his life not just up until then but also well into his next
decade.

Isherwood in Transit is an effort to understand the challenges Isherwood faced as a consequence of all this travel—the inherent rootlessness
and feelings of dislocation and even desperation—that ended with his settling in Los Angeles and becoming an American. We see this volume as a
follow-up to our previous book, The American Isherwood (2015), in which
we make the case for Isherwood as an American writer. He became a U.S.
citizen in 1946 and spent the rest of his career exploring his own version
of the American vernacular. He also contributed significantly to the literary legacy of Los Angeles. But much wandering occurred before he finally
settled down in Southern California. Indeed, even after he found his new
home, he remained rather unsettled for another decade. His transit during
that time was spiritual and personal rather than geographical.

Isherwood left England for Germany before he was twenty-five. He
wrote and published his Berlin books in the 1930s. After he left Berlin, he
lived in England briefly and then moved through much of Europe, searching for a safe place for himself and his German boyfriend, Heinz Neddermeyer, who was trying to evade service in Hitler's army. In his midthirties,
with his close friend and writing partner W. H. Auden, he left England for
New York, and a few months after that, he moved to Los Angeles, where
he would live for the rest of his life. Forty years later, after the film Cabaret
(1972) made him wealthy and better known, he revisited this era of his life
in nonfiction. As he was beginning to write what became Christopher and
His Kind (1976), he told the scholar Carola M. Kaplan:

> I'm actually engaged at the moment in just starting a book which is, as
> you might say, an autobiography, that is to say it's absolutely true, not fic-
> tion at all. . . . It's a sort of book of the period of my life which Germans

call *Wanderjahren*. It's about going to Berlin and covers the time until I'd been in this country about four or five years and it became kind of my home. I don't mean that there's a great big thing about that, but it's that the wandering stopped.[1]

The wandering may have stopped, but Isherwood never stopped moving, evolving, growing. These are the aspects of his legacy and his journey that the essays in this volume are exploring.

Indeed, as he explained to Kaplan, revisiting that part of his life was fascinating for him because "it involved going through some of this material from a different angle. It's very interesting to me, at least, doing it, because quite different things come out." Not to put too fine a point on it, but one of those things was, in fact, Christopher Isherwood. He had "come out" in print a couple of years earlier, in *Kathleen and Frank* (1971), which he called a biography of his parents. He had included homosexuality in much of his work, most notably in his novel *The World in the Evening* (1954), which features a gay couple, one of whom rails against the recent antihomosexual policy of the U.S. military. Surely that is one of the first instances of such protest in American literature or even in American culture. He addressed homosexuality as a "theme" in his works in public lectures throughout the 1960s but stopped short of explicitly identifying himself as gay. Isherwood was "out" in his life but not as much in his work. However, in the autobiography in progress that he refers to in the conversation with Kaplan, *Christopher and His Kind*, he is blunt. On the bottom of page 2 he declares, "To Christopher, Berlin meant boys." His new openness came as the world changed. Coming out in print was a significant part of his transitioning—from a self-described "individualistic old liberal" to gay "advocate" (*Conversations* 57). We continue to write about and celebrate his work and legacy in part because of the ways in which he spent the final twenty years of his life engaged with his "kind."

OUR KIND

Isherwood relished the double entendre of the title of the memoir: it's his tribe, our tribe, and it's his "kids," in the German sense of *Kinder*. One of the biggest beneficiaries of Isherwood's kindness, his mentoring, and his wisdom is Armistead Maupin, author of *Tales of the City* (1978), who contributed a foreword to our first book, *The Isherwood Century* (2000). Maupin's work was important enough to us that we invited him to be the keynote speaker at a two-day symposium called "'My Self in a Transitional State': Isherwood in California," which was held at the Huntington Library in the fall of 2015. We organized the conference to assess Isherwood thirty years after his death, to showcase scholarship on Isherwood that had been done using the archive at the Huntington, and to get scholars working on various aspects of Isherwood's life and career into the same room. We are pleased to include essays by many influential, established scholars, alongside some newer voices. More and more people are interested in Isherwood, and that for us is an exciting and fortunate development.

The keynote address, "My Logical Grandfather," was provocatively delivered by Maupin, who has subsequently included it in his memoir, *Logical Family* (2017). In his remarks, Maupin was candid, insightful, funny, and a little bit risqué for the staid Huntington. He set the perfect tone for what was to come in the brilliant talks at the symposium. Much of what follows in this volume began as work delivered at that event.

A highlight of Maupin's presentation was an anecdote about the night the young writer met Isherwood at an Oscar party in West Hollywood in the late 1970s: "Isherwood struck me as the obvious tribal elder for our new breed of open queers. He *called* himself queer, in fact, way back then, believing that the blithe use of the word was the way to embarrass our enemies. . . . He was sassy in his public presentation, but never bitchy. Kindness, in fact, seemed important to him" (254). Quite a tribute to a mentor and a friend.

Maupin's fellow novelist Christopher Bram captures the spirit of Isherwood in his foreword to this book, "A Fan's Notes." Bram's perspective is ideal for insights into Isherwood's influence in American literature, especially among LGBTQ writers. Bram is perhaps best known for *Father of Frankenstein* (1995), which was adapted into the compelling, Academy Award–winning film *Gods and Monsters* (1998). But Bram is also a literary critic. His book *Eminent Outlaws: The Gay Writers Who Changed America* (2012) assesses Isherwood's place in contemporary literature. Writing about the 1950s, Bram points out that "Isherwood spent much of his life as an exile. He was, among other things, a citizen of love without a country" (55). He found the country, and he found the love, finally, in Don Bachardy. Bram also recognizes the significance of the film *Cabaret* (1972) to Isherwood's staying power, especially when it is coupled with his classic 1964 novel, *A Single Man*. As Bram puts it, "For all its faults, *Cabaret* helped to keep Isherwood's name alive until the world had changed enough that it was ready for the real Isherwood. A novel is such a small thing, but *A Single Man* has endured, like an early mammal surrounded by dinosaurs" (*Eminent Outlaws* 116). That metaphor is stirring. It asserts what we have always believed about Isherwood's work: that he was a pioneer, thematically and stylistically. The world, at last, caught up to him. And, because of Bram's acumen, we asked him to write his foreword, incorporating what he hadn't been able to use in *Eminent Outlaws*. As we suspected, he still had a few gems, and we are grateful for how elegantly his essay sets up the trajectory of *Isherwood in Transit*.

As we argued in *The American Isherwood*, Christopher Isherwood self-consciously became both an American writer and a California writer in the second half of his life. Beginning with *Prater Violet*, he not only explored the American vernacular but also used his insider/outsider position to think about, critique, and in some ways embrace his new homeland. Regarding that homeland, it is fitting that a writer of Isherwood's stature, who spent half his life in Southern California, should have his archive housed at the Huntington. The vast collection of manuscripts, notebooks, photographs, and ephemera has been open for use for over a dozen years. As our conference demonstrated, the depth and breadth of work on Isherwood and his circle have grown substantially due to the availability of this material. Young scholars and future scholars will find a treasure trove in the Isherwood papers, and this rich source will keep Isherwood's work alive in ways we are only just starting to imagine.

The archive has been beautifully organized, cataloged, and stewarded by one of our contributors, Sara S. (Sue) Hodson, who has now retired from her position as an archivist at the Huntington. Her essay in this volume provides a helpful overview of Isherwood's movements across Europe and the United States, especially as she elaborates on his fulfillment of his own version of the California Dream. Having worked so intimately over a period of several years with the papers, photographs, letters, and ephemera in the collection, Hodson knows better than anyone how much potential remains to be explored.

In part because we ourselves value collaboration, we're pleased that several of the essays here focus on Isherwood and other writers he worked with. One of Isherwood's longest relationships was with his childhood friend, the writer Edward Upward. The two young men conspired during their schooldays at Cambridge on the "Mortmere" stories, and Katharine Stevenson explores the subversiveness of these often-overlooked early works. Both Wendy Moffat, author of the important Forster biography *A Great Unrecorded History* (2010), and young scholar Xenobe Purvis explore the long friendship between Isherwood and E. M. Forster. Forster's work inspired Isherwood to become a (better) writer, and praise from his friend meant a great deal to him. As he wrote in *Christopher and His Kind*, "Christopher was fond of saying, 'My literary career is over—I don't give a damn for the Nobel Prize or the Order of Merit—*I've been praised by Forster!*'" (105). Whereas Purvis focuses on Forster's philosophical and ethic influence on Isherwood, Moffat takes a more theoretical and historical approach. Exploring the intricacies of the "queer archive," she reminds us of what has heretofore been "lost" and how careful, creative searching can reveal truths of queer lives, past and present.

Lois Cucullu examines Isherwood's "journey" and his literal and imaginative transit during the 1930s from a queer theory perspective. The restlessness in that period of his life fostered some of his important early work, including the travel writing he did with his other lifelong friend and collaborator, the poet W. H. Auden. Our essay "Fellow Travelers" explores the geographical, religious, and personal scope of the fifty-plus-year relationship between these two major twentieth-century writers.

Lisa Colletta, the editor of *Kathleen and Christopher: Isherwood's Letters to His Mother* (2005), discusses what we can learn about Isherwood through his travel writing, a nonfiction form that he helped pioneer. Her essay focuses especially on *The Condor and the Cows* (1949), which has up to now been largely neglected in Isherwood studies. Robert L. Caserio, whose work on literary modernism has been influential for many years, explores *The World in the Evening* (1954), which Isherwood considered marginally successful at best. Like Caserio, we hold that novel in higher esteem and are happy to see it getting serious scholarly attention again. Given his expertise in modernism and in the twentieth-century novel, Caserio is in a strong position to make an affirmative case about the significance of this undervalued book.

By the 1960s, Isherwood's fiction was at its peak; he had found his voice and his subject matter. Carola M. Kaplan, who wrote the first-ever dissertation on Isherwood and has spent her career writing about modernism, offers a psychoanalytically inflected take on *Down There on a Visit* (1962). Calvin W. Keogh, whose dissertation and forthcoming book examine Isherwood's status as a "minor" writer using the theoretical paradigm of Gilles Deleuze and Félix Guattari, offers an analysis of *A Single Man* in terms of citizenship and what it was to be a "foreigner" in the United States in the 1950s and 1960s. In particular, Keogh explores the tensions between the utopian mythos of Southern California, including the changing demographics in the ever-expanding city of Los Angeles, as it clashes with the personal, intimate sadness of George in the wake of the recent sudden death of his lover, Jim.

Jaime Harker, whose book *Middlebrow Queer* (2013) is a major contribution to Isherwood studies, is a skilled archivist and literary historian. She focuses here on Isherwood's fascination with Asia, in part through his correspondence with the queer Japanese writer Yukio Mishima. Harker's essay is an excellent companion piece to Colletta's, as both authors consider Isherwood in a more comparative, global context.

Two contributors read Isherwood directly from the point of view of LGBTQ writers and writing. Edmund White, one of the most prominent queer authors of the past forty years, contemplates and pays tribute to the influence Queer Isherwood had on gay people of the next generation. Reading Isherwood mattered to people invested in what queer life and art looked like before the gay liberation movement escalated, and White's essay provides an incisive perspective on the Isherwood legacy from that era. Writer Barrie Jean Borich, who has not published on Isherwood before, offers insights into his groundbreaking nonfiction, especially in the memoir form. Borich, author of *My Lesbian Husband* (1999) and *Body Geographic* (2013), is one of the best theorists of creative nonfiction, so she is the perfect writer-critic to contextualize what Isherwood did to help create that significant literary form. We believe Isherwood's influence as a writer, especially in his nonfiction, is finally getting the attention it merits. His prodigious diary keeping is one part of what he has left us to think about, but it's his integrated approach, the way his diaries and his life fed into, indeed nurtured, his work, that is perhaps most instructive to future writers.

Some of the most inspirational writing in Isherwood's career comes from the strong presence of Vedantic Hinduism in the second half of his life. Vedanta in the West (a title Isherwood used for some of his early spiritual writing) emerged in Southern California in the 1920s and '30s. Through his friends Aldous Huxley and Gerald Heard, Isherwood joined that community, and in Swami Prabhavananda, he found the spiritual guide he needed. The final essays here—those by Bidhan Chandra Roy, Victor Marsh, and Jamie Carr—add important insights into ways Isherwood's devotion to Vedanta challenged and comforted him and influenced his fiction and nonfiction alike.

As we neared the end of our editorial process on *Isherwood in Transit,* we discovered an interview from 1979 conducted by D. J. (Dennis) Bartel. The piece was published in a small Los Angeles–based magazine, but it is otherwise unknown. We chose to end this volume with the man himself, in a freewheeling conversation on the cusp of the publication of his final book, *My Guru and His Disciple* (1980). The interview is perhaps the last one he gave prior to his cancer diagnosis in 1981, and it captures a key valedictory moment in which he reflects on his past, his work, and his current situation as a robust, active seventy-five-year-old. The interview reveals a lot about his state of being and about where he saw himself, and, for that reason, it's our perfect ending.

We discovered this interview through our friends Tina Mascara and Guido Santi, the brilliant filmmaking team who gave us *Chris & Don: A Love Story* (2007). They contributed an essay called "Labor of Love" about their film to *The American Isherwood.* We were devastated to find out that, on February 4, 2019, as we were finishing this collection, Guido died suddenly, at the age of fifty-six. Everyone in this volume, indeed anyone who is part of the Isherwood-Bachardy community, owes a tremendous debt to Tina and Guido, and we are honored to dedicate *Isherwood in Transit* to the two of them, with love and with much sadness.

TWENTY YEARS AND COUNTING

Christopher has been kind to us throughout the years we have spent working on him. It's rather uncommon for humanities scholars to work together. Our collaboration started on a walk around Lake Harriet in Minneapolis on a sunny, cold Sunday afternoon. (In Minnesota, you go outside, wrapped up, whenever the sun shines between Halloween and Mother's Day.) In

1995, since we were living in the same city, we thought maybe it would be fun to do some work together. But what would the topic be? Perhaps E. M. Forster? We both loved him, but a new book had just come out on him. Then who? Isherwood! We struck gold: no one in the nascent field of queer studies seemed to be paying him any attention.

This collaboration among Jim and Chris and Christopher has taken us many places. Most significantly, in 1997, we traveled together to Southern California to meet Isherwood's longtime partner, the artist Don Bachardy. At our first meeting with Don, he put us in touch with many who knew Isherwood, and we were able to spend time with their friends and associates, some of whom would write essays for *The Isherwood Century* and our other books. Our collaboration on *The Isherwood Century* culminated in a trip to Chicago together in May 2001: we brought home a Lambda Literary Award in Gay Studies for that book.

On that first journey together to Los Angeles, we were able to explore significant Isherwood locations. We went to Trabuco Canyon, to the Vedanta Center in Hollywood, and to Santa Monica Canyon in order to get a sense of the spiritual and geographical path Isherwood followed for the second half of his life. Those locations spoke to us; we could feel what drew Isherwood to them.

Twenty years and several books later, we too have been much in transit. Like Isherwood, we fell in love with Southern California, which led to our eventual departure from Minneapolis: Chris moved to West Hollywood in 2005, followed a couple of years later by Jim's move to Palm Springs. Jim now lives and works in New York, a city Isherwood rejected after only one winter. Perhaps Jim has solved that problem by making regular pilgrimages back to the California desert.

Is *Isherwood in Transit* the end of our partnership? We don't think so. But for now, as we wrap up this twenty-year chapter, we are nothing but grateful to Isherwood, to Don, and to so many friends, scholars, and students with whom we have shared Isherwood. One thing we know for sure: the quality and range of the material in this volume demonstrate that Isherwood's legacy is in good hands, and we are confident that new theoretical and historical work will be done in the coming years, thanks to the Huntington archive, to the Christopher Isherwood Foundation, and through the groundwork established by the scholars assembled here.

We are, all of us, proud to be his kind.

NOTE

1. Carola M. Kaplan, "The Wandering Stopped: An Interview with Christopher Isherwood" [1973], in *Conversations with Christopher Isherwood,* ed. James J. Berg and Chris Freeman (Jackson: University Press of Mississippi, 2001), 119.

SARA S. HODSON

1. Christopher Isherwood and the California Dream

Late one night at the end of January 1939, Christopher Isherwood gazed out the window of his room in New York's George Washington Hotel. He had just arrived on board the *Champlain*, as an immigrant to the United States. Studying the scene outside, he wrote a short essay called "Midnight in New York." It opens with these words: "Well, here you are. Here, for the moment, is your home, your shelter from the night. In your thirty-fifth year, at the age when Dante met the leopard, when your Father got married, this is the place to which thousands of miles of wandering have brought you. Twelve months ago, you were in Hankow; twenty-four months ago, you were in Brussels; thirty-six months ago, you were in Lisbon. This time next year, you will quite possibly be dead. You certainly get around."[1]

As we know, Isherwood wasn't dead by the following year. Rather, he headed west to California within just three months of writing these ruminations on his wanderings. Once in California, he made the Golden State his adopted home for the rest of his life. How did he arrive at this point of transition? What led him on the path of an émigré, from England to the United States? What was the California Dream, and did Isherwood find it?

Isherwood was born on August 26, 1904, at Wyberslegh Hall, a fifteenth-century manor on the Bradshaw-Isherwood estate in Cheshire. He was the son of Kathleen and Frank Bradshaw-Isherwood. An officer in the York and Lancaster Regiment, Frank served in the Boer War and

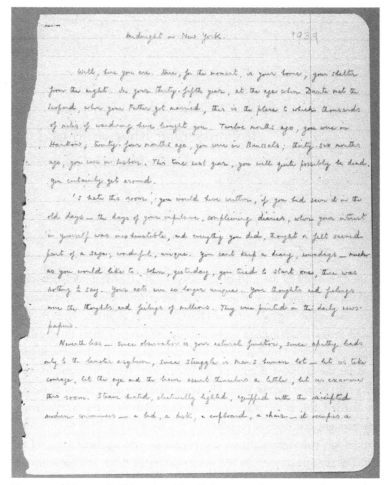

First page of Isherwood's "Midnight in New York" autograph manuscript. Courtesy of Don Bachardy.

in the First World War, where he was killed in action at Ypres in 1915, when Christopher was eleven.[2] While a student at Repton, Isherwood met Edward Upward, who would become a lifelong friend. There are some 301 letters from Upward to Isherwood housed in the Christopher Isherwood Papers in the Huntington Library. Upward was a schoolmaster and writer, and the correspondence with Isherwood ranges over both of their literary projects, with comments and criticisms from each about the work of the other. The story of Isherwood's schooling is told in his 1938 autobiography

Lions and Shadows. While a student at St. Edmund's, he met W. H. Auden, but the two did not become close friends until they were reintroduced ten years later, in 1925, when Auden was at Oxford. Isherwood, two years older, became Auden's mentor and literary partner, and the more than one hundred Auden letters in the library's collection attest to Isherwood's extensive role as teacher, mentor, and demanding critic of Auden's poetry.

That same year, 1925, Isherwood, ever a rebel who chafed at the establishment, deliberately failed his exams and left Cambridge University. He went to work as secretary to André Mangeot, a prominent violinist who headed a string quartet. Isherwood entered fully into Mangeot's chaotic professional life as he endeavored to keep the quartet organized and functioning efficiently. In an ill-advised effort to launch himself in a profession—any profession—Isherwood attended medical school in London but dropped out after just six months. The first novel from his pen, *All the Conspirators,* was published in 1928, and his second, *The Memorial,* in 1931. Isherwood took Auden's advice and moved to Berlin in 1929. As Isherwood later wrote, "To Christopher, Berlin meant boys" (*Christopher and His Kind* 2). Specifically, it meant that he could live more freely and openly as a gay man than he could in England. Berlin also meant getting away from his mother and her expectations, and it meant acquiring friends and experiences that would appear in the book for which he is perhaps best known, *The Berlin Stories.* He met people like Jean Ross, the inspiration for Sally Bowles, and Gerald Hamilton, the basis for Mr. Norris—both vivid, memorable characters. *The Berlin Stories* were the basis for the play *I Am a Camera* and for the musical *Cabaret.*

As the Nazis rose to power and Berlin became dangerous, Isherwood left in 1933, taking with him his lover, Heinz Neddermeyer. For much of the 1930s, the two traveled throughout Europe, often meeting up with Auden and with Stephen Spender. Isherwood and Auden collaborated on several experimental plays: *The Dog Beneath the Skin* (1936), *The Ascent of F6* (1937), and *On the Frontier* (1938). Auden, Spender, and Isherwood together were viewed as the most important young literary voices of their generation. Their friendship is captured in a famous photograph, taken by Spender using a timed cable release.

Isherwood commented that "Stephen, in the middle, has his arms around Wystan and Christopher and an expression on his face which suggests an off-duty Jesus relaxing with 'these little ones.'" Isherwood also noted that he himself looks as if he is standing in a hole (*Christopher and His Kind* 82). These are the three young men who, as Evelyn Waugh noted, "ganged up and captured the decade."[3] The critic Cyril Connolly described Auden as England's "one poet of genius today," and referred to Isherwood as "a hope of English fiction."[4]

In 1938, Isherwood and Auden, under contract with the publisher Faber and Faber in England and with Random House in the United States, left England for the Far East to write and report on the war between China and Japan. At this time both men had attained considerable fame as writers and had been much in the public eye, especially for their literary innovations. As public figures of note, they were wined, dined, and housed in consular luxury much of the time, but they also tramped through battlefield trenches and felt the earth shudder from nearby barrages and bombings. Both writers kept diaries, and the two they wrote jointly, containing drafts of poems by Auden, as well as apt, sometimes snarky, depictions of their fellow shipboard travelers, are in the Huntington. These diaries were the basis for the book Isherwood and Auden wrote together, *Journey to a War* (1939).

Back in England from China after a brief sojourn in the United States, Isherwood and Auden worked on a number of literary projects, both individually and jointly. The imminent war posed a greater danger than ever and dominated their lives. Both writers were pacifists, and they felt deeply disturbed by the coming conflict even as they perceived its threat and its direct effects on them. They watched as trenches were dug in Hyde Park, gas masks were issued, the numbers of servicemen burgeoned, and people began to hoard food against anticipated shortages. As Isherwood wrote, "Nothing matters but this crisis—nothing. We are all mad, and drowned with madness. . . . At a moment like this it seems utterly impossible to understand why one was 'unhappy' in the old days. The memory now seems almost impossibly sweet and lovely. I had better think about them a good deal, now—if I want to keep some last shreds of sanity."[5] Intertwined in all the war madness was Isherwood's grief at being apart from his partner, Heinz, who had been forced to return to Germany, where he faced conscription. The mere possibility of serving in the armed forces and being forced to kill German soldiers, some of whom he might have known and one of whom could be Heinz, was intolerable. Coinciding with his despair over the war and being apart from Heinz, Isherwood realized that his considerable fame was hollow and that Isherwood the writer was possibly interchangeable with, and indistinguishable from, Isherwood the protagonist of his novels and stories. Isherwood further realized that his readers could not truly distinguish between him and his fictional character. As a result, he began to see himself as a "character" who performed a role in public, and he began to wonder who, if anyone, was actually within his public persona.

In turmoil himself, just as Britain and Europe were, Isherwood had clearly reached a turning point. On January 19, 1939, he and Auden sailed for America, where their ship, the *Champlain*, docked in New York at the end of the month. Unfortunately, at least for the moment, the United States proved no more salubrious for Isherwood than Britain had. He was disappointed to find that Americans didn't know his Berlin stories, despite his enormous fame in Britain and Europe, so he had trouble finding literary projects. It was dispiriting for him to look on as Auden thrived in New York, landing a teaching post in New England, gathering writing assignments, and relishing his growing renown among American readers. Moreover, Auden quickly met Chester Kallman, who became his life partner. For Isherwood, missing Heinz and not knowing whether they would ever meet again, it was difficult in the extreme to watch Auden's happiness, when he felt so empty and unhappy. Add to all this the fact that he roundly disliked New York, writing in a letter to John Lehmann, "Oh, God, what a city! The nervous breakdown expressed in terms of architecture. The skyscrapers are all Father-fixations. The police-cars are fitted with air-raid sirens, specially designed to promote paranoia. The elevated railway is the circular madness."[6]

Isherwood decided to leave, and, on May 6, just three months after landing in New York, he hopped on a Greyhound bus with his boyfriend Vernon, bound for California.[7] Why California? What did Isherwood hope to find there? The eminent historian Kevin Starr, in his multivolume history of the Golden State, writes of the California Dream and what it means. In his first volume, fittingly titled *Americans and the California Dream, 1850–1915,* Starr traces the development of the concept of a California Dream: "Certainly an ideal California—a California of the mind— underwent composite definition: the elusive possibility of a new American alternative; the belief, the suggestion (or perhaps only the hope), that here on Pacific shores Americans might search out for themselves new values and ways of living. In this sense—as a concept and as an imaginative goal—California showed the beginnings of becoming the cutting edge of the American Dream."[8] The California Dream, then, is the ultimate American Dream. Immigrants flocked to America in search of a fresh beginning, opportunity, success, a freer way of life, and the freedom to believe and live as they wished. In time the same goals inspired people to head farther west, to California, the Land of Golden Dreams, as it has been characterized. As Starr explains, "California provided a special context for the working-out of this aspiration [that is, for a better life], intensified it, indeed, gave it a probing, prophetic edge in which the good and evil of the American dream was sorted out and dramatized" (443–44).

For Isherwood, as for so many seekers of opportunity and freedom to live as they wished, California was indeed the promised land. We can identify three areas in which he sought fulfillment of the California Dream. He hoped to continue growing as a writer; he sought to live free from society's strictures on his sexuality; and he wanted spiritual freedom to believe as he chose. Let's consider these in turn, beginning with the last area identified—the quest for spiritual freedom.

One of the most immediate attractions of California for Isherwood was the presence there of another émigré, Gerald Heard. An Irish writer, broadcaster, and philosopher, Heard had met Isherwood in London in 1932. He had gone to California in 1937, and he and Isherwood corresponded while Isherwood was in New York. Most of their letters focused on pacifism, but Heard also wrote of the mysticism and yoga he was sampling, and he urged Isherwood to come to the West. Isherwood does not appear to have been consciously seeking spiritual grounding, but it isn't hard to imagine, given the personal and professional emptiness he had felt in Britain and New York, that he would find Heard's accounts of spiritual rewards to be an inviting prospect and that he would hope to achieve some of the same fulfillment Heard had attained. Isherwood also was drawn to Aldous Huxley, who had moved to Los Angeles in 1937. Like Heard, he had embraced Eastern mysticism and had published *Ends and Means,* an important pacifist text.

On arriving in Los Angeles, Isherwood connected with Heard, who began teaching him about Eastern mysticism and its connections to pacifism. The time was perfect for Isherwood's education. He had long ago turned his back on Christianity, rejecting a God of justice and punishment, and he had embraced his own individualism rather than allegiance to any political cause or philosophy. Most recently, with the approaching war, he had realized that he was a pacifist. Now, Heard taught him that, in order to become a true pacifist, he must find peace within himself. But Isherwood was at war with himself; he had rejected much of mainstream society, had written critically and satirically of that society, and had reacted with anger and discontent to society's strictures. An even taller order from Heard was that Isherwood should meditate for six hours a day, become celibate, avoid alcohol and other stimulants, and find sustenance in such foods as raisins, carrots, and tea. As Isherwood's biographer Peter Parker notes, "A skeptical, sybaritic, chain-smoking, egotistical and morally confused homosexual atheist such as Isherwood can hardly have seemed the most likely convert to the rigorous self-discipline Heard was advocating" (433).

Heard taught Isherwood that one must search for and understand one's true nature. He invoked the tenets of Vedanta, which espoused the divine nature of man. Isherwood struggled with this, asking how, if he does possess an essential nature within himself, he is to realize it and enjoy it. The answer was "by ceasing to be yourself." The challenge here is obvious: it would be especially difficult for Isherwood, whose life and nature were so entwined in his writings. But Isherwood accepted the challenge. As he wrote to Lehmann in July 1939, "I am so utterly sick of being a person— Christopher Isherwood, or Isherwood, or even Chris. Aren't you, too? Don't you feel, more and more, that all your achievements, all your sexual triumphs, are just like cheques, which represent money, but have no real value? Aren't you sick to death of your face in the glass, and your business voice, and your love-voice, and your signature on documents? I know I am. . . . Don't be alarmed. . . . I am just trying to tell you, quite sanely, how I feel. And maybe why I'm not writing, just now. I'm just tired of strumming on that old harp, the Ego, darling Me" (436).

But, noting that he will always see the world from a personal viewpoint, he went on to write to Edward Upward, "I don't belong in any movement; and I cannot really take sides in any struggle. My only integrity can be to see the members of both sides as people, only as people, and to deplore their sufferings and crimes as personal sufferings and personal crimes" (445).

As Isherwood struggled to find his essential nature and to reject his individualism, he joked that he was like "the ground under California . . .

there is a 'fault' inside me which may produce earthquakes" (442). Clearly, he had become a true Californian.

After studying with Heard for some months, Isherwood was taken to meet Swami Prabhavananda, the spiritual leader of the Vedanta Society of Southern California. They hit it off immediately (helped by their short stature and shared chain-smoking habit), and Isherwood began to study with the swami. He was drawn more deeply into Vedanta and, in February 1943, he moved into the society's quarters on Ivar Avenue in Hollywood. There, he noted that he was "hanging on by the eyelids" as he fought his worldly habits and thought about becoming a monk.[9] The regimen of meditation, celibacy, and forswearing alcohol were intensely difficult for him, and he despaired, writing, "I haven't said a real prayer in weeks, or meditated in months. . . . At present I have no feeling for the sacredness of the shrine and not the least reverence for Ramakrishna or anybody else. If you ask me what I want, I reply: Sex, followed by a long sleep. If you offered a painless drug which would kill me in my sleep, I would seriously consider taking it: and I've never played much with thoughts of suicide before" (*Diaries* 306).

Recognizing that he was not cut out for the life of a monk, Isherwood left the Vedanta monastery. He had, however, found the philosophy and spiritual support that would resonate for him the rest of his life. He wrote that Swami Prabhavananda "offered me personally a solution and a way of life which I desperately needed, and which seems to work, and within which I can imagine living for the rest of my life with a feeling of purpose and lack of despair" (*Diaries* 366).

Swami enlisted Isherwood to help with translating several texts, including the Bhagavad Gita. Isherwood wrote a treatise called *What Vedanta Means to Me* (1951). Prompted by his religious doubts (but not inspired by the swami) is Isherwood's final novel, *A Meeting by the River* (1967), in which two brothers question their lives. Set in India, the book is largely epistolary with Patrick and Oliver engaged in a dialogue about their beliefs and life choices. It can be seen to represent Isherwood's own struggle between his religious and worldly lives, but the novel is much more than that. His final completed book was a biography of Prabhavananda, titled *My Guru and His Disciple* (1980). All of these are highly personal statements in which Isherwood sought to convince readers not of the truth of Vedanta but of its truth for *him*.

In finding Vedanta, Isherwood found a philosophy and spiritual support that would resonate with him for the rest of his life. If it didn't give him a complete understanding of his own nature, it did provide him with guidance and structure in which he could search for that inner nature in a meaningful way.

Isherwood's search to understand his own nature leads to the second of the three areas in which he sought fulfillment of the California Dream—his desire to live free of society's strictures on homosexuality. Upon arriving in Los Angeles on May 20, 1939, he called Heard's partner, Chris Wood, who declared, "How wonderful to hear an effeminate British voice!" (*Diaries* 20). Isherwood had indeed come to the place where he would be able to live freely as a gay man. California was, as it still is, a land of tolerant folks, and Los Angeles boasted multiple communities of like-minded people who could find a place to belong. His joy at discovering this openness and tolerance shines in a letter to his mother, where he exults, "We all live openly, in the great eye of the sunshine—and if you appear dressed in red velvet, or leading a baby puma, nobody bats an eyelid."[10] Having come from England, where homosexual acts were outlawed, and then finding freedom in Berlin only to see it disappear with the rise of the Nazis, Isherwood had found the place where he could live as a gay man. (Homosexual acts were also outlawed in pre-Nazi Germany, but officials generally winked at the laws, and Berlin was a city in which gays congregated.) He had long held the firm conviction that the individual should have the freedom to live his own life without any official interference, so California presented a land of openness and opportunity. Here, although society still largely disapproved of homosexuality, he felt that he would not have to worry that the state would come knocking at his door. On one occasion, however, December 4, 1947, Isherwood and his boyfriend Jim Charlton were caught up in a raid on the Variety, a bar on Pacific Coast Highway, formerly for both hetero- and homosexuals, but now entirely homosexual. In the raid, Isherwood and Charlton were taken to the police station and questioned about whether they were queer and whether they were involved with one another. To his chagrin, Isherwood denied being gay. Writing later about himself in the third person in *Lost Years,* Isherwood noted, "Even as I write these words, I feel bitterly ashamed of him for not having said that he was queer."[11]

The strength of Isherwood's belief in the right of the individual to live life as he wishes is evident in his writings, and this conviction burned strongly and deeply within him. Witness this angry passage from *Christopher and His Kind*: "Damn nearly Everybody. Girls are what the State and the Church and the Law and the Press and the Medical profession endorse, and command me to desire. My mother endorses them, too. She is silently, brutishly willing me to get married and breed grandchildren for her. Her will is the Will of Nearly Everybody, and in their will is my death. My will is to live according to my nature, and to find a place where I can be what I am. . . . But I'll admit this—even if my nature were like theirs, I should still have to fight them, in one way or another. If boys didn't exist, I should have to invent them" (12).

California enabled Isherwood to live according to his nature, and he met and had relationships with a large number of young men, in a much freer way than he could in either England or Berlin. Isherwood had an important, long-term relationship with Bill Caskey, a photographer. Caskey was a rakish fellow who was arrested a few times, and Isherwood's life with him was volatile, disorderly, and unsettled. Eventually, Isherwood realized that they could not go on together. In 1952, at Will Rogers State Beach in Santa Monica, Isherwood met Don Bachardy through his older brother, Ted.[12] A few months later, on February 14, 1953, Isherwood went to the beach with Ted and Don. That night, Chris and Don spent their first night together. Isherwood was forty-eight, and Don was eighteen.[13] The difference in their ages initially stunned Isherwood's friends, but both men recognized and openly acknowledged that the father–son relationship was an important aspect of their need for one another. They became life partners. Don went on to attend Chouinard Art Institute and is a renowned portraitist and artist whose works are collected by such institutions as the Smithsonian, the National Portrait Gallery, and the Huntington.

Isherwood and Bachardy became one of the best-known gay couples in Los Angeles, and their home on Adelaide Drive in Santa Monica was a gathering place for dinners, parties, and other events. It was also a mecca for countless troubled young gay men seeking counsel. Both were recognized as leaders in the gay community, and they opened their door to welcome gays seeking advice and acceptance. The mature Isherwood, as a very well-known author and, in his later years, a lecturer and visiting faculty member at universities in the greater Los Angeles area, was in great demand to write and to speak, as, for example, at an event hosted by *ONE Magazine*, where his topic was "A Writer and a Minority." Isherwood became a kind of guiding "uncle" for the gay movement (Parker 764). For Armistead Maupin, Edmund White, and other gay writers, Isherwood demonstrated that writing openly about homosexuality was no longer "some sort of career suicide." In turn, Isherwood's books developed a readership of gays, which enhanced his fame and book sales.[14]

As we have seen in the passage quoted from his book *Kathleen and Frank,* Isherwood was vehement in his demand to live according to his nature. His 1976 book *Christopher and His Kind,* in which Isherwood wrote of himself in the third person as "Christopher," was his strongest statement about homosexuality. The British edition's publisher, Methuen, warned on the dust jacket, "Christopher is a born minority-member. He rages against The Others in all their manifestations, including the heterosexual dictatorship" (quoted in Parker 793). In notes for the book, Isherwood had written, "For the homosexual, as long as he lives under the heterosexual dictatorship, the act of love must be, to some extent, an act of defiance, a political act."[15] The book, which appeared during the height of the gay liberation movement, was angry, a work of belligerent rebellion. Isherwood had spoken out, loudly and urgently, and his ringing cry for a free and open life reached gays everywhere. As one reader wrote in a birthday greeting to Isherwood, "Our gay pride is built upon the dignity of your life and work" (*Liberation* 570).

The third area in which Isherwood sought fulfillment of the California Dream was in his writing. As we have seen, in 1939 he had reached a turning point in both his life and his writing, and he wanted to search for new ways and modes of writing, or at least to evaluate his approach to writing. We saw that Isherwood had not found his path in New York, as Auden did, and he looked farther afield, not only for a place to live and work but also for a place where he could earn money to replenish his diminishing purse. Hollywood and the lucrative film industry beckoned, offering him the opportunity to be paid generous sums for screenplays. Isherwood loved films and had long been an avid devotee of the big screen. Not only did Isherwood love films, but he had already gained experience when he was hired as script doctor and general assistant to an Austrian director, Berthold Viertel, for a British film called *Little Friend.* He reveled in life on the film set, with its camaraderie, quirky characters, and oversized egos. Isherwood satirized his experience in a superb, hilarious novel, *Prater Violet,* published in 1945.

Thus, it was inevitable that Isherwood would be drawn to Hollywood and its attendant money and excitement. Soon after arriving in Southern California in 1939, he began to meet some of the stars he had most admired, and he made inroads in the rich social and intellectual mix of Hollywood. At a picnic in November, he mingled with Aldous and Maria Huxley, Berthold and Salka Viertel, Anita Loos, Bertrand Russell, Krishnamurti, and Greta Garbo—quite a heady array of star power for the dazzled young man. Early the following year, Isherwood's contacts paid off as he acquired a full-time job writing for MGM, at the pay rate of $500 per week. Salka Viertel, despite having been fired by MGM, called on her influence with the other émigrés at the studio to secure the job for him. Thus began his on-again, off-again work as a scriptwriter in Hollywood, a career that brought him welcome income at needful moments, but that also confirmed his initial observations when he worked with Berthold Viertel about the looniness of the film world and its often ridiculous adaptations and creations for the big screen. His experiences afforded Isherwood abundant opportunity to learn how powerless writers are when sucked into the great grinding mill of the studios.

In 1955, under contract with MGM, Isherwood worked on the script for *Diane,* about Catherine de Medici, Henri II of France, and Diane de Poitiers, starring Lana Turner, Roger Moore, Marisa Pavan, and Pedro Armendáriz. The actors were a casting misfire of mammoth proportion, and not even the vision of Roger Moore in tights could save the film. A film with more potential was an adaptation of *The Loved One,* Evelyn Waugh's 1948 satire of the legendary Forest Lawn cemetery and the funeral industry in Southern California. The distinguished cast of John Gielgud, Robert Morley, Margaret Leighton, Rod Steiger, James Coburn, and Milton Berle also boasted Isherwood himself in a cameo part as a graveside mourner.

Isherwood had much better luck with both the film and dramatic adaptations of his *Berlin Stories.* In 1951 John van Druten adapted the stories as the play *I Am a Camera,* starring Julie Harris as Sally Bowles. Isherwood initially had reservations about the play and its star, but those concerns vanished. He later recalled first meeting Julie Harris: "Now, out of the dressing room, came a slim sparkling-eyed girl in an absurdly tartlike black dress, with a jaunty little cap stuck sideways on her pale flame-colored hair and a gay, silly, naughty giggle. This certainly wasn't Miss Harris (who is a married lady of serious tastes and a spotless moral reputation); it was

Sally Bowles in person—my unserious, somewhat shop-soiled but always endearing heroine. Miss Harris was more essentially Sally Bowles than the Sally of my book, and much, much more like Sally than the real girl who, long ago, gave me the idea for my character" (Parker 606).

Subsequently, writer Joe Masteroff teamed with composer John Kander and lyricist Fred Ebb to turn the play into a musical, *Cabaret*. Bob Fosse's 1972 film version, which was much closer than the play to Isherwood's original stories about Berlin, was a huge popular and critical hit. It earned eight Academy Awards, including Oscars to Liza Minnelli for Best Actress, to Joel Grey for Best Actor, and to Bob Fosse for Best Director.

The ongoing success and renown of the play and musical based on his *Berlin Stories* provided a link for Isherwood to his earlier writing life, before emigrating, but in California he looked to the future and how he might adjust or alter his approach to writing. As we have seen, Isherwood had reached a turning point in his life and writing at the time he arrived in New York. He doubted himself as a writer, as he wondered whether he had reached a plateau or ending point in his approach to writing. In New York, he had mused in a letter to his mother about his writer's block and what it might mean: "I wish I could write novels, real ones, but perhaps I can't. Maybe I have come to the limit of my talent, and shall just go on being 'promising' until people are tired of me. Of course, I secretly feel there is something more inside me; but it won't come out. I could describe anybody, anything in the world; but I can't make it all into a pattern. Perhaps that's the penalty you pay for not believing in anything positive. Perhaps it's a certain lack of vitality. Perhaps it's only New York. Wystan, on the other hand, flourishes exceedingly. Never has he written so much" (March 26, 1939).[16]

In California, Isherwood continued his efforts to write novels. The novel that gave him the most difficulty was *The World in the Evening*, finally published in 1954 but which he worked on from about 1947. Initially conceived as a novel about war refugees, set in a hostel near Philadelphia operated by Quakers, the book was first titled *The School of Tragedy*. It was to feature three pairs of lovers, both hetero- and homosexual. Because one of the characters rejects the hostel and the Society of Friends people running it, Isherwood's private, humorous title for the book was "Too Queer to Be Quaker." Ultimately, he narrowed the scope of the novel, reducing the number of main characters and dropping most of the refugee story.

Isherwood had nothing but trouble in writing this novel. It changed back and forth between first and third person; the number and genders of his main characters changed; and the plot elements shifted repeatedly. This was the first novel in which his protagonist would not be a "Christopher," that is, some form of himself. This was new territory for him, and the taxing demands of this new approach to writing are vividly apparent.

For much of the seven years he struggled with the book, he wrote of his woes in a large ledger volume that he called his "Writing Notebook." He also wrote multiple partial drafts in this notebook and separately in loose pages. Throughout this tortuous process, his close and valued advisers were his friends Dodie Smith (author of *The Hundred and One Dalmatians*) and her husband, Alec Beesley. The patient couple read all the drafts, endlessly discussed the novel with Isherwood, and helped him shape his novel and characters. In gratitude for this great help, he dedicated the novel to them, and he had the final draft (which Don typed) bound in full green morocco and presented it to them.

The final version of the novel is a troubled work. Isherwood was never happy with it. In a letter to Dodie Smith, he called it "awful and false and bogus" (Parker 599), and he was brutally honest about its failings when he mentioned it in his lectures. Critics were generally, but not completely, unhappy with it as well. Flawed though it is, the novel holds an important, transitional place in Isherwood's writing career, as his first experiment in changing his approach. In addition, it has strengths and is quite readable.[17]

The Writing Notebook I mentioned also includes notes, beginning in about 1955, for *Down There on a Visit*.[18] Envisioned as a novel set in Mexico, it was to feature "a central character who avoids the weaknesses of Stephen in 'The World in the Evening.' Someone who is more relaxed, less ashamed, more amusing, more outrageous, more despotic.... So no more apologies. No more repentances and regenerations."[19] Isherwood drew upon some of his own experiences after Berlin. The finished novel is divided into four sections, each titled after an influential person in Isherwood's life.

One of the great treasures in all of twentieth-century literature is Isherwood's novel *A Single Man*, published in 1964. Impressed by reading *Mrs. Dalloway*, by Virginia Woolf, and by the works of Willa Cather, he was intrigued by the idea of creating a novel focusing narrowly on one life, in the span of just one day in that life. He thought at first to write of a war bride coming to the United States and would call the book "The Englishwoman." But as he continued to work on the idea and to write notes for it, he changed his protagonist to a gay man and decided to take Don's suggestion for the title, *A Single Man*. The novel is a gem, beautifully and gracefully written, that explores a day in the life of George, a gay lecturer at a Los Angeles university, after he has lost his life partner to an auto accident.

Reviewing Isherwood's writing career after he settled in California, we can observe that he did advance his writing technique while at the same time staying largely true to his long-standing, largely autobiographical approach. In examining what he knew best—himself—he was able to tease out meaning that could speak for others as well. His characters were drawn from life, but they also were his own creations. He had long believed in truth, as distinct from facts. That is, one can, and sometimes must, stretch and alter the literal facts in order to arrive at the truth behind and within them. He told an interviewer, "I do try to convey, if it doesn't sound too pompous, the inwardness of experience. . . . You cut corners, you invent, you simplify; you heighten certain lights and deepen certain shadows, as you might in a portrait."[20] In a lecture titled "Writing as a Way of Life," Isherwood elaborated on this concept: "You only use the experience to create the myth which corresponds to the inner reality. . . . That explains why what is really truthful in art is not the same as what is truthful in a newspaper report of a fire or a murder and is not the same as your autobiography told in completely factual terms."[21]

Isherwood's place in Anglo-American letters is assured and his stature continues to grow. Since his papers came to the Huntington in 1999, scholarly publications have burgeoned, and his own books continue to be reprinted. Did Isherwood attain his California Dream? I think we can assert a resounding *yes*. Through his belief in Vedanta, he developed his ability to discover his own nature and to live according to it. In the greater freedom of life in California, he was able to live much more openly as a gay man, and he met his life partner, Don Bachardy. Finally, he produced works of fiction that reached scores of readers with their combination of creativity and experience. Isherwood knew how important California was for him. He described the Golden State as the place "where we make the mistakes first and then learn from them" (Parker 833), and he certainly did this. At the end of his life, he was beginning to work on an autobiography. Its working title was "California." It was never completed, but the rest of his remarkable works are there for us, acclaimed by both critics and fans. Alan

Wilde, in his biography, *Christopher Isherwood,* observed that Isherwood "has been one of the period's most original ironists and one of its most subtle moral thinkers as well."[22] Isherwood's favorite fan letter said, "You try to describe what it's like to be alive." It's a grand, outsized claim, but he did that for all of us, and we will all benefit from, and be enriched by, his works for many years to come.

NOTES

1. Christopher Isherwood, "Midnight in New York," autograph manuscript, January 1939, Christopher Isherwood Papers, CI 1102, Huntington Library, San Marino, California.

2. See chapter 2 of Peter Parker's biography for more on Frank, especially his death. His body was never recovered, and it was several months before his death was officially acknowledged. Peter Parker, *Isherwood* (London: Picador, 2004).—Eds.

3. Evelyn Waugh, "Two Unquiet Lives," review of *World within World,* by Stephen Spender, and *Saints and Parachutes,* by John Miller, *Tablet,* May 5, 1951. Reprinted in Donat Gallagher, ed., *The Essays, Articles and Reviews of Evelyn Waugh* (London: Methuen, 1983), 394–98.

4. Cyril Connolly, *Enemies of Promise* (Boston: Little, Brown, 1939).

5. Christopher Isherwood, "Diary, 1935–1938 and 1947," autograph manuscript, CI 2751, Huntington Library.

6. Quoted in Parker, *Isherwood,* 430.

7. Isherwood used the pseudonym "Vernon" or "Vernon Old" when writing about his boyfriend from this era. Both Lisa Colletta, in her edition of the letters between Isherwood and his mother, and Richard Zeikowitz, in his edition of the letters between Isherwood and Forster, use his real name, Harvey Young. This use of pseudonyms is instructive in terms of Wendy Moffat's essay in this volume on the "archival I" and queer history's erasures. See also the glossary of names in *Lost Years,* in which Katherine Bucknell provides more information on "Vernon," including the fascinating fact that his "painting career was increasingly successful, and in the late 1950s he tutored Don Bachardy." Christopher Isherwood, *Lost Years: A Memoir, 1945–1951,* ed. Katherine Bucknell (New York: HarperCollins, 2000), 338.—Eds.

8. Kevin Starr, *Americans and the California Dream, 1850–1915* (Santa Barbara, Calif.: Peregrine Smith, 1981), 46.

9. Christopher Isherwood, *Diaries,* vol. 1, *1939–1960,* ed. Katherine Bucknell (New York: HarperCollins, 1996), 272.

10. Christopher Isherwood to Kathleen Bradshaw-Isherwood, March 23, 1939, CI 1280, Huntington Library. See Colletta 134.—Eds.

11. Isherwood, *Lost Years*, 217. Reflecting on this painful incident almost twenty-five years later, Isherwood remarked, "Even as I write these words, I feel bitterly ashamed . . . for not having said that [I] was queer" (217).

12. For more on the chronology and nature of Isherwood's relationship with Ted Bachardy, see *Lost Years*. The passage concludes with Isherwood saying that the "weak link of acquaintanceship" was sufficient to "draw its attached chain of beautiful and incredible consequences into Christopher's life—the first of them being Christopher's meeting with Ted's four-years-younger brother, Don" (212–13n1).—Eds.

13. The story of the beginnings of this relationship is recounted in chapters 19 and 20 of Parker's *Isherwood* and in the documentary by Tina Mascara and Guido Santi, *Chris & Don: A Love Story* (Asphalt Stars Productions/Zeitgeist Films, 2007).—Eds.

14. See Edmund White's essay in this collection, chapter 12, "Becoming Gay in the 1960s: Reading *A Single Man*," for more on Isherwood's role as mentor to younger gay men and writers.—Eds.

15. Christopher Isherwood, *Liberation: Diaries*, vol. 3, *1970–1983*, ed. Katherine Bucknell (London: Chatto & Windus, 2012), 522.

16. Lisa Colletta, ed., *Kathleen and Christopher: Christopher Isherwood's Letters to His Mother* (Minneapolis: University of Minnesota Press, 2005), 131.

17. See the essay by Robert Caserio in this volume, chapter 8, for more on the significance of *The World in the Evening*.

18. For a fuller description of the Writing Notebook, see Sara S. Hodson, "A Writer at Work: The Isherwood Archive," *The American Isherwood*, ed. James J. Berg and Chris Freeman (Minneapolis: University of Minnesota Press, 2015), 243–58.

19. Christopher Isherwood, Writing Notebook, CI 1158, Huntington Library, 94.

20. *Conversations with Christopher Isherwood*, ed. James J. Berg and Chris Freeman (Jackson: University Press of Mississippi, 2001), 42.

21. Christopher Isherwood, "Writing as a Way of Life," typescript with autograph corrections, February 10, 1965, CI 1186, Huntington Library, 5.

22. Alan Wilde, *Christopher Isherwood* (New York: Twayne, 1971), 5.

2. "Rejecting the Real World Outright"

The Shared Fantasy of Mortmere

*T*h*e Mortmere Stories* exist today as a volume published in 1994 by Enitharmon Press, edited by Katherine Bucknell and made possible by her collaboration with Edward Upward. In referring to the Mortmere stories as a body of work in this project, I will use the formal title *The Mortmere Stories* only in specific reference to the 1994 published work, which contains the existing Mortmere material that Bucknell found coherent enough for publication and that Upward was comfortable making available. The Mortmere stories as they existed in the lives of the two authors are a separate entity, including material that was lost, material that the authors destroyed, material that was planned and discussed but never put into writing, and material that existed only in the authors' imaginations. Additionally, the phenomenon of "Mortmere" is not merely a series of stories but also an atmosphere, an attitude, and a period of time in Isherwood's and Upward's lives. When I reference "Mortmere" and "the Mortmere stories," I attempt to encompass the complex web of content and nebulous significance that these words held for the authors.

Scholarly work on *The Mortmere Stories* is thin on the ground. This is in part because the stories existed as mere myth for such a long period of time, sitting unpublished in Isherwood's and Upward's private papers from the 1920s until the early 1990s. Additionally, Upward destroyed a fair amount of his own work after joining the Communist Party during the 1930s, including at least some of his own completed contributions to Mortmere. Upward did, however, retain many of Isherwood's stories that were in his possession, and these make up the bulk of the published material. In his final letter to Isherwood before Isherwood's death in 1986, Upward wrote:

> I have been plagued at intervals for some time by Mortmere addicts who want to read your Mortmere stories. There seems to be a growing Mortmere cult. Would there be any possibility of your having them published in the U.S. and/or the U.K. in a small edition with perhaps illustrations by David Hackney [sic] and/or Don? I have been re-reading them recently and they have seemed as marvellously funny as ever and have sent me into fits of laughter such as I have not had for a long time. I can easily get them all photocopied and can send them to you.[1]

These "Mortmere addicts" learned of the stories in two ways: from Isherwood's description of them in *Lions and Shadows* and from Upward. Interest in Isherwood had picked up in the late 1970s and early 1980s as Brian Finney's *Christopher Isherwood: A Critical Biography* was released and several Isherwood novels, including *All the Conspirators* and *Lions and Shadows,* were reissued. Upward had been in contact with Isherwood's biographers Finney and Jonathan Fryer, who had asked him for information on Isherwood's life and work, and who had visited Upward. Upward's letters also indicate another reason why *The Mortmere Stories* have been given so little scholarly attention: the belief that they are mere "childishness," thoughtless means of passing the time at Cambridge, rife with juvenile jokes and tiresome prep-school slang.

What Upward's letters show is that Mortmere remained an important part of Isherwood's and Upward's lives and friendship forever. They also illustrate the change that occurred in the Isherwood–Upward friendship after the Cambridge years passed: while Isherwood really did seem to leave Mortmere behind him, embarking on new, successful writing projects and even on a new life in the United States, Upward continued to return to Mortmere in the hopes that it could somehow restore the creative powers that had flourished in him during the 1920s and that had been stifled and lost after he took up school teaching and especially after he joined the Communist Party. For Isherwood, Mortmere really was a youthful dalliance in pure fiction, whereas for Upward it was the pinnacle of his creative career. The idea of being able to "return" to Mortmere, as Upward believed he could, also highlights the fact that Isherwood and Upward thought of

Mortmere as a place. Despite its imaginary nature, they often wrote of it as a physical location to which they could travel, and it was closely tied to the idea of the British countryside as Isherwood experienced it in his youth: a slightly sinister landscape representative of the repressive social traditions he longed to escape, secretly rotten with sexual deviance and crime. In this sense, Mortmere served as an important physical and imaginative point of departure for Isherwood in particular, the platform from which he jumped into new forms of writing and for which he eventually left England forever.

Upward was most obsessed with Mortmere during the 1920s, most particularly in 1926, when he was tutoring in Cornwall after graduating from Cambridge. Although it is difficult to tell with only Upward's letters to go by, Isherwood seemed equally engaged with Mortmere at this point; their correspondence apparently included short Mortmere fictions and ideas for a book-length Mortmere epic. But by 1928, mentions of Mortmere drop off sharply in Upward's letters. By then, Isherwood was working on *The Memorial* and traveling to Berlin, while Upward was miserable in his teaching positions and was struggling desperately to produce works of poetry and fiction that did not leave him even more dissatisfied than writing nothing. It was also in 1928 that Upward made his first mention of the Communist Party in a letter to Isherwood, and over the next few years, his involvement in politics began to take up more and more of his spare time. During this period, Upward viewed the process as a necessary and noble sacrifice of his creative work to his political beliefs, a view that would later change. Between 1928 and 1971, Upward mentioned Mortmere mainly to describe events, people, and places in his everyday life: a school building is "Mortmerish," or a colleague has a face like one of the Mortmere characters from the 1920s. Upward connected his feeling of being far from Mortmere directly to his inability to write well, feeling that if he could "go back to Mortmere," he could regain his youthful creative energy:

> To-day there is snow in the garden behind our flat, and like Kathy [Katherine Mansfield] I look at it and try to think of Mortmere. But only the curtest, most algebraic memories return. Was it for this? Yes, it was. No reprieve. (CI 2447)

Throughout this long period from 1928 to 1971, Upward attempted some "Mortmere fiction" but felt that he could no longer summon up Mortmere convincingly. Yet when he tried to avoid the subject of Mortmere, he was equally unsuccessful. In 1950, in the midst of slogging work on a never-finished novel (possibly a piece that would later become part of *The Spiral Ascent*), Upward wrote:

> My trouble is that I have been trying to write something as different as possible from Mortmere, something austerely originating in actuality (ie the trivial experiences of my own life), but no matter how I wangle it and try to unify the quite interesting separate incidents I can't soberly see it as anything but a string of rather static sketches. Probably my only hope is to start from the abstract, to invent a <u>story</u> no matter how fantastic and Mortmerish provided it's exciting, and then try to adapt it to what actually happened. (CI 2468)

Upward never displayed the natural talent for autobiographical fiction that Isherwood had. In shunning creative fiction for didactic pro-communist writing during the 1930s, Upward lost the imaginative spark that ignited the Mortmere fantasy and inspired both himself and Isherwood to become lifelong writers and friends. Whereas for Isherwood Mortmere was a starting place, the fantastical jumping-off point of a successful creative career, for Upward it became a sort of never-never land, a place where he had once known a magic he could no longer access.

By far the most insightful and useful piece on Mortmere is Katherine Bucknell's introduction to the published version of the stories, written with input from and materials provided by Edward Upward, who was ninety-one when the stories were finally published in 1994. Aside from explaining Mortmere and its complicated origins and afterlife, Bucknell begins to delve into its significance for Isherwood and Upward. Bucknell summarizes Upward's creative struggles after his graduation from Cambridge and his commitment to communism, and she points out that Mortmere helped to free Isherwood from the youthful puritanism that held him back creatively before he and Upward were reunited at Cambridge. Most important, Bucknell acknowledges and skillfully outlines the authors' personalities in relation to Mortmere, which are so clearly demonstrated by their attitudes toward Mortmere as they aged:

> Upward's relation to Mortmere was far more problematic. If Isherwood's imagination, according to Nietzsche's symbolism, was in some sense Apollonian—light, measured, disciplined to observe the real world—

then Upward's was Dionysian—dark, passionate, morbid, and unruly.
In youth, Upward took imaginative risks, and was apparently capable of
complete self-absorption and uncontrol; Isherwood was pragmatic and
absolutely sane.[2]

This dichotomy is clear in Isherwood's portrayal of his friendship with
Upward in *Lions and Shadows*, from the Mortmere stories themselves,
and from the friends' correspondence. It can also be seen in a class photograph of Repton taken in 1921, which hangs on the wall of Don Bachardy's
kitchen above his own Los Angeles class photograph from the 1950s:
Isherwood smiles at the camera with his light hair messy, looking like a
carefree Tom Sawyer; Upward gives the camera a dark, disgruntled smirk,
half-hidden behind the boy in front of him.

It is tempting to say that Isherwood and Upward changed completely
after leaving Cambridge: Isherwood suddenly became the more capable,
more adventurous, more confident young man whereas Upward, formerly
in the ascendant, sank into obscurity without warning. Bucknell's analysis helps to clarify that Isherwood was *always* the more balanced and self-
confident of the pair, and that he influenced Upward more than Upward
influenced him once they reached their Cambridge years. Bucknell writes,
"Without the excitement and inspiration of Isherwood's constant compan-
ionship, Upward lost faith in his talent and in his imagination," and thus
began his downward spiral into creative sterility (19). I will follow Bucknell's analysis to its conclusion and examine how Isherwood, by shattering
the Mortmere fantasy with one Mortmere-like and apparently uncharac-
teristic act of rebellion, made it possible to utilize pieces of Mortmere as
tools for writing and for living, instead of encapsulating and venerating the
fantasy and making it inaccessible to himself, as Upward did.

Their Mortmere stories became Isherwood and Upward's means
of expressing their disdain for three main perceived antagonists in their
young lives: institutions (their public school and Cambridge), war (the
Great War, the fear of future war, and the "idea" of war), and what I will call
"tradition." The last of these three is the most amorphous, encompassing
the young men's negative feelings about their families, older generations
of authors, the Edwardian ideals they felt were still being pressed upon
them in the 1920s, and their vague feelings of resentment and distaste for
the expectations that they associated with the middle-class British society
whence they came. In this sense, Mortmere is representative of transit and

travel in Isherwood's and Upward's lives: it became a means of metaphorical escape before they were old enough to attempt a literal escape.

Mortmere is first mentioned publicly in Isherwood's 1938 autobiographical novel *Lions and Shadows,* in which he described the "discovery" of the imaginary English village. At Cambridge together, the private world of the Isherwood–Upward friendship had already become populated by literary influences and by "the Watcher in Spanish." Mortmere was the next logical step in their semiserious game of being beset by the forces of the Combine:

> One evening, as we were strolling along Silver Street, we happened to turn off into an unfamiliar alley, where there was a strange-looking, rusty-hinged little old door in a high blank wall. Chalmers said: "It's the doorway into the Other Town." This idea of "The Other Town" appealed to us greatly; for it offered a way of escape from Cambridge altogether. . . . Here was a world which the dons didn't even dream existed.[3]

Just as the Watcher in Spanish evolved, so did the idea of the Other Town. Immersed in the atmospheric language that helped to keep their friendship deep and exclusive, Upward came up with a phrase to describe "the inmost nature of the Other Town": "The Rats' Hostel" (*Lions and Shadows* 47). This phrase evolved over time into the simple adjective "rats," and came to describe the entire atmosphere of the early Isherwood–Upward friendship:

> a certain atmosphere, a genre: the special brand of medieval surrealism which we had made our own. . . . Soon we began to describe as "rats" any object, animal, scene, place or phrase which seemed connected, however obscurely, with our general conception of the "Rats' Hostel." . . . We used the word more and more loosely and indiscriminately, until it came to mean, simply, "romantic" or "quaint." (48)

Isherwood simplified the meaning of the word "rats" in *Lions and Shadows.* "Rats-ness" is one of the central "conceits" that gave rise to the existence of Mortmere, providing Isherwood and Upward with a private piece of slang with which to describe anything that fit into this imaginary world and enhanced its atmosphere. Made possible by their mutual game playing, this single word was representative of the intricacy and depth of their shared imagination, which Isherwood could not—or would not—fully articulate in this relatively early published work.

Glimpses of the importance of this piece of slang, in combination with the rest of Isherwood and Upward's shared language, are visible in Upward's letters to Isherwood during the 1920s. The first mention of the word "rat" comes in Upward's fourth letter to Isherwood, while Isherwood was still at Repton. It is featured in a quote from Wilfred Owen's "A Terre," Owen being one of the pair's biggest early influences and a central figure in their literary pantheon:

> I am never happy unless I am either hating or loving; here there is both-ing [sic] to hate, so one has to fall back on love. And a damn poor substi-tute it is. It attacks the stomach, whereas hate attacks and fries the brain. "O Life—Life, let me breathe—a dug-out rat!" (CI 2291)

By June 1925, "rats" had taken on its Mortmere meaning. In a letter writ-ten during June of that year, Upward contemplates (not too seriously) the possibility of committing suicide. A long-running playacting in these early letters is Upward's desire to kill himself with a pistol that Isherwood supposedly owns, without casting suspicion of murder on Isherwood. This scenario does not seem to have been discussed in much depth. I was unable to find corresponding mentions of it in Upward's archive in the Brit-ish Library, and the irony that Upward lived to be over one hundred years old is never mentioned in either author's work or archive. The following poem was written by Upward to suggest a Mortmere-like alternative to self-destruction:

> . . . Meanwhile I ask you seriously
> To find a lodging house for me
> Somewhere in London, where the bats
> Swoop nightly, and it's very rats.
> And if not rats, well, <u>rattable</u>,
> With lavatory chains that do not pull
> But can be used for strangling newts
> And climbing roofs, and dangling boots
> Down where in waters turgid and deep
> The ever-hungry shit-sharks sleep. (CI 2313)

Isherwood apparently took this request seriously, since later that same year, after a tryst with a woman that Isherwood had arranged in London, Upward wrote, "How rats to think that no word of mine can change the new history of that little high bedroom in London. Forgive my corps boots; I am fresh from the slime. One should always be in love" (CI 2318).[4] And in a fragment of a work written in 1926, Upward revealed that he and Isherwood toyed with calling Mortmere "Ratsmere," so important was the concept of "rats-ness" to the atmosphere of the fictional village.

This atmosphere was not merely "romantic" or "quaint" but also surreal in a slightly sinister way, influenced by Dürer engravings and the work of Edgar Allan Poe, Beatrix Potter, the Brothers Grimm, and *Alice in Wonderland*. Isherwood wrote that "graveyards were 'rats' and very old gnarled trees, and cave mouths overhung with ivy" (*Lions and Shadows* 48). In the context of Mortmere it became clear that "rats" did not simply mean "romantic" or "quaint": it had a sinister connotation that was integral to the setting of Mortmere, a hybrid "romantic-sinister" quality that permeated Isherwood and Upward's shared imaginings.

It is tempting to call Mortmere "an alternate reality" owing to its origins as a "metaphysical University city" hidden within Cambridge. As it evolved, however, it became less an alternate reality and more a fictional place to which Isherwood and Upward could be transported as their Mortmere alter egos, Starn and Hynd. Rather than over- or underlying the real Cambridge as Isherwood and Upward knew it, Mortmere became a separate town in a remote part of the English countryside, removed from Cambridge not only by harsh reality but also by physical space. It evolved from a fiction along the lines of Philip Pullman's His Dark Materials series in which Cambridge is partially altered and made magical, into a fiction much more like *Midsomer Murders,* in which a madcap and murder-ridden county exists in a vague location in the south of England. One reason for this change was probably that a separate Mortmere was less complicated than the idea of an altered Cambridge: if Mortmere were entirely separate, it could be structured and arranged however the authors' fancy struck them, unconfined by the framework of the real city. A more important reason was that Isherwood and Upward wanted Mortmere to be an escape from Cambridge, a place of total freedom, not a place somehow hidden within and therefore subjugated to oppressive Cambridge and its dons.

One of Isherwood and Upward's poems from the 1920s, "The Recessional from Cambridge," illustrated the physical removal of Mortmere from the university town. The poem was written to a figure called "Laily," a representation of the slimy, social-climbing future dons whom Isherwood and Upward particularly loathed at Cambridge: the type of student

Isherwood's mother wished he could be. It is clear from the following stanzas of the poem that the authors once imagined the characters who populated Mortmere walking the streets of Cambridge too:

> And yet, not quite alone. A certain few
>   Chosen companions, a jolly troop
>   Come with us, such as would most gladly stoop
> To eat dog's excrement like Irish stew,
>   To savour cat's urine like caviare,
>   Rather than blaspheme the Beauty which they are . . .
>
> These shall be with us in the third-class carriage
>   Drinking and playing cards the whole night long.
>   Welken will entertain us with a song,
> Gunball will ask Miss Belmare's hand in marriage,
>   Claptree will spit and swear and tell foul rhymes,
>   Moxon will masturbate behind a copy of The Times.
>
> While the enormous engine, mad with fear
>   Tears southward in a swirl of flying sparks
>   Through silent hamlets where no watch dog barks
> Past farms whose cocks cry that the dawn is near
>   By many a lichenous and low arched tunnel
>   At whose mouth waving grasses brush against the funnel.
>
> Until the morning lights along the hills
>   And the train slackens, winding out and in
>   Between the cushion downs and larks begin
> And the green cutting is wild with daffodils
>   Till one by one the villages are passed
>   And the low station comes—Mortmere at last. (CI 1131)

In this scenario, Isherwood and Upward leave Cambridge behind and escape to Mortmere permanently. The poem positions Mortmere as a physical destination and its denizens, along with Isherwood and Upward, as in transit to it as a separate location. Over the course of the fantasy, Mortmere was changed from a secret or magical aspect of Cambridge to an entirely separate destination, an imaginary village in an imaginary county that could only be reached by means of a "mad" train from Cambridge, and then only by those "certain few" who understood and appreciated its meaning.

As evidenced by the Watcher in Spanish, Isherwood and Upward's imagined characters and locations involved a cooperative performance, carried out for the actors' mutual amusement and, at least subconsciously, for the purpose of maintaining the relative exclusivity of their friendship. This performativity was not limited to Isherwood and Upward's conversation, but extended itself into their writing, into their letters, and into the production of the Mortmere stories. Like the Watcher in Spanish, Mortmere was a private form of entertainment between Isherwood and Upward, begun as "a series of indecent stories" left by the authors on each other's breakfast tables in their Cambridge rooms. Isherwood and Upward often appeared in these stories, but not as their usual selves. The narrators Edward Hynd and Christopher Starn stood in for Edward Upward and Christopher Isherwood, and would introduce the story and occasionally appear as characters in it. Hynd and Starn were not merely pseudonyms but alter egos: although they were both former Cambridge students, they were now pornographers who had to flee London for the English countryside, presumably due to legal troubles in the city (*Mortmere* 41). The importance of the use of these fictionalized second selves cannot be overstated. Isherwood glossed over this aspect of the stories in *Lions and Shadows,* and Upward did not dwell upon it in his letters, but it suggests that the Mortmere stories should not be read, as they almost always are, as novelties or as pieces of schoolboyish juvenilia entirely separate from Isherwood's and Upward's adult ouevres. The Mortmere materials are significant precursors to the strange methods of self-representation and unstable uses of genre that we see in Isherwood's and Upward's later works.

The Mortmere alter egos bring up important questions about self-representation and the nature of the authors' relationships with reality and fantasy at this early point in their writing careers. Why create alter egos to narrate Mortmere at all? Mortmere, being entirely fictional, would seem to be a risk-free space in which to allow the subconscious free play without fear of the consequences. My theory of Isherwood's and Upward's Mortmere alter egos is closely tied to the performativity of their friendship. Despite the closeness of their relationship, Isherwood's and Upward's primary modes of interaction during the 1920s were mutual entertainment and the exchange of criticism, not self-revelation. Isherwood and Upward began trading pieces of poetry for critique before they began trading pieces of fiction for entertainment, and it was this interaction that led them to think of themselves as writers and to establish a friendship based in large part on shared literary tastes and shared uses of language. Although drawn closely together in their likes and dislikes and in their opposition to the Cambridge Combine, Isherwood and Upward kept certain aspects of their personal lives hidden from one another. The most notable hidden element in their early friendship was Isherwood's sexuality. Isherwood did not give Upward his short story "The Old Game" to be criticized like most of his other work; this story is about a young man seducing an even younger male lover. "The Old Game" is written in manuscript within the same notebook as "The Hero," a short story Isherwood discussed with Upward in person and by mail when they were apart (CI 2302). It is clear from Upward's letters to Isherwood that Upward was unaware of his best friend's sexuality until sometime in 1925 or 1926. Before Isherwood arrived at Cambridge, Upward referred to the university as "a hot-bed of homo-sexualism" (CI 2291), and once he was working as a tutor and schoolmaster, he made endless jokes about "buggery":

> The masters bugger one another and probably bugger the boys too—though only one case of this has definitely come to my notice. The boys bugger one another and tell the masters all about it. The headmaster cures frigging by sleeping with anyone caught frigging. He also massages the boys' stomachs after rowing. He also sticks nude photos of boys on to three-ply wood and cuts them out with a fretsaw. (CI 2314)

In 1926 it became clear that Isherwood's homosexuality had been revealed to Upward only after five or more years of friendship, although it is mentioned only obliquely in the entire collection of their correspondence. Upward's references to homosexuality are never entirely comfortable; often he is joking or half joking about sleeping with boys himself, asking Isherwood for advice on seducing his students or approaching boys in various settings, and showing something approaching timidity when he asks Isherwood serious questions about his sex life. On a holiday in Surrey, he wrote to Isherwood, "The boy was pretty, the man had the head of a foetus. I thought of you, my partner and my quick: What would you have done?— 'Boy, I give you these downs,' I should have said" (CI 2318). As a schoolmaster in Worcester, he ended a letter with, "But there is one boy with pallid freckles who would soon alter my sex. None of the masters are homos"

(CI 2330). And during a summer in Cornwall he asked Isherwood, "Have you ever tried to meet a boy at a fair?" (CI 2351).

This distance between the two friends was directly related to the assumption of the "Hynd" and "Starn" identities in Mortmere, and to the ongoing performativity of their life writing. This connection is most obvious in how Isherwood and Upward address each another in their letters. Isherwood explains in *Lions and Shadows* that their correspondence had no conventional salutations nor endings because they "were still shy. Such was the influence of public school convention upon two declared rebels of using each other's Christian names. It was years before I could call Chalmers 'Allen' or he could call me 'Christopher' without a trace of self-consciousness" (*Lions and Shadows* 45). Because Mortmere extended into Isherwood's and Upward's everyday life at Cambridge, their Mortmere pseudonyms served the purpose of covering any of the awkwardness they felt in admitting their importance to one another. Upward addressed Isherwood as "Starn" especially when expressing sentiments that could be construed as embarrassing or, in Mortmere-speak, "quisb":

> Ah, my poor Starn. I miss you sadly. I am cut off from humanity and emotional truth. Do not pay me back in my own coin but write, and tell of your plans, the Hero [an unpublished short story by Isherwood], and when we return to the sorrowful dark—the twilight of youth Cambridge night. (CI 2302)

Despite his insistence on rejecting the conventions they were taught at public school, Upward was too embarrassed to tell Christopher that he was sorely missed; Hynd and Starn, on the other hand, were not subject to these social constraints.

Another reason why these second selves were so necessary is apparent in the invented backgrounds of Hynd and Starn: they were pornographers who had to flee London because it became too hot to hold them (*Mortmere* 41). In other words, they were true social outcasts, open and unashamed deviants, of the type that the young Isherwood and Upward longed to be. Just as the two authors were ashamed of their helpless adherence to some social conventions, like the avoidance of Christian names, they were also slightly ashamed of their ability to fit in with the poshocracy and other conventional, upper-middle-class social groups (for instance, Upward's ability to socialize with the bourgeoisie he eventually tutored for). And they were certainly ashamed of any pleasure they derived from the company and the approval of these conventional groups. Hynd and Starn, unlike Upward and Isherwood, had no desire whatsoever to please or propitiate anyone else. Unbound by middle-class morals, traditions, families, or financial concerns, they had no disapproving dons, no nagging mothers, no dead fathers, and no sexual mores; they were the versions of Isherwood and Upward who could be their genuine selves without guilt, fear, or loss of face, and Mortmere was a setting handcrafted for the exploration of their most deviant desires and the exorcism of their deepest resentments.

At one point in the evolution of Mortmere, Isherwood and Upward toyed with combining their two alter egos into a single entity called "Edward Hearn," his last name a portmanteau of "Hynd" and "Starn." Hearn was referred to as a "cipher," a cursory means of eliminating Hynd and Starn and having one consolidated narrator of the Mortmere stories. However, Hearn appeared in very few of the Mortmere materials and seems to be a relic of Isherwood and Upward's idea of a long novel based on their Mortmere stories, an idea that never came to fruition. Despite their almost telepathic connection as young men, Isherwood and Upward were distinct even in the world of Mortmere. Hynd's stories are noticeably different from Starn's, and even one long story narrated by Hearn, "The World War," has elements of each author that can be easily discerned by an experienced reader.

Until 1925 Mortmere existed primarily as a private performance between Isherwood and Upward, most of its content merely imagined. But in the spring of Isherwood's tripos year at Cambridge, the imaginary world of Mortmere started to bleed over into reality, with fateful consequences for Isherwood: he was thrown—albeit very gently—out of Cambridge. This incident marks not only the beginning of a period of relative dissipation for Isherwood, but also the beginning of a marked shift in Isherwood and Upward's relations to each other, and the beginning of a long series of shifts in Isherwood's physical location. During his youth, Isherwood had come to see himself as crafty, timid, people-pleasing, and weak in principle compared to Upward, whom he viewed as morally and ethically steadfast, strong, and rebellious. Being dismissed from Cambridge, however, put Isherwood at a level of rebelliousness that Upward never reached, and from that point forward, Isherwood emerged as the much more fearless, intrepid, and even the more modern of the two men. After being dismissed from Cambridge, Isherwood began his travels to Germany, Greece, China, and more: his Mortmere-like act of rebellion could be said to have precipitated the series of events that eventually led him to America.

Isherwood describes in detail his final weeks at Cambridge in *Lions and Shadows*. He had never been successful at the university; from the very beginning, he struggled to concentrate on his lectures, failed to write the way his tutors expected, and made no real effort to catch up with the other students. This last point is most important: Isherwood's self-sabotage began long before he consciously considered it. He had been slowly making his way out of Cambridge since the moment he arrived there, in part by mentally transporting himself to Mortmere on a regular basis. Isherwood hereby marked himself as distinct from Upward: "Suppose I stayed on and did, somehow, get a degree: what would become of me? I should have to be a schoolmaster. But I didn't want to be a schoolmaster—I wanted, at least, to escape from that world" (*Lions and Shadows* 91). Upward would never be able to make this escape. Bucknell writes, "Responding to Upward's lead, playing the Mortmere game to its extreme, Isherwood acted himself into a real rebellion, and wrested his future away from conventional institutional life" (*Mortmere* 17). While Isherwood spent the rest of his life traveling the world and finally settled in Los Angeles, Upward remained in England as a schoolteacher.

Isherwood effected his escape by writing his tripos exam in the form of riddles, poems, and insults. The idea was conceived in conference with Upward, who did not think Isherwood was serious about failing the exam; he was apparently treating Isherwood's "plans" like the rest of the Mortmere stories, an amusing mutual performance. In their discussions, the two thought of Isherwood's hypothetical actions as taking a sort of stand, remembering the "two sides" of the Cambridge social Combine, the tyranny of Laily, and the superiority of Mortmere. But when Isherwood was called to meet with his tutor and discreetly sent down, Mortmere evaporated around him:

> What was there to say? My act now seemed more than ever unreal to me: failing the Tripos had merely been a kind of extension of dream-action on to the plane of reality. How was I to tell the tutor that we had often plotted to blow him sky-high with a bomb? How was I to tell him anything? The tutor wasn't the tutor: he was a kindly but aggrieved middle-

aged gentleman. . . . How could I talk to this perfect stranger about Mortmere and Hynd and Starn and the Dürers and Laily? (*Lions and Shadows* 98)

For Isherwood, this was the beginning of the end of Mortmere. "The Mortmere enthusiasm carried him out through the college gates into the world" (*Mortmere* 17), where he would wander, struggle, learn, and eventually become far more successful than Upward, who suddenly looked timid and conventional beside him. The blending of fiction with reality that Isherwood describes during his tripos exam has important implications for his later work, most of which blends fiction with autobiography.

Upward, on the other hand, exited Cambridge to do exactly what Isherwood so frantically distanced himself from. In 1925 Upward wrote, "I am determined now that whatever comes I WILL NOT WORK. (Damn Laily.) . . . If I schoolmaster in due season, it will only be in order to gain a small capital on which to idle somehow" (CI 2328). But within a year, Upward was tutoring for upper-class families and living in abject misery. His letters were more full of Mortmere lore than ever:

> Another Laily sonnet:
> Shall I compare thee to black whorls of shit?
> Thou art more poignant and more glutinous.
> Rough faeces oft reveal a mermaid's tit,
> And flushing down the evacuated pus . . .
> But thy, etc . . . (CI 2339)

> As for Mortmere—the method I'm trying to use is all wrong. The first chapter cannot open quite calmly in Mortmere. That village is too holy. I've decided that the first part at least of the story must be told by Hynd to Starn. Hynd knew Heaven at Mortmere. (CI 2341)

This second excerpt particularly illustrates how Upward seemed to *need* Mortmere whereas Isherwood was able to merely play at it. Isherwood wrote much later:

> But Chalmers needed Gunball, at all costs. I did not. That, as writers, was the essential difference between us. . . . He could never afford to abandon [Mortmere] altogether; if he did so, he was lost. He was to spend the next three years in desperate and bitter struggles to relate Mortmere to the real world of the jobs and the lodging-houses; to find the formula which would transform our private fancies and amusing freaks and

bogies into valid symbols of the ills of society and the toils and aspirations of our daily lives. (*Lions and Shadows* 273)

This is a piece of remarkable insight on Isherwood's part, showing just how telepathically close the two young men were. But Isherwood had no way of knowing that, decades later, Upward would *still* be desperately grappling with the characters and the fantasies of the 1920s, while Isherwood himself would have moved on to other, more successful literary pursuits.

The most moving and revealing example of Mortmere's importance is visible in letters between Isherwood and Upward in mid-1939, when Upward was deeply interested and involved in the Communist Party and when Isherwood was already living in the United States. These letters also illustrate the transition between the youthful Mortmere stories and the more mature fictionalized autobiographies both authors produced. Perhaps most important, they help illustrate the changes in the Isherwood–Upward friendship that occurred after Isherwood's exodus from Cambridge and his subsequent success as an author.

Before leaving England in 1939, Isherwood destroyed diaries that apparently dated back through the 1920s and were stored at his mother's house. According to Don Bachardy, who was "horrified" to learn that Isherwood had done that, Isherwood feared that a second disastrous global war was on its way, and that in the event of their discovery in a certain political climate, his diaries could be used against him and his family members. Hence Isherwood's first published diaries begin with his arrival in America with W. H. Auden in 1939. Isherwood expected to be met with the same success as Auden upon his arrival in New York. Looking back on 1939 in 1946, Isherwood wrote:

> Certainly, at that time, I had every reason to believe in the favourable aspect of my star. . . . In private, to my intimate friends, I boasted, with a vulgarity that still makes me squirm as I write these lines. Auden, particularly, disliked my attitude; it hurt him because he was really fond of me. . . . Edward Upward, now only an occasional visitor, didn't say much. Something was broken between us. I couldn't meet his faintly ironical eye. When we were together, I covered my embarrassment with an awkward heartiness.[5]

This break between Isherwood and Upward is obvious from Isherwood's papers: there was a gap in their correspondence between 1936 and 1939.

It seems that Isherwood's departure from Cambridge only strengthened their friendship, but that Isherwood's commercial and social successes in the 1930s put great strain upon it. In New York, Isherwood found himself again, as he had been after leaving Cambridge, in a sort of intellectual and spiritual crisis, unable to continue the "heartiness" and boastfulness he described above and unable to continue ignoring the reality of looming war. It was at this time that Isherwood experienced a life-changing epiphany about his own belief systems:

> Edward had always said, quite rightly, that my mind was unfitted for abstract ideas; it could only grasp concrete examples, special instances. Anti-Nazism had been possible for me as long as Nazism meant Hitler, Goering and Goebbels, the Gestapo, and the consuls and spies who potentially menaced Heinz on his travels. . . . Suppose I have in my power an army of six million men. I can destroy it by pressing an electric button. The six millionth man is Heinz. Will I press the button? Of course not. (*Diaries* 7)

Sometime before July 23, 1939, Isherwood sent a letter to England declaring himself a pacifist. He apparently addressed the letter to Olive Mangeot but knew perfectly well that Upward would see it, since Olive was Upward's mistress for many years; they remained close even after Upward's marriage to his wife, Hilda. Upward's immediate response to the letter was scathing:

> I have seen your letter to Olive. Shocked isn't the word for what I felt when I read it. And the appalling thing is that for all I know you may feel the same about this letter. I don't think so, however, because you knew beforehand what to expect from me.
>
> I wish I could convey what I want to write by grimaces and inaudibilities instead of by crude statements at a distance.
>
> In brief, I feel much as we once imagined one of us would feel if the other turned Roman Catholic. I can't really believe you've done it. At least, I couldn't at first.
>
> I never expected you to become a Marxist. If you had I should have felt slightly embarrassed. Theoretical Marxism is not in your line. Nor is any other theory or system of opinions in your line. Your strength as a writer has always been and always will be in your ability to see and understand persons and things. If you now start foisting a theory—no matter what theory—on to your writings you will ruin them. I don't think you will do it, and that's what I mainly care about. Commit any other

crimes you like, but if you commit a crime against your writing I will never forgive you. (CI 2455)

Upward followed with a long and well-thought-out discussion detailing his own objections to pacifism and his reasons for opposing fascism at all costs, including the cost of innocent human lives. Isherwood's response to Upward's eight-page letter is not available, but Upward's reaction to it was what permanently reunited the estranged friends even across the Atlantic. Upward displayed an emotional intelligence in his next letter that was not present in most of his rather dry adult writing:

> Your letter would have melted a heart of stone.
>
> I understand all, and I blame only myself—for having momentarily suspected that you had betrayed everything. What you wrote to Olive terrified me partly because it suggested that you were about to join or allow yourself to be made use of by a semi-political movement, and a movement which I believe to be profoundly wrong. But I recognize now that you will never deliberately do that. However, your letter to me still contains hints that you are looking for a way to reform the world, even if only by changing people's hearts. But there is only one way to reform the world, and that is by first of all changing material conditions, and I believe that in your bones you know it. You refuse to plunge into the horrors through which and out of which this way leads. Very well, I respect your refusal. I still have and always will have half a foot in Mortmere. But Mortmere did not try to reform the world. That was its strength. It was wholehearted, not a mushy compromise between the real and the ideal. It rejected the real world outright and created a more satisfying imaginary one. (CI 2456)

Here Upward laid out his objections to pacifism, and, as we will soon see, to yoga: he believed that the world could be changed, but only by "changing material conditions." He had rejected the notion, which Isherwood came to believe in even more strongly, that a personal, internal revolution could have any positive effect on the outside world. But most importantly, Upward had defined the function of Mortmere: to serve as an imaginary world more satisfying than the real one. The irony of Upward's statements became apparent over the next few decades, during which he continually tried to "return to Mortmere" and recapture its inspiration after becoming disillusioned with the "material" aims of the Communist Party. He elaborated in 1939:

Take up yoga by all means, provided you take it up in a Mortmere manner, in the manner for example in which we invented our wonderful card game. But if you start converting other people to it you will vitiate and debase it, just as we debased Mortmere when at Cambridge we made Laily read The Horror in the Tower and The Little Hotel. And worse, if you start converting other people you will be starting a "movement," and a movement—besides vitiating the true quality of Mortmere—must inevitably become mixed up with politics. A movement, no matter whether you intend it to do so or not, must inevitably help or hinder one or other—but never both—of the two main political forces which are in conflict all over the modern world. And Mortmere—or yoga—if it became a movement would tend to help fascism rather than communism.... Let your theory, your doctrine, your philosophy, be a Mortmerish (or Yogish) escapism. You needn't mention it in your writings. In fact you will rigidly avoid mentioning it, and for the same anti-quisb reasons that you avoided mentioning in *Goodbye to Berlin* your motives for going to Germany. (CI 2456)

This turn to pacifism in 1939, so closely tied to Isherwood's permanent departure for America, stands out from the many other sharp turns in Isherwood's life: his dismissal from Cambridge, his departure for Germany, his venture to China, his success with Auden in the London theaters. Isherwood's move to America and his turn to pacifism not only had the unlikely effect of knitting back together his relationship with Edward Upward. It also marked the beginning of a life of semipublic, semiprivate self-reflection that would make possible his best works of fictionalized autobiography. Mortmere, although only a fictional place, served as the imaginative jumping-off point from which Isherwood realized success as a writer and realized the personal fulfillment that eventually came from leaving behind his life in England.[6]

NOTES

1. Edward Upward to Christopher Isherwood, 1985, Christopher Isherwood Papers, CI 2588, Huntington Library, San Marino, California.

2. Christopher Isherwood and Edward Upward, *The Mortmere Stories*, intro. Katherine Bucknell (London: Enitharmon, 1997), 18–19.

3. Christopher Isherwood, *Lions and Shadows* [1938] (London: Vintage Books, 2013), 46.

4. Isherwood seems to have arranged for Upward to meet women or a woman at a London flat during the mid- to late 1920s. Upward would also carry on an affair with Olive Mangeot for several years; they met through Isherwood, who worked as secretary to Olive's husband after leaving Cambridge.

5. Christopher Isherwood, *Diaries*, vol. 1, *1939–1960*, ed. Katherine Bucknell (New York: Vintage, 2011), 4.

6. For more on the complex relationship between Upward and Isherwood, see Benjamin Kohlmann, "Christopher Isherwood and Edward Upward," in *The American Isherwood*, ed. James J. Berg and Chris Freeman (Minneapolis: University of Minnesota Press, 2015).—Eds.

3. "A Faith of Personal Sincerity"

Christopher Isherwood's Debt to the
Individualism of E. M. Forster

"Heinz and I wistfully looked up Malaga on the map and decided
that 'some day' we would 'travel,'" Isherwood writes in a letter from
Berlin to Stephen Spender. "Yes really," he continues, "perhaps even as far
as München."[1] The note, written in November 1932, is consciously silly,
brushing over Spender's decision not to dedicate his *Poems* to Isherwood
after all. It is also unconsciously affecting. Its "some day" came sooner than
supposed, and its longed-for "travel" grew much more urgent, much less
frivolous, than hoped. Isherwood prepared to leave Berlin for good only
five months later, and would spend the next four years with his boyfriend
Heinz Neddermeyer in a state of itinerancy, searching for a place safe from
Nazi conscription.

Of course, Isherwood had been roaming long before he wrote this
letter to Spender, and would continue to roam long after. His correspondence throughout the 1930s, adorned with exotic postmarks, testifies to
this intrepid streak—although he is quick to ridicule any suggestion of
heroism in these expeditions. "We think continually of the great travellers," Isherwood writes on a postcard sent to William Plomer during his
and W. H. Auden's brief stay in Colombo in 1938 (he alludes to Plomer's
own far-reaching travels, but the riff on Spender's "I think continually of
those who were truly great" is also clear).[2] The accompanying specter of
the "great travellers" is made real in China in the figure of Peter Fleming:
"With Fleming to the Front" becomes the title for an "imaginary travel-

book" composed by the pair.³ The actual travel book cowritten during this trip to the Far East, *Journey to a War* (1939), was largely well received, and Isherwood's other books that have at their heart the experiences of a tourist—*Mr Norris Changes Trains, Goodbye to Berlin,* and *Down There on a Visit*—were widely praised. Although no "great traveller" himself, Isherwood naturally inhabited the outsider's perspective.

But Isherwood's travels in 1939 elicited a very different response. Sailing to New York with Auden was an attempt to "escape,"⁴ a "flight,"⁵ and a grave act of "desertion."⁶ They had "abandoned what they consider to be the sinking ship of European democracy" (Connolly 69). Cyril Connolly describes this emigration in ideological terms: the "departure of Auden and Isherwood to America," he writes, "is the most important literary event since the outbreak of the Spanish War" (68). It was a "symptom of the failure of social realism as an aesthetic doctrine" (70).

This was not the first time commentators collated Isherwood's physical restlessness with an ideological one, nor would it be the last. Indeed, the language of travel is often employed in discussions of his life. "Throughout the 1930s," Peter Parker observes, "he frequently gave the impression that he was not so much a fellow traveller as someone who was simply coming along for the ride" (Parker 419). "Fellow traveller" seems a fitting appellation for the itinerant Isherwood; in fact, it is a Trotskyite term— "poputchik" in Russian (meaning, literally, "one who travels the same path")—describing someone with communist sympathies. In a piece in *Horizon* titled "Traveller's Return," Louis MacNeice describes Isherwood and Auden's change of heart since moving to America, using the imagery of travel to illustrate his point:

> "But Auden and Isherwood," people say, "were always preaching the fight against Fascism." So what? I had many conversations with Auden this autumn, and he still is anti-Fascist, but he is no longer in any way a "fellow traveller"; since getting off that particular train, he had decided—as he told me in March 1939—that it was not his job to be a crusader, that this was a thing everyone must decide for himself, but that, in his opinion, most writers falsified their work and themselves when they took a direct part in politics.⁷

Isherwood subscribed to the conception of his journey across the Atlantic as ideological: "I have suddenly realised that I am a pacifist, pure and simple," he writes home from New York City in April 1939.[8] In a later letter to Edward Upward, he paints his new position with a darker palette. "What remains to me but pacifism of some kind? And what revolution can I attempt to promote but a revolution inside myself?" he asks. "All I can tell you is, I can see no other way out of my little personal valley of despair. I hear behind me the cries of Forster, frankly lost in the desert . . . and I feel: No. I am not going back."[9]

Isherwood would soon make the journey across America to California. Despite the home he found for himself in Los Angeles and the comfort he would take in Vedanta, the accusations of ideological restlessness that had haunted him in Europe in the 1930s would continue to trouble him in the 1940s. For many, this—his first full decade in the United States—seems to embody the height of his political and personal lostness.[10]

And yet, notwithstanding this impression of lostness and ideological itinerancy, there is a consistent thread to Isherwood's thoughts and actions in this period and beyond which deserves a second look. This thread—a Forsterian strain of individualism—is made especially obvious in a letter he wrote at the close of his lost decade, in April 1949.

The Cultural and Scientific Conference for World Peace, organized by the so-called National Council of the Arts, Sciences and Professions, was to be held in March 1949 at the Waldorf Astoria in New York City. In a climate of growing political tension between the Soviet Union and the United States, the conference was a bid, in Arthur Miller's words, for "the piano players, composers, playwrights and anthropologists" to "appeal over the bureaucracies' head for common sense."[11] Numbered among its supporters were such luminaries as Albert Einstein, Norman Mailer, Charlie Chaplin, Thomas Mann, Clifford Odets, Aaron Copland, Nicolas Nabokov, and Dmitri Shostakovich. The two-day conference was steeped in controversy, with protestors packed outside the Waldorf Astoria's entrance for its entirety—and not without reason. The violence of Stalin's regime, embodied in the purges and trials he had conducted throughout the 1930s and '40s, was no secret to Western intelligentsia. Indeed, many deemed this conference to be an endorsement of the Stalinist system.

In *The Noise of Time,* his recent fictionalized account of Shostakovich's participation in the conference, Julian Barnes makes vivid the composer's predicament:

[Shostakovich] knew, when he had agreed to attend the Cultural and Scientific Congress for World Peace, that he had no choice. He also suspected that he might be displayed as a figurehead, a representative of Soviet values. He had expected some Americans to be welcoming, others to be hostile. . . . All this was foreseeable. What he had not prepared himself for was that New York would turn out to be a place of the purest humiliation, and of moral shame.[12]

Shostakovich's "purest humiliation" came at the hands of Nabokov, who asked him if he "personally subscribe[d] to the banning from Soviet concert halls the works of Hindemith, Schoenberg and Stravinsky" (Barnes 102).[13] In perhaps the most distressing moment of Barnes's novel, Shostakovich admits that he did, in spite of the "love and reverence" he felt for Stravinsky (132).

Stravinsky had had the foresight not to attend the conference, for obvious reasons. In a "snubbing and well-publicised telegram" (64) sent to Olin Downes, music critic for the *New York Times,* he explains that his absence was a matter of principle: "Regret not to be able to join welcomers of Soviet artists coming to this country. But all my ethic and esthetic convictions oppose such gesture."[14] Despite his sponsorship, Einstein would subsequently voice doubts about the conference, noting in a letter of April 7, 1949, that

> from what I have observed concerning the recent congress in New York, I have the strong impression that this kind of procedure does not really serve the cause of international understanding. The reason is simply that it is more or less a Soviet enterprise and everything is managed accordingly.[15]

And so to Isherwood, who, on the same day, was writing a letter of his own, this time to the Southern Californian chapter of the National Council of the Arts, Sciences and Professions, which appeared to have been planning a local conference to mirror the one taking place in New York. Isherwood declined the invitation to attend, putting forward his reasons in a letter that was, as he notes in his diary upon revisiting the episode, "very well constructed," made "telling points," and had a "main accusation [that] is really unanswerable" (*Lost Years* 189).

This letter was doubly preserved by Isherwood: first, in his personal collection of papers, and second, in the pages he devotes to its composition in *Lost Years*, his reconstructed diary. Although it was a private piece of correspondence, Isherwood intimates near the letter's close that he will publish it if "somebody—on either side of this dispute—takes the trouble to misquote me." He quotes from the letter at length in his diary:

> Strict pacifism is total and neutral. It condemns all use of armed force, both in foreign and domestic politics, and it seeks to find an alternative, non-violent approach to the world's social and political problems. You do not pretend to be total pacifists, and I'm not going to try to convert you to that position. What I am now concerned with is your neutrality. . . .
>
> I am . . . basing my opinion . . . on your own leaflet, your "call" to the Conference. . . . [A] whole paragraph is devoted to Washington's misdeeds and mistakes. I agree with much of what is said in this paragraph. But where is the paragraph which ought, in fairness, to follow it—the paragraph dealing with the misdeeds and mistakes of Moscow? You imply—or seem to me to imply—that the "cold war" (and hence the "hot war" which will probably follow it) must be blamed entirely on the U.S. government. This is simply not true.
>
> There is, of course, the obligation of hosts to be courteous. If we invite guests from overseas, we should not greet them with accusations. We should be humble and dwell most upon our own shortcomings. . . . Nevertheless, I must suggest that such politeness hopelessly confuses the issue. You dissociate yourselves from the aggressive and militaristic aims of your own Government and yet, by refraining from criticism of Soviet militarism and aggression, you imply that your guests are associated with it and that, therefore, you mustn't hurt their feelings. Isn't this the very opposite of courtesy. Isn't it, in fact, an accusation?
>
> A well-founded accusation, I fear. Consider the facts. The greatest police-state on earth permits some of its prominent citizens to come over to this country and take part in a peace conference. Such a conference implies—or ought to imply—a condemnation of all the governments whose nationals are involved; since these governments have failed to establish peace. . . . If these Russian delegates had come with genuinely neutral, pacifistic aims, they would be condemning Soviet militarism. Their lives would be in danger. They could never return to their own country. . . .
>
> I am forced to believe that the Russian delegates were permitted to come to this country because the Soviet Government intends to

exploit . . . your whole Conference for propaganda purposes. I believe that your Conference, despite its admirable intentions, will be used as a weapon in the cold war. Worse still, I fear that its findings and resolutions . . . will inspire militarists within the Soviet Union with the most dangerous confidence that the intelligentsia of the United States are actually on their side; that the cold war is already half-won and should therefore be pressed to the utmost. . . .

I hope I am wrong about all this. But that is how I see things at the moment—and, believe me, I have thought this matter over very carefully. It isn't pleasant to find myself disagreeing, even temporarily, with men and women I deeply respect.[16]

There are several notable Isherwoodian themes here, the most obvious being his concern for the Russian delegates and his understanding of their role in the "greatest police-state on earth."[17] A decade earlier, he observed to Upward that "theories have never been in my line. People are the volumes in my library."[18] His sympathy with people rather than systems had led to the monumental success of *Goodbye to Berlin,* which examined the impact of Nazism at street level. His interest in the organizers of the conference is also illuminating, particularly in the language of duty he uses ("the obligation of hosts to be courteous"; "we should not greet them with accusations"; "we should be humble"), which will be explored later in this essay. Finally, the influence of Forster on this letter is marked and testifies to Isherwood's long-standing debt to the values by which Forster lived.

Isherwood's pacifism was not that of Forster. The pacifist ideas Isherwood brought with him to California were enriched by his commitment to Vedanta, a religious conviction Forster could not comprehend ("What I don't follow is your belief that when you are in trouble . . . God will help you," Forster writes to Isherwood in 1943. "You may be right, of course, but I can't imagine the belief").[19] Forster, on the other hand, "to the extent that he was a pacifist, was so by instinct rather than settled conviction," according to P. N. Furbank.[20] It is not, therefore, in the letter's pacifist argument that Isherwood shows the influence of Forster but rather in the writing and sending of the letter.

On January 11 of the same year, 1949, the BBC broadcast a talk by Forster titled "I Speak for Myself." "I try to speak for myself," Forster says at the start. "It is impossible to speak for someone else—one cannot get inside another person's skin—and it is dangerous to speak on behalf of a group or community, though most of us do that at times. A man is only safe and straight when he realises he is an individual and speaks for himself."[21]

He goes on to admit that while the world "was always difficult," it "can never have been so full of movements as it is today—so full of appeals to the individual to sink his individuality and allow some organisation or movement to speak for him" (402). In Forster's view, this would be "a dereliction of duty." The affinities between the action recommended here and Isherwood's private dissociation from the Southern Californian Peace Conference are obvious. Although it is unlikely that Isherwood would have read Forster's talk by the time he wrote his letter (his mother had sent a transcript of a previous lecture by Forster; it is unclear whether she did so for this one),[22] this kind of individualism was not a new refrain for Forster. Indeed, he had voiced a similar sentiment to Isherwood as early as February 1934: "All that I can do is to work out a private ethic which, in the outbreak of a war, might be helpful to me. The individual is more than ever the goods. . . . I am O.K. personally, as we call it."[23] As his recent biographer Wendy Moffat puts it, "*Personally* was the watchword" (242).

In his BBC lecture, Forster frames his appeal in terms with which both men would have been familiar. In speaking for himself, Forster says a man is "fulfilling the purpose for which he was born into this troublesome and difficult world."[24] His emphasis on "duty" and "purpose" sounds decidedly dharmic: a concept Forster had addressed in "Hymn Before Action," his commentary on the Bhagavad Gita, published in *Abinger Harvest* in 1936.

The notion of dharma had been preoccupying Isherwood since the First World War (partly as a result of his efforts with Swami Prabhavananda to translate the Gita), but he first encountered it in "Hymn Before Action"; he had reviewed *Abinger Harvest* in March 1936. In 1944, he puzzles over the question of duty in a letter to Spender:

> Krishna says we all have to do our duty—"the duty imposed by our nature"—but how are we to find out what that duty is? Arjuna belonged to the warrior-caste, he had got his people in the war, and his duty was as plain as Churchill's. But for most people, at any given moment, "duty" isn't so clear.[25]

His allusion to Churchill is interesting. Churchill, for Isherwood, seems continually to represent an example of positive dharmic fulfillment. As early as November 1936, while noting that the "idea of me as a platform speaker with dynamic gestures raises terrible dream-pictures and temptations," he writes that

> as Winston Churchill said as he left for London just before the beginning of the battle of Arras: "My heart was with my old regiment, but my duty sternly called me elsewhere." I shall go to Mexico, or wherever it is, and salve my conscience by getting involved to the fullest possible extent.[26]

Despite his oblique admiration for Churchill, Isherwood is clear on the difference between their temperaments ("Come off it—you're not Hitler or Churchill. Nobody called on you to make a statement," he observes in his diary on January 1, 1941).[27] He remained uneasy with propagandizing, admitting in an earlier diary entry that "the whole essence of my 'position' is not to make statements. I am the only silent member of a community of all-too-noisy prophets" (*Diaries* 55).

It would be a shock, then, when Forster appeared to become one of these "all-too-noisy prophets." In 1940, Forster published his pro-war pamphlet *Nordic Twilight*, an unabashed piece of propaganda. Gravely disappointed, Isherwood wrote in his diary that "Churchill, from his point of view, is absolutely right when he says [that life would be worse under the Nazis]. . . . But from Morgan, our philosopher, we expect something more" (136).

Isherwood perceived Forster to have betrayed his individualism through an act of propaganda, confusing his personal dharma as philosopher with that of Churchill as politician. But how did Isherwood envisage his own duties—not as a propagandist or politician, but as a writer, a pacifist, and a homosexual? And how did he square these duties with the Forsterian need for individualism and speaking for oneself? In a lecture delivered in the 1960s, which Isherwood called "A Personal Statement," he considered the duty of the writer: "In discussing this question of the writer's dharma, I've found myself again and again using the convenient term: 'the outsider.'" He goes on to observe that "when a writer writes, he writes for an *x* number of individuals—maybe for millions and millions. But he writes for each individual as an individual. This is, I believe, one of the differences between art and propaganda."[28]

This emphasis on individual communication informs the discreet acts of protest Isherwood undertook in his correspondence, illustrated in his letter of April 1949. His archive gives us a number of other examples of this movement toward a kind of private activism, but two further letters, both held at the Huntington Library, are particularly striking. The first was sent in response to a letter by one Martin S. Curtler from Massachusetts, published in June 1949 in the *Saturday Review of Literature*. The columns in that journal, Curtler observes, "have not up to now aired the problem of another minority which suffers from its position in society in somewhat the same way as the Jews and Negroes. I refer to homosexuals."[29] In his own letter to Curtler, Isherwood describes how he was "moved to write and tell you how much I appreciated the humanity and good sense of your letter." He goes on to mention the "prejudice of the average heterosexual against homosexuals," and concludes by noting that "every time the word 'homosexual' (rather than 'pervert,' 'moral degenerate,' etc) appears in print, that is a tiny step forward."[30]

Another letter, addressed to "Mr President," was sent in April 1965 to Lyndon Johnson at the White House. "I feel that I ought not to remain silent," Isherwood writes—the language of duty impressing itself upon him once again—"so I am sending you this private letter. It is a protest against our military presence in Vietnam but also an expression of sympathy for you and faith in your goodwill at this time of crisis."[31] This personal appeal, and Isherwood's decision not to "sign open letters" attacking the president's policy in Vietnam, further attests to his need to make his protest known without resorting to public broadcast. In doing so, he stays faithful to the advice put forward by Krishna in the Gita: "You have the right to work, but for the work's sake only. You have no right to the fruits of work. Desire for the fruits of work must never be your motive in working."[32] Isherwood first encountered this instruction in Forster's summary in "Hymn Before Action": "The saint may renounce action, but the soldier, the citizen, the practical man generally—they should renounce, not action, but its fruits. It is wrong for them to be idle; it is equally wrong to desire a reward for industry."[33]

For Isherwood, the recognition that comes with speaking publicly is the perceived "reward," the deliciousness of the "terrible dream-pictures and temptations" he described, albeit facetiously, to Spender in 1936. Despite Krishna's advice and Forster's moral scrutiny, however, he was not entirely successful in subduing his desire for recognition. "My greatest vice: an increasing, really horrible vanity," he comments in his diary on March 4, 1952. "I'm eaten up with it" (*Diaries* 442).

The extent of Forster's influence on Isherwood is already well documented. In her introduction to *Lost Years*, Katherine Bucknell notes that "it was Forster's moral character which made Isherwood feel the need to judge himself. Isherwood writes in the reconstructed diary that 'he thought of Forster as a great writer and as a particular master'" (xxviii). Such a master, in fact, that he determined to publish a memoir of Swami with one of Forster. The resulting book "would be a Tale of Two Gurus, as it were" (xxviii). What elevated Forster to the position of "guru" in Isherwood's eyes? It was the fact, in Zadie Smith's words, that he "made a faith of personal sincerity and a career of disingenuousness."[34] ("You are incapable of telling a lie," Isherwood wrote to Forster in 1944.)[35] In his actions, particularly in moments of unpublicized activism, Isherwood demonstrates the hold Forster's ethical system, his "faith of personal sincerity," had over him.

Isherwood's debt to the individualism communicated to him through Forster's essays, lectures, and letters endured throughout his life. It fed into his fixed belief in pacifism and complemented his understanding of dharma. His relationship with Forster was to be the overture to his embrace of Vedanta and the "virtue" of "truth-telling" he discovered in that religion.[36] Although restless at times, and often conflicted, Isherwood seemed constantly to value this debt, disproving accusations of his ideological itinerancy in doing so. His postwar decades were founded on a bedrock of Forsterian sincerity, a basis of which he was entirely aware: Forster, he asserts, "was a true and beloved father figure in my life."[37]

NOTES

1. Christopher Isherwood to Stephen Spender, November 14, 1932, MS. Spender 53, Bodleian Library, University of Oxford.

2. Christopher Isherwood to William Plomer, postcard, February 3, 1938, Plomer MSS, PLO/109, Archives and Special Collections, Durham University Library.

3. W. H. Auden and Christopher Isherwood, *Journey to a War* (London: Faber & Faber, 1939), 214.

4. Stephen Spender, "Letter to a Colleague in America," *New Statesman and Nation*, November 16, 1940, 490.

5. Cyril Connolly, "Comment," *Horizon,* February 1940, 70.

6. Peter Parker, *Isherwood* (London: Picador, 2004), 420.

7. Louis MacNeice, "Traveller's Return," *Horizon,* February 1941, 113–14.

8. Isherwood to Spender, April 28, 1939, MS. Spender 53, Bodleian Library, Oxford.

9. Christopher Isherwood to Edward Upward, August 6, 1939, Edward Upward Papers, Add MS 72688, British Library.

10. Isherwood's "lostness" in this period is a main theme of *Lost Years,* a diary that Katherine Bucknell points out in her introduction he "reconstructed" with the intention "to recapture a lost period following World War II when he had all but abandoned his lifelong habit of keeping a diary." *Lost Years: A Memoir, 1945–1951,* ed. Katherine Bucknell (London: Vintage Books, 2001), vii.

11. Martin Gottfried, *Arthur Miller: His Life and Work* (Cambridge, Mass.: Da Capo Press, 2003), 159.

12. Julian Barnes, *The Noise of Time* (London: Jonathan Cape, 2016), 95.

13. Composer and music lecturer Nicolas Nabokov was born in the Russian town of Lubcza in 1903 and became a U.S. citizen in 1939. He would go on to become secretary-general of the Congress of Cultural Freedom; in 1966, the CCF was exposed to have been funded by the CIA.

14. Robert Craft, ed., *Stravinsky: Selected Correspondence,* vol. 1 (London: Faber & Faber, 1982), 358.

15. David E. Rowe and Robert Schulmann, *Einstein on Politics* (Princeton, N.J.: Princeton University Press, 2007), 481–82.

16. Christopher Isherwood Papers, CI 1-4085, Huntington Library, San Marino, California. [After discussing this letter in his diary, Isherwood reflects on how much the situation was complicated by the Senator Joseph McCarthy–led Red Scare in U.S. politics at the time. See *Lost Years* (189–90), for more on this murky issue. —Eds.]

17. Isherwood knew too well the actions of this "police-state." In *Christopher and His Kind,* he makes clear that his brief period of "fellow travelling" was curtailed by the decision of Stalin's government to make "all homosexual acts punishable by heavy prison sentences" (London: Vintage Books, 2012), 346. Writing of his past self in the third person, he continues: "He now realized he must dissociate himself from the Communists, even as a fellow traveler. . . . He must never again give way to embarrassment, never deny the rights of his tribe . . . never think of sacrificing himself masochistically on the altar of that false god of the totalitarians, the Greatest Good of the Greatest Number—whose priests are alone empowered to decide what 'good' is" (346).

18. Isherwood to Upward, August 6, 1939, Edward Upward Papers, Add MS 72688, British Library.

19. Richard E. Zeikowitz, ed., *Letters between Forster and Isherwood on Homosexuality and Literature* (New York: Palgrave Macmillan, 2008), 118.

20. P. N. Furbank, *Forster: A Life*, vol. 2 (London: Secker & Warburg, 1978), 1.

21. Mary Lago, Linda K. Hughes, and Elizabeth MacLeod Walls, eds., *The BBC Talks of E. M. Forster, 1929–1969: A Selected Edition* (Columbia: University of Missouri Press, 2008), 401–2.

22. Christopher Isherwood to Kathleen Isherwood, April 20, 1946, thanking his mother for sending "the Forster lecture," Christopher Isherwood's Letters to His Family, GEN MSS 345, Beinecke Rare Book and Manuscript Library, Yale University.

23. Wendy Moffat, *E. M. Forster: A New Life* (London: Bloomsbury, 2011), 241.

24. Lago, Hughes, and MacLeod Walls, *BBC Talks of E. M. Forster*, 402.

25. Isherwood to Spender, March 20, 1944, MS. Spender 53, Bodleian Library, Oxford.

26. Isherwood to Spender, November 15, 1936, MS. Spender 53, Bodleian Library.

27. Christopher Isherwood, *Diaries*, vol. 1, *1939–1960*, ed. Katherine Bucknell (London: Vintage Books, 2011), 132.

28. Christopher Isherwood, "A Personal Statement," https://archive.org/details/a-personal-statement-christopher-isherwood.aN3liu.popuparchive.org, accessed February 4, 2017. [A version of this talk is printed in James Berg, ed., *Isherwood on Writing* (Minneapolis: University of Minnesota Press, 2007), 243–44.—Eds.]

29. Martin S. Curtler, "Homosexual Minority," *Saturday Review of Literature*, June 4, 1949, 25.

30. Isherwood Papers, CI 1–4085, Huntington Library.

31. Isherwood Papers, letter of April 5, 1965.

32. *Bhagavad Gita: Song of God*, trans. Christopher Isherwood and Swami Prabhavananda (Hollywood: Vedanta Press, 1944), 46.

33. E. M. Forster, "Hymn Before Action," *Abinger Harvest* (London: Edward Arnold, 1936), 333.

34. Zadie Smith, *Changing My Mind: Occasional Essays* (London: Hamish Hamilton, 2009), 14.

35. Zeikowitz, *Letters between Forster and Isherwood*, 139.

36. Katherine Bucknell, "Why Isherwood Stopped Writing Fiction," *On Modern British Fiction*, ed. Zachary Leader (Oxford: Oxford University Press, 2002), 146.

37. Daniel Halpern, "A Conversation with Christopher Isherwood," *Antaeus*, no. 13–14 (Spring/Summer 1974): 370.

4. The Archival "I"

Forster, Isherwood, and the Future of Queer Biography

You shall not look through my eyes either, nor take things from me,
You shall listen to all sides and filter them from your self.
—WALT WHITMAN, *SONG OF MYSELF*

GENERATIONAL ENCOUNTERS

The first meeting between the British novelists E. M. Forster and Christopher Isherwood in the early 1930s marks a seminal moment in gay literary history. I describe it in my biography of Forster:

> When Christopher first met Morgan [Forster] . . . he was already yearning to be his "disciple." Here was a gay mentor, a novelist who had found "the key to the whole art of writing." Christopher admired Morgan's technical skill, but he was awed by his humility. He reminded Christopher of a Zen master. . . . They met in the [London] flat that Morgan had rented . . . as an occasional escape from the suburban surveillance of his mother. . . . Christopher was so bowled over that he barely recalled their conversation. But the pleasurable sense of being invited into a circle of the elect was palpable.[1]

Christopher left the flat clutching Forster's contraband copy of T. E. Lawrence's *Seven Pillars of Wisdom*. At their second meeting six months later, "in a gesture that became a ritual of intimacy," Morgan showed Christopher the typescript of his unpublished and to him "unpublishable" gay novel *Maurice* (15). Christopher was touched by reading this story of committed love between two men—and the imperative of its happy ending. He was

Left to right: E. M. Forster, Christopher Isherwood, Jean Delaite, and Gerald Hamilton, near Brussels, 1937. Courtesy of Don Bachardy.

moved, too, by Forster's bravery in writing the novel, that the power of his imagination could take root in arid Edwardian England. "The wonder was Forster himself," Isherwood wrote four decades later in *Christopher and His Kind*, "imprisoned within the jungle of pre-war prejudice putting those unthinkable thoughts into words" (126).

Even at the time, Isherwood recognized the moment's proleptic power. To become a "disciple," Isherwood knew, was to undergo a psychic transition knitting oneself into the great chain of queer kinship. Isherwood had traveled from Germany to England for a paternal blessing from Forster, a connection not only to these forbidden books but a temporal transition to the moment when the "pioneer heroes" of gay history who lived openly, like the Victorian sexual guru Edward Carpenter and his working-class partner George Merrill, similarly inspired Forster in the generation before. To use Armistead Maupin's figuration quoted in Freeman and Berg's introduction to this volume, Isherwood sought out the "tribal elder for [his] new breed of open queers." As a young man, Forster had approached Carpenter as a "saviour," he tells us in his author's note to *Maurice*.[2]

These generative, intergenerational encounters were transformative rather than strictly reproductive. *Maurice* was conceived when the "spark" of a queer touch awakened a "creative spring": "George Merrill touched my backside—gently and just above the buttocks. . . . The sensation was unusual and I still remember it. . . . It seemed to go straight through the small of my back into my ideas, without involving my thoughts" (215). Forster's intimacy with Isherwood adopted the currency of books and manuscripts furtively passed from hand to hand rather than a sexual spark. But more deeply both of these generational encounters shared a mythic quality of spiritual recognition, an epistemology of awakening to what in some sense you already know. For Isherwood, steeped in Vedanta, the concept of knowledge that is not formed cerebrally was amenable. It opened new narrative possibilities to what Robert Caserio calls Isherwood's "liberatory, as yet unrealized visions" and the "alternate possibilities" of queer narrative forms.[3] Queer literary kinship animated both the brain and heart of the fatherless Christopher: just as Christopher Isherwood is Armistead Maupin's "logical grandfather," so Forster and Carpenter, and indeed Carpenter's mentor Walt Whitman, became in an instant Isherwood's queer forefathers.[4]

The friendship between Forster and Isherwood gains mythic potency because we know it has a *future* and it has ties to a queer past. Looking backward, readers of queer history stand in a rewarding temporal location to appreciate the meaning of this chain of influence. (So queer literary history affords transitional identities—time travel and the transformation from reader to author and back.) In a satisfying inversion of generations, Isherwood the child became father to Forster the man by shepherding the dream of *Maurice*'s coming out for forty-seven years. The letters between the writers, many of them in the archive at the Huntington Library, repeat a pattern. In 1938, 1948, again in 1952, Forster demurred, "ashamed at shirking publication" but fearful that coming out by publishing the novel would hurt those he loved—first his mother, then his lover the policeman Bob Buckingham, and Buckingham's wife, May.[5] For his part, Isherwood continually encouraged publication. Eventually, Forster, quite literally imagining an afterlife, agreed to posthumous publication, and arranged for Isherwood to enact his plan. A teenager when Oscar Wilde was sent to prison for "gross indecency," Forster died the year after the Stonewall riots. *Maurice* was published the following year, in 1971.

Isherwood's editorial enterprise in turn contributed to Forster's renewed composition and revision of the *Maurice* manuscript. These twinned histories are suspended in dialogic equipoise, like the encircling strands of a double helix. As Philip Gardner demonstrates in his careful textual histories, this tension proved fruitful to the novel.[6] Goaded by Isherwood to rethink *Maurice,* Forster returned to the manuscript again and again, revising and polishing, inserting new sex scenes, always staying true to the essential structure—that Maurice Hall and his lover, Alec Scudder, would stay together and be happy, in spite of it all. And since its posthumous publication, *Maurice* has become recognized as the generative seed for so much great gay writing that followed.

This sounds very romantic. The truth was, to the younger man's ear on first reading, Forster's writing about sex in *Maurice* sounded antique and prudish. There were good reasons for this. The first version of *Maurice* was drafted during the Great War and set in a nebulous Edwardian world untouched by that impending cataclysm. When Forster wrote the novel, he burned with sexual desire, but Merrill's brief comradely touch was the sum of his sexual contact with another human being. Both the sex and the possibility of queer intimacy were constructed almost wholly out of Morgan's yearning imagination. No wonder he elided the mechanics of actual lovemaking in the novel. When he read the scene where Maurice announces that he's slept with Alec, Isherwood "grimaced and wriggled his toes with embarrassment" (*Christopher and His Kind* 126). But the younger man was ready to forgive the solecisms and euphemisms in *Maurice* precisely because they sprang from Morgan's powerful belief in a happy queer future.

For his part, Forster's greatest fear and vulnerability in showing the manuscript to his younger friend were that it would seem paralyzingly *uncool.* Isherwood recounted this scene with pathos and generosity more than forty years later:

> This time the Pupil was being asked by the Master, quite humbly, how *Maurice* appeared to a member of the thirties generation. "Does it date?" Forster was asking. To which Christopher, I am proud to say, replied, "Why *shouldn't* it date?" (126)

This was precisely the right question. In the moment, it engendered a perfect, human response. Forster leaned forward, "his eyes brimming with tears," and kissed Isherwood on the cheek (126). The generosity of the question cemented their friendship for life.

THE ARCHIVAL I

"Why *shouldn't* it date?" was a tender question. But it was also a prophetic one. It was the right question to reassure Forster; it was also the right question for queer literary history. Isherwood understands time. Things *should* date. Isherwood's insistence on temporality opens new paths for the future of queer history. Insisting on the meaning of queer ideas *in time* helps us resist an uncritical progressive attitude: it does *not always get better,* much as we hope to encourage the young.[7] Isherwood's question demands that we do our homework and situate the experience of sexual minorities in the context of the world in which they lived. His turn to the new world and a new sexual homeland sharpened this idea for Isherwood. Thinking about this question redirects our attention away from the stylistic contrasts between these writers (the closeted, timid Forster versus the sexually liberated Isherwood; Forster's warm tone versus Isherwood's cool) that have become a staple reading of their relations. It invites us, rather, to attend to the bedrock fact of their collaborative work as custodians of queer history. Both writers spent lifelong energy recording and preserving the truth of queer lives. They developed a complex subject position to undertake this task: experimental, self-aware, generically fluid, open to readers in a distant future. I call this subject position the *Archival I.*

To parse a few key aspects of what marks the Archival I requires a reconsideration of the narrative of the birth of *Maurice.* Forster's and Isherwood's queer sensibility depends on two interlinking elements: the concept of the Archive—the *what* and *how* evidence of queer history is preserved—and the "I"—the *who,* the visionary Self that perceives, records, and has the authority to interpret that history. I have pieced together what sounds like a coherent narrative of the birth of these writers' friendship and collaboration. But in fact this story comes to us as pastiche, from reams of papers scattered in archives from northern England to Los Angeles. It's easy to elide the fact that we know the story of the birth of *Maurice* only because it was carefully preserved, reported, and repeatedly examined in writing by both men. My particular scholarly contribution has been to show how painstakingly Forster sought to preserve the record of his sexuality, and how central it was to what he viewed as his life's story. It's important to acknowledge how fractured and vulnerable the queer archive continues to be.

Another queer in transit, the theorist and writer Neil Bartlett, argues that the construction of queer literary history is intertwined with the construction of gay identity, that inquiry and identity necessarily shape each other.[8] Bartlett is the author of the remarkable memoir-meditation on his own youthful search for the generative spark—*Who Was That Man? A Present for Mr Oscar Wilde*. Adrift from sources of queer kinship, Bartlett came to London in the 1980s searching for evidence of the queer past. At that time, all books pertaining to gay history, including J. A. (John Addington) Symonds's writing, were classified as obscene and kept in a locked cabinet in the British Library. Would-be readers were obliged to offer bona fides to consult the works. Bartlett notes:

> The place I started looking for my story was not the city, but the library. . . . I pursued texts with the dogged energy I usually reserve for cruising; I became excited by the smallest hints; I scrutinized every gesture for significance. . . . I went to the most unlikely places.[9]

Depicting the British Library with a queer eye—it is indeed an unlikely place for cruising—Bartlett turns the tables on what might have been a humiliating scene.

Bartlett's hunger for a legible past is linked slyly to more corporeal desires. Cruising and paying close attention to the queer archive are interwoven avenues of inquiry, and both lead to the discovery of a queer Self. Bartlett's search for his queer story has two modes: looking (cruising) and *sharing the vulnerability of being seen to be looking*. He understands that the social conditions of gay desire—whether for history or sex or love—mean that the act of discovery is always an act of risk taking. Bartlett writes that, in searching for the gay past, "we are always held between ignorance and exposure" (99). This suspended place—"between ignorance and exposure"—in Bartlett corresponds to ways of reading and knowing.

To "read" is to risk making connections. In a homophobic world, to be seen reading, or to share secret readings, courts the danger of being *seen to be looking*. These are concrete dangers in safety for a queer man looking for an archive of experience. As Bartlett notes, the very mechanism of self-protection isolates him from seeking others of his kind and, occasionally, even from himself. So, incompleteness, both singular and collective, amplifies and reinforces itself. Bartlett's "we" can't be "ourselves" without a gay culture, because we can't recognize "ourselves"; and "we" are always suspended between being alone and finding a community. The shared moment of risk when Forster showed Isherwood the *Maurice* manuscript is an instantiation of the promise and peril of this scene of queer recognition.[10]

Bartlett's subject—the gay man trolling for a past—is a reader locked in a paradox of knowing too little and too much. The perceived "safety" of incomplete or historically undercontextualized reading obfuscates the collective activity of gay culture and *writes* erasure. That is why queer writers and scholars of queer history must keep discovering literary history over and over again: suspended between overdetermination and underdetermination, the gay past is always simultaneously being forgotten and rediscovered. And the record of this past, Bartlett argues, will always exist in the form of a "scrapbook," fractured and fragile: "The scrapbook is the true form of our history, because it records what we remember, and embodies in its omissions both how we remember and how we forget our lives" (99). Piecing together the scrapbook is an archival act, at once political and creative.

Christopher Isherwood knows this and enacts this constant transition into queer being into his writing. Think about how often he constructs queer lives in the form of the scrapbook—the recording of history in fragments of letters and diaries, the fractured shape of the narrative of *Down There on a Visit,* most explicitly in the generic mosaic of *Christopher and His Kind.* Even when his object is to piece together the bits of evidence of queer life, Isherwood reminds readers of their contingent, fragile nature. He painstakingly builds an account of an "imperfectly patched up quarrel" between himself and Stephen Spender, which is anticlimactically robbed of its dénouement:

> "I am an entirely impossible character [he writes to Spender]; unstable,
> ill-natured, petty and selfish. . . . I have the virtues of my defects. But I
> can't imagine that I ever could or should be able to live intimately with
> an equal for long." . . . Christopher may have explained himself further;
> the next page of the letter is missing. (*Christopher and His Kind* 114–15)

For Isherwood, as for Bartlett, the evidence of the queer archive cannot be separated from the search for that evidence: subject and the subjectivity are intertwined, like a second double helix. This insight returns us to the creation of *Maurice.*

The story of the long creation of *Maurice* is inextricably interwoven into Isherwood's many accounts of the story. Isherwood repeatedly examined and revised accounts of the origin of his friendship with E. M. Forster over many years and in many forms. A version of it appears circa 1938 in *Lions and Shadows*, his first autobiography; in 1962 in the fractured autobiographical novel *Down There on a Visit*; in the 1976 memoir *Christopher and His Kind*; in dairies and letters, and—I would argue—in *A Single Man*, his 1964 masterpiece. This is only a partial account of Isherwood's fragments. We should also add Richard Zeikowitz's fine 2008 edition of the full correspondence of the two writers on "homosexuality and literature."[11] These fragments do not supplant each other. In queer scholarship of this sort, new instantiations are not "corrections."

So far, I've been considering the *form of the archive*. But we need to attend to the other strand of this oscillating thread, the "I" who explores it, the Archival I suspended in time, in search of the generative spark that is being created by the act of exploring. Some scholars have misread Isherwood's oeuvre as a form of narcissism. But the singularity of his Archival I is better understood as the proper tool to both interpret and embody the epistemology of the queer fragmented archive. This Archival I also has queer literary ancestors. I'll begin by quoting from James J. Berg's archival project, the 2007 collection *Isherwood on Writing*. In "A Last Lecture," Isherwood described the task of the writer beautifully and simply: "to follow his experience, to try to understand what it means, to try not to lie to himself about its meaning, and that is all."[12] This troika places Isherwood squarely in the tradition of his spiritual grandfather, Walt Whitman.[13] Note the temporal and ethical arc of this process of discovery: to follow his experience (to be in the present with eyes open), to try to understand what it *means* (to look at the past from the perspective of a later time), and to try not to lie about its meaning (to resist mythmaking or self-serving in the act of recording). Here is the Archival I at work. Because the Archival I exists in time, it can be its own interlocutor—both Whitman's "you" and Whitman's "me":[14]

> You shall not look through my eyes either, nor take things from me,
> You shall listen to all sides and filter them from your self. (Walt Whitman, *Song of Myself*)

"Who Was That Man?" is a question about identity formation in and shaped by time, a question Isherwood continually poses in his fiction and nonfiction. It is a question for an individual, as well as a question about another. This split can occur in the same person over time. Who among us has not searched for the strange self in a childhood photo? Who was that I? For Isherwood, the self can be simultaneously conscious and aware that it must compose itself, like an archive, into a coherent state. The beginning of *A Single Man* is a brilliant demonstration of this process:

> Obediently, it washes, shaves, brushes its hair, for it accepts its responsibilities. . . . It knows what is expected of it. . . . [He] has become already more or less George—though still not the whole George they demand and are prepared to recognize. (11)

As "it" coalesces into "George," as George wakens and faces his day, the self emerges both as series of temporal layers (embedded in time) and as a singular man fixed in a moment who sees himself—in the mirror—from the outside, as others see him:

> Staring and staring into the mirror, it sees many faces within its face— the face of the child, the boy, the young man, the not-so-young man—all present still, preserved like fossils on superimposed layers, and, like fossils, dead. Their message to this live dying creature is: Look at us—we have died—what is there to be afraid of? (10)

Here Isherwood creates a genuinely illuminating metaphor, the fossil self. Nothing *dates* like being a fossil. Accreted in sedimentary layers, the queer self is simultaneously lost and preserved. This sedimentary self is both the subject and the method in Isherwood's last meditation on his friendship with Forster. Isherwood's self becomes "Christopher" in *Christopher and His Kind,* the almost-alienated younger self whose motives and thoughts are parsed from the distance of decades later. Isherwood described this distancing process among his "selves" in different contexts, but it is perhaps best encapsulated in a 1977 conversation with Studs Terkel, who remarks about the memoir, "You are looking at yourself now and saying here is the real Christopher Isherwood, not the one you read about earlier. In a sense you are still outside looking at yourself." Isherwood expands on Terkel's assertion: "There are actually three, aren't there? There's the author, now, seventy-two; there's the character who appears in *The Berlin Stories,* in his thirties, and there's also the real Christopher—not as he's presented in *The Berlin Stories*—in his thirties. Those are three quite different people."[15]

Forster also playfully invokes the divided Archival "I." Less well known because of its peculiar (non)publication history—but well before Isherwood's temporal splitting of the Archival I in *Christopher and His Kind*—Forster was likewise fascinated with the possibilities of queer self-consciousness. In 1927 he wrote a witty speculative piece displacing his literary persona into the future.[16] Some of the evidence is still effectively in the archives at King's College Cambridge. Around 1924 Forster wrote an autobiographical piece to read aloud to his queer friends at the Memoir Club. In "My Books and I," Forster laughed at his prudish frightened younger self from the perspective of his older, more knowing self—the two conjoined and separated by the watershed of his sexual awakening in Egypt during the First World War.[17] He described his twenty-three-year-old self as being "horrified" and "disgusted" when his more knowing friends discerned the homosexual subtext in his early fiction. Looking back, Forster acknowledged that "I had been [sexually] excited as I wrote and the passages where [my friends] had thought something was up had excited me most." (Bartlett's primal scene of self-discovery deliberately echoes Forster's.) It's not known whether Isherwood knew of Forster's self-revelatory memoir, which he read aloud as a queer testimony to Lytton Strachey and Leonard Woolf in the early 1920s.[18] But *A Single Man* shares Forster's distinctive double narrative—the Archival I as a single authorial self, reflecting on itself.

Significantly both Forster and Isherwood share a belief in the queer self as an *individuated* consciousness. Here is Forster, in his great essay "What I Believe":

> As for individualism—there seems no way of getting off this, even if one wanted to. The dictator-hero can grind down his citizens until they are all alike, but he cannot melt them into a single man. . . . The memory of birth and the expectation of death always lurk within the human being, making him separate from his fellows and consequently capable of intercourse with them.[19]

Forster's phrase resonates a quarter-century later in the title of Isherwood's masterwork.[20]

The single self is the focal point to follow, understand, and be truthful about human experience. And yet it is a beautiful paradox in Forster that the possibility of generation, of sexuality and community, can thrive only in this knowledge of the solitude of our separation from each other. Like Whitman, Forster always understood the queer self to be in dialectic with an *other*—a *you*. But Forster's sense of self-in-time was not as benign or sympathetic as Whitman's.[21] There is a particular *oppositional pressure* embedded within Forster's queer self—a knowledge that the identity is always set against and shaped by social attitudes of homophobia and conformism.

In his author's note to *Maurice,* dated 1960, Forster faced this double-ness pointedly—simultaneously giving readers rare insight into his own writing process, and starkly framing the novel against prevalent attitudes toward homosexuality over the course of almost half-century of composition. He explicitly undermines the progressive narrative:

> Since *Maurice* was written there has been a change in the public attitude: a change from ignorance and terror to familiarity and contempt. . . . We had not realised that what the public loathes in homosexuality is not the thing itself but having to think about it. (220)

Here Forster deliberately revisits the advice he gave Isherwood in 1933— "the more one meets decent & sensible people, of whom there are now a good few, the more does one forget the millions of beasts and idiots who still prowl in the darkness, ready to gibber and devour."[22] Of course, where the story begins is connected to who reads it. My biography of Forster opens with an edict from Christopher Isherwood: "Unless you start with the fact that he was homosexual, nothing's any good at all."[23] *Start* with the fact. Begin with the queer subject. Some reviewers of my life of Forster thought they knew what this statement meant and the story it implied: their emphasis was on the *homosexual.* But Isherwood intended to empha-size the word *start.* Even in the original moment of transcendent discovery, he was self-consciously situated in time. He wanted to set the frame of reference toward the queer.

And yet both Forster and Isherwood understood that in creating an Archival I they shared an expansive opportunity for life to read differently in the future. Even Isherwood's earliest manifestation of Forster has the possibility of a happier year built into his sedimental self. In 1938, Isher-wood described his friend this way:

Well, my "England" is E. M.; the antiheroic hero, with his straggly straw
mustache, his light, gay blue baby-eyes and his elderly stoop. . . . While
the others tell their followers to be ready to die, he advises us to live as if
we were immortal. (*Down There on a Visit* 162)

Both writers seem comfortable imagining a posthumous self. As Isherwood writes in *A Single Man,* "Look at us—we have died—what is there
to be afraid of?" (10).

So Isherwood spent his life building a self that could grow and reflect,
a self that was supple enough to become a "transitional state." These writers
are collaborators and narrative innovators in writing queer history; they
leave their scrapbook open to readers like us, in a far-distant time. While
embedded in the past, both of them are forward-looking precisely because
of their yearning to revise, their attentiveness to truth, their preservation of
records of the intimate and the ordinary, and their resistance to genre. They
point us to the future, paradoxically, by inviting us back into the archive to
look at the past. In a recent essay on the importance of queer biography, I
argue that we "can't rush on the future of queer studies because we don't
know the story yet." When I was writing my book on Forster, I spent more
than a decade shuttling between the sliver of text, the piece of ephemera in
the archive, and the larger cultural inquiry that would reveal a new story.
Indeed, I believe that "the future of queer theory is in the past. It will come
in queer life work." I assert:

> Sexual biography is reparative work because it is so full of surprises. It
> consistently punctures our theoretical "understandings." We have so
> much work to do going backwards. I can tell you that we really are just
> beginning to know these stories. Then, once we have more real stories of
> sexuality, we can resume theorizing them.[24]

In that essay and in this one, I am, in part, making a plea for preservation
and for attention to the quotidian queer. Many people—almost all now
dead—talked with me about their friendship with Forster for the first
time, not because they were closeted but because they did not believe their
queer lives were important. Be sure to leave your record so that the young
Moffats and Bartletts of the world will be able to read it in the future. I am
encouraged by the ONE National Gay and Lesbian Archives at the University of Southern California in Los Angeles, by Yale's Beinecke Rare Book
and Manuscript Library, and by the Huntington Library in collecting the

fractured archives of queer lives. The space suspended between ignorance and exposure should be supplanted by an open queer archive.

The history of *Maurice* and the friendship of these two writers is a rich occasion for queer narrative possibilities because it's such a contained version of the problems and possibilities of the Archival I—as subject, object, and ethos all in one. Isherwood was rightly proud of his place in opening a queer future in his conservation and his innovative narrative forms. But he won't allow the final word to sound portentous. Occasionally his impish spirit enters, whether invited or not. When I left the college library with a light sketch of this argument and a full satchel, I was temporarily blinded by the burst of brightness at the lintel and accidentally walked into a supporting column on the building's porch. I bruised my forehead on a poster inviting me to join a Buddhist monk from Sri Lanka for a meditation on campus. It read **Be. Here. Now.** As Isherwood knew better than anyone, sometimes you cannot make this shit up.

NOTES

1. Wendy Moffat, *A Great Unrecorded History: A New Life of E. M. Forster* (New York: Farrar, Straus and Giroux, 2010), 13, 14.

2. E. M. Forster, "Notes on *Maurice*," *Maurice* (London: André Deutsch, 1999), 215.

3. From notes taken at Robert Caserio's talk delivered at the Huntington conference on Isherwood in November 2015, a revised version of which is reprinted in this volume.—Eds.

4. The phrase originates in Armistead Maupin's lecture at the Huntington Library, "My Logical Grandfather," November 2015. See also Maupin, *Logical Family: A Memoir* (New York: HarperCollins, 2017).

5. E. M. Forster to Christopher Isherwood, June 25, 1948, Isherwood Papers, Huntington Library, San Marino, California. Many of the letters from Forster to Isherwood are reprinted in P. N. Furbank and Mary Lago, eds., *Selected Letters of E. M. Forster,* 2 vols. (Cambridge, Mass.: Belknap Press of Harvard University Press, 1985).

6. See Philip Gardner, "The Evolution of E. M. Forster's *Maurice,*" in *E. M. Forster: Centenary Revaluations,* ed. Judith Scherer Herz and Robert K. Martin (London: Macmillan, 1984), 204–24.

7. In the fall of 2010, after several well-publicized suicides by gay teens, activist and columnist Dan Savage and his partner, Terry Miller, launched the "It

Gets Better" campaign on YouTube to encourage troubled LGBTQ youth. See, for example, https://well.blogs.nytimes.com/2010/09/22/showing-gay-teens-a -happy-future/ for more.

8. Alan Sinfield makes the case that Bartlett's choice of "we"—a pronoun directed at an exclusively gay audience—is a seminal moment in the history of queer scholarship. Alan Sinfield, *Gay and After: Gender, Culture, and Consumption* (London: Serpent's Tail, 2000), 4. Sinfield seems to have forgotten the "we" in Forster's 1960 author's note on *Maurice*, published in 1971.

9. Neil Bartlett, *Who Was That Man? A Present for Mr Oscar Wilde* (London: Serpent's Tail, 1988), 26, 28.

10. A portion of the following two paragraphs was published in a slightly different form as "E. M. Forster and the Unpublished 'Scrapbook' of Gay History: 'Lest We Forget Him,'" *English Literature in Transition* 55, no. 1 (2012): 19–31.

11. See Christopher Isherwood, *Down There on a Visit* (London: Methuen, 1962); Christopher Isherwood, *Christopher and His Kind, 1929–1939* (New York: Farrar, Straus and Giroux, 1976); Christopher Isherwood, *A Single Man* (New York: Simon and Schuster, 1964); and Richard E. Zeikowitz, *Letters between Forster and Isherwood on Homosexuality and Literature* (New York: Palgrave Macmillan, 2008).

12. James J. Berg, ed., *Isherwood on Writing* (Minneapolis: University of Minnesota Press, 2007), 140.

13. It is useful to recall here that Forster found the title *A Passage to India* in *Song of Myself.*

14. Jesse Matz argues that this layered temporality that I associate with the Archival I is also central to Forster's *Maurice*: "Even as it waits for its future, Maurice looks to the past." Jesse Matz, "*Maurice* in Time," *Style* 34, no. 2 (Summer 2000): 188.

15. Studs Terkel, interview with Christopher Isherwood (1977), in *Conversations with Christopher Isherwood,* ed. James L. Berg and Chris Freeman (Jackson: University Press of Mississippi, 2001), 168.

16. E. M. Forster, "My Own Centenary," in *Abinger Harvest and England's Pleasant Land* (London: Edward Arnold, 1936), 60–63.

17. The literary history of this important little essay is telling: "My Books and I" remained unpublished except as an appendix to the expensive Abinger edition of his novel *The Longest Journey.* It has since been published as an appendix to the Penguin reprint of *The Longest Journey* and discussed in S. P. Rosenbaum's *The Bloomsbury Group Memoir Club,* ed. James M. Haule (London: Palgrave Macmillan, 2014)—but this rare autobiographical fragment has not received the analysis it deserves.

18. Even now, the normalized myth of Forster exerts power. Philip Gardner's edition of Forster's journals and diaries published in 2011 omits almost all the significant reflections on his sexual feelings. Isherwood, who thought that the whole of literary history would be upended by the publication of *Maurice*, saw to his chagrin how puny his efforts to reframe the Forster myth were. See Philip Gardner, ed., *The Journals and Diaries of E. M. Forster* (London: Pickering & Chatto, 2011).

19. E. M. Forster, "What I Believe," in *Two Cheers for Democracy* (New York: Harcourt Brace, 1951), 76.

20. Lois Cucullo astutely explores the literary intertwining of *A Single Man* and *Maurice*. See *"A Single Man* and the American *Maurice,"* in *The American Isherwood,* ed. James J. Berg and Chris Freeman (Minneapolis: University of Minnesota Press, 2015), 5–23.

21. This separation within identity is a manifestation of desire. The echo of Whitman in the title *A Passage to India* and the novel's figuration of desire remind us how Forster prefigures Bartlett's gay subject position. Forster's realization that the negative space of the human connection he sought was the gap of desire itself engendered in him a franker and more homoerotic reading of personal relations than he had held heretofore. The people of the novel are always wanting, in the twin senses of the word: lacking and desiring. Into the gap Forster places an antidote to Mrs. Moore's nihilism in the form of Professor Godbole's curious song of invitation, which simultaneously represents the desire to connect and the impossibility of doing so:

"'I say to Shri Krishna, "Come! Come to me only." The god refuses to come. I grew humble and say: "Do not come to me only. Multiply yourself into a hundred Krishnas, and let one go to each of my hundred companions, but one . . . come to me." He refuses to come. This is repeated several times.'

"'But He comes in some other song, I hope?' said Mrs. Moore gently.

"'Oh no, he refuses to come,' repeated Godbole. . . . 'I say to Him, Come, come, come, come, come, come. He neglects to come.'" E. M. Forster, *A Passage to India* (London: Edward Arnold, 1978), 85.

22. E. M. Forster to Christopher Isherwood, July 16, 1933, Isherwood Papers, Huntington Library.

23. John Lehmann, *Christopher Isherwood: A Personal Memoir* (New York: Henry Holt, 1988), 121.

24. For more on my thinking about queer biography and the Archival I, see my essay "The Narrative Case for Queer Biography," in *Narrative Theory Unbound: Queer and Feminist Interventions,* ed. Robyn Warhol and Susan S. Lanser (Columbus: Ohio State University Press, 2015), 225.

5. A Queer Progress

Christopher Isherwood, Sexual Exceptionalism,
and Berlin in the Thirties

Christopher was certainly more a socialist than he was a fascist,
and more a pacifist than he was a socialist. But he was a queer first
and foremost.
—CHRISTOPHER ISHERWOOD,
LOST YEARS: A MEMOIR, 1945–1951

Oh, darling Chrissikins! . . . You know, you really are a tourist, to
your bones.
—CHRISTOPHER ISHERWOOD, *DOWN THERE ON A VISIT*

Goodbye to Berlin may well remain Christopher Isherwood's most popular book. Yet it wasn't until well after its publication in 1939 and the consecutive successes of, first, John van Druten's play adaptation, *I Am a Camera,* and then its stage and film musical adaptation, *Cabaret,* that his 1976 memoir, *Christopher and His Kind,* gave readers insight into the intimate side and personal cost of his transit from post–World War I London to Weimar Berlin as a promising young writer in his twenties. In this later work, his readers began to grasp the liberation, transience, and turmoil, dare I say even heartbreak, that Isherwood both witnessed and experienced in writing his farewell to that vibrant, doomed city.

With that backdrop, let me offer two scenes to ground this essay:

Scene one: Berlin, June 1937, Heinz Neddermeyer, German lover of the young writer Christopher Isherwood, was tried and convicted following his arrest for draft evasion and for acts of mutual onanism with the English Isherwood. His thirty-six-month sentence and ultimate conscription into the German army foreclosed his relationship with the writer and their frantic attempts to find asylum outside Nazi Germany.[1]

Scene two: Berlin, June 2010, queer theory pioneer Judith Butler publicly refused the Civil Courage Prize awarded by Berlin Pride and chastised organizers for what she considered their racial exclusion of groups representing queer nonnormative nationalities.

With the scenes of Neddermeyer's trial and Butler's public stance on nonnormative nationalities, this essay aims at putting into conversation recent work by Jasbir Puar on homonationalism and Lisa Duggan on homonormativity to investigate Christopher Isherwood's narratives as a queer English writer in the Berlin of the 1930s.[2] The object is twofold:

1. To consider how an emancipatory sexual identity can also reiterate markers of privilege through aspects of their instantiations. Neglect of these marks of privilege—in the case of Isherwood, inscriptions of class and of national identity—can lead to the reproduction of other forms of oppression. Such is the case of Isherwood's sexual exceptionalism of the 1930s that I shall be laying out.

2. To trace as well that which, for want of a better term, is the "queer progress" I find in Isherwood's writings of the 1930s and in his decision at the end of that decade, with Europe on the brink of war, to immigrate to

Heinz Neddermeyer and Christopher Isherwood in Sintra, Portugal, circa 1936. Courtesy of Don Bachardy.

America and to Los Angeles. On the face of it, the terms "queer" and "progress" would appear in direct opposition. There is, on one side, the heavy denotative and connotative weight of the word "progress," which offers a teleology of improvement, of betterment, the Enlightenment's great ambition for its Western pilgrims, whether the pilgrim is John Bunyan or Oliver Twist. On the other, there is the recent reclamation of the pejorative deployment of the word "queer" from the nineteenth century. Queer points now, as Eve Sedgwick in *Tendencies* notably contended, to "the open mesh of possibilities, gaps, overlaps, dissonances and resonances, lapses and excesses of meaning when the constituent elements of anyone's gender, of anyone's sexuality aren't made (or *can't be* made) to signify monolithically."[3] Queer progress suggests, then, a hopeful yet probing approach to Isherwood's writings that will put in a more nuanced perspective his long-standing persona as the English evangelist par excellence of the 1930s demimonde of Weimar Berlin.

To begin with the vignettes of *Goodbye to Berlin*, we are led, perforce, to confront his camera as narrative stratagem in the narrator's oft-cited opening declaration: "I am a camera with its shutter open."[4] We note that Isherwood's narrator assumes the position not of a photographer but of the device itself—therefore, mechanical, indiscriminate, reflexive, uncontrived—a picture-taking instrument merely. The narrator becomes "the automatism of an apparatus," if I may riff on Stephen Melville's suggestive phrase.[5] Its images will reinforce the documentary note struck in the opening vignette's title "A Berlin Diary (Autumn 1930)." And what this camera-narrative device records is not the extraordinary but the routine, the mundane, the quotidian: "the man shaving at the window opposite and the woman in her kimono washing her hair" (1). For the purpose of this essay, one means to situate Isherwood's conceit of this narrating apparatus is to reference Friedrich Kittler's canny reflection on the many mechanical innovations of the nineteenth century. In his concluding chapter of *Discourse Networks*, Kittler contends that "machines do away with polar sexual difference and its symbols."[6] Although Kittler refers explicitly to the typewriter, we might also include such devices as the modern camera.[7] Applied to Isherwood's camera ruse, we might say that Isherwood's narrating device, pace Kittler, is nonsexual.

Indeed, this result is not far from the effect Isherwood's camera-narrator had on at least one contemporary reader of *Goodbye to Berlin*. Isherwood subsequently recollects in his memoir *Christopher and His Kind* that one reviewer cast his narrator as a "sexless nitwit" (186). While "nitwit" isn't likely the impression Isherwood attempted to convey, that of a *sexless* narrator is not far from his stated intent. Reflecting back on his 1930s narrator in his memoir, Isherwood explains that, while he used autobiographical material from his diary accounts of his friends and acquaintances to populate the episodes of *Goodbye to Berlin*, he was chary of presenting a first-person narrator strictly identified with himself as a homosexual. As he put it in his memoir, "Although his own life as a homosexual was lived fairly openly," he explains, "he feared to create a scandal" (185). Given the persistent repressive political and juridical climate in England for any sexual unorthodoxy, such a scandal was all too likely. His chariness also had a literary motive. He feared readers' attention would focus not on the images of his narrating camera but on himself as homosexual, a narrator at odds with established norms. Conversely, however, Isherwood refused to make the narrator overtly heterosexual. As he explained in his memoir, "That, to Christopher, would be as shameful as pretending to be a heterosexual himself" (186), a point I shall return to below. The consequence was Isherwood's "sexless nitwit."

Yet, as much as the writer may have wished to carry off this nonsexed, impersonal, recording device, Isherwood, rarely camera shy himself, does not even manage to have his narrator stay in character till the end of the first page. After several more snapshots of the street, our narrating camera doffs its disguise to appear full blooded and alive, center frame as the character Christopher Isherwood. What draws him out and into view is the seductive whistling he hears of the young men in the street below calling up to their lovers. Their echoing whistles, he confides forlornly, are not alas for him as he now reveals himself to be on his own, far from home in a foreign city. The note of loneliness strikes a sympathetic chord. However, along with disclosing his loneliness is the noticeable remark that the city, Berlin, is foreign. The city and not he, the visiting Englishman, is the oddity.

This newcomer's withholding his homosexuality but not his nationality is significant: for what comes to the fore is the narrator's privileged Englishness. But for this Englishness, his readers might well question whether this narrator is equipped to serve as their conductor now bidding Berlin good-bye. Yet, safely in the hands of a knowing *English* narrator, readers are prepared to begin their journey with this tour guide formerly inert camera, who is, to be blunt, an English visitor, a mere tourist. What's more, as later disclosed in *Christopher and His Kind*, this Christopher is, in reality, a sex tourist. Notably, at the beginning of his memoir, Isherwood baldly admits that he wanted to travel to Berlin for one overarching reason. As he frankly puts it, "To Christopher, Berlin meant boys" (2). As an upper-class, shy, twenty-six-year-old homosexual, Isherwood confesses, he "couldn't relax sexually with a member of his own class or nation." Given the climate of repression and the illegality of any consensual liaison in England between members of the same sex—romantic, casual, or pecuniary—his admission isn't surprising. To overcome his sexual inhibitions, he asserts, "He needed a working-class foreigner" (3). Thirties Berlin, its demimonde, and espe-cially its "foreign" proletariat then, are to function as the instrument of his sexual liberation. His 1976 memoir chronicles again and again the problem-atic relation he initially sought, as a privileged, educated, English national, with Berlin and with the young men he befriended in the working-class boy bars of this tolerant but economically encumbered postwar German city. To offer one notable example from his memoir, Isherwood describes his rapture at his first conquest, Berthold Szczesny, a Czech boy nicknamed Bubi. "By embracing Bubi," he states, "Christopher could hold in his arms the whole mystery-magic of foreignness, Germanness. By means of Bubi, he could fall in love with and possess the entire nation" (4). This euphoric possession of working-class boy and of foreign national essence, "German-ness," is more evident still as he describes trolling the bar scene with an English friend, the archaeologist Francis Turville-Petre, then residing in Berlin. Isherwood writes in his memoir:

> In the bars, Christopher used to think of Francis and himself being like traders who had entered a jungle. The natives of the jungle surrounded them—childlike, curious, mistrustful, sly, easily and unpredictably moved to friendship or hostility. The two traders had what the natives wanted, money. (28)

Now surely there is in Isherwood's memoir, written four decades after his Berlin sojourn, some exaggerated bravura, as Norman Page has pointed out.[8] Still, we have Isherwood describing boy-bar Berlin in the discourse of what amounts to an imperial fantasy. A pair of would-be English adventurers appear to step out of some knockoff Rider Haggard thriller to exercise their rights, in this case sexual, as Englishmen over a primitive foreign band of working-class boys described as childlike, entranced, wary, and, above all, poor.

Nor is Isherwood alone in deploying such a trope. Other English writers used similar language to describe the events of their emancipation at the same haunts that Isherwood frequented. For instance, in his 1976 novel *In the Purely Pagan Sense,* Isherwood's friend, the writer and editor John Lehmann, describes his protagonist Jack Marlowe's excursion to Berlin at the urging of English friend William. As other scholars have noted, Marlowe's friend William is a fictional character whose background and circumstances bear a striking resemblance to Isherwood.[9] In point of fact, it was Isherwood who had urged Lehmann to visit Berlin and then had undertaken Lehmann's introduction to Berlin's bohemian bar scene. In Lehmann's novel, this primer on nightlife is exactly what transpires. His protagonist Marlowe explains, "One of the first things William did to further my education was to take me on a tour of the homosexual bars and night-clubs."[10] Moreover, as Marlowe reveals, tour guide and imperial adventurer William launches his conscript's initiation "at one of the most popular non-smart *lokals,* the 'Cosy Corner,'" the very neighborhood bar in the proletarian southeast section of the city favored and made famous by Auden, his "bugger daydream," and in Isherwood's writing.[11] At another bar, in appraising the collection of patrons, an accommodating William confidentially instructs Marlowe: "'You can have any of them. They're all pretty well on the rocks, but they won't expect more than so many marks and they're completely honest. Besides, whether they're queer or not, they're mad about blond Englishmen'" (Lehmann 45). Ready money and fair-haired Englishmen are the necessaries of the trade in this exotic quarter. Here, the issue of capital is critical to note. Before beginning their nighttime jaunt, tour guide William examines the good luck charm that Marlowe superstitiously carries with him. He reads the French inscription it bears: *"Monnaie fait tout"*— money is everything. Marlowe then expressively affirms, "There was no denying its relevance to life as it was lived in Berlin at that time" (44). The relative wealth of these blond English traders financed their sexual emancipation among the boys living in an economically beleaguered Berlin hit hard in the aftermath of the Great War and subsequent Great Depression, which put any paying job, even sexual liaisons, at a premium.

Not only were impecunious youths a target of Isherwood's privilege, so, too, was Berlin itself a habitation fertile for literary sowing. After three years in Berlin, Isherwood, now the sure-footed imperial interloper, "regarded Berlin as his territory." Berlin becomes his material to write about and his resource to extract. He even recalls his fears that English friend and fellow Berlin sojourner Stephen Spender "would scoop him by writing Berlin stories of his own and rushing them into print!" (*Christopher and His Kind* 107). Moreover, on returning from Germany later in 1932 to England, Isherwood recalls how he enjoyed his role as "the self-exiled mysterious 'Man from Berlin'" (109). Despite the ironic humor, the hegemonic language reveals a callous turn. Berlin and its unemployed males serve as imperial spoils for the privileged Isherwood and his friends to plunder literarily and sexually.

In fairness to Isherwood, it is quite true of Berlin that, in addition to its liberal treatment of queer sexualities, which made the city a mecca of sexual tolerance, the Weimar capital was also far more liberal in terms of censorship, especially compared to London. As such, Berlin was a particularly appealing destination not just for well-heeled cosmopolitans drawn to the prospect of imbibing its lurid nightlife. It was also an appealing destination for writers, artists, and filmmakers, as well as homosexual and political activists. As Robert Beachy has documented in *Gay Berlin*, "The Weimar Republic [had] eased laws, permitting far greater freedom for Berlin's press and print media, film industry, art institutions, and entertainment venues."[12] Yet, given Berlin's liberal policies for gays and artists, Isherwood's opening conceit in *Goodbye to Berlin* of an impartial camera-narrator turned tour guide and the sexual colonialism of *Christopher and His Kind* are difficult to defend. The pilgrim Isherwood may be revered for promoting Berlin's openly hedonic homosexuality, but this site is also one he opportunistically exploited.

Indeed, Isherwood would come to regret his cavalier manner and to recant the sexual exceptionalism to which he had felt entitled as an upper-class and educated Englishman. He would later write:

> The "wickedness" of Berlin's night-life was of a most pitiful kind: the kisses and embraces, as always, had price-tags attached to them. . . . As for the "monsters," they were quite ordinary human beings prosaically engaged in getting their living by illegal methods. The only genuine

monster was the young foreigner who passed gaily through these scenes of desolation, misinterpreting them to suit his childish fantasy.[13]

In this passage, Isherwood acknowledges *himself* as the foreigner and monster and his imperial fantasy a *childish* one.

Although Isherwood's repudiation arrives belatedly, there are in *Goodbye to Berlin* frames of reference in which to view a far more profound trespass on Berlin than that of his emancipating pilgrimage. The vignettes of *Goodbye to Berlin* advance in time from the fall of 1930 to the winter of 1932–33. They proceed to the more ominous closing episodes of "The Nowaks" and "The Landauers." In these, we encounter, on one hand, a working-class family of five, the Nowaks, living hand to mouth in close attic quarters of a tenement building. On the other, there is the well-to-do, educated, Jewish family, the Landauers, headed by a business magnate who owns an upscale Berlin department store managed by his nephew Bernhard Landauer. At these two extremes, working-class and haute-bourgeois, the understated change in the camera-narrator's manner from bemused and campy observer to aware witness becomes more pronounced as he observes these families' efforts to survive in the city disintegrating around them as the National Socialists seize power. Notably Frau Nowak, who works as a charwoman and suffers from tuberculosis, worries over her elder son Lothar who has joined the Nazi Party. She complains to Christopher about how restless he has become with all the ideas the Nazis have put in his head (*Goodbye to Berlin* 109). "The Landauers" begins with a Nazi action against Jewish shops in the Leipzigerstrasse and concludes with a conversation Christopher overhears in Prague in which he learns that Bernhard Landauer has died suspiciously of a heart condition, one that might well have resulted from a bullet to the chest. Christopher's premonition at an earlier gathering at Bernhard's lake house proves eerily accurate. Observing the party guests, he pronounces, "All these people are ultimately doomed. This evening is a dress-rehearsal of a disaster" (177). In choosing to present the everyday lives encountered, what transpires in *Goodbye to Berlin*, especially as the narrative moves into 1933, makes, as Isherwood remarks in *Christopher and His Kind*, "not only the bizarre seem humdrum but the humdrum seem bizarre" (188).

The brutality of Hitler's coup and the financial collapse of Berlin, however, come home more personally in those autobiographical events that

Isherwood's narrator-camera does not record on the pages of *Goodbye to Berlin*. These he chronicled in his unpublished diary held at the Huntington Library, some details of which subsequently appear in *Christopher and His Kind*. In both diary and memoir, Isherwood recounts his meeting and his falling in love with another working-class boy, Heinz Neddermeyer, in March 1932. From 1933 to 1937, with Hitler and the Nazi Party now in control, Isherwood records his and Neddermeyer's decisive exit from Germany, fatalistically represented in *Christopher and His Kind*. Gone is Isherwood's earlier Berlin fantasy, and in its place are the pair's peripatetic attempts over five years to find sanctuary for Heinz in another country to avoid his conscription into the German army. These military orders for Neddermeyer's return to Germany, however, do eventually catch up to him in June 1936. In his June 26 diary entry, a distraught Isherwood confides regarding Neddermeyer's conscription orders: "Yesterday, at last it happened." And continues: "At present, my only reaction is a fierce warm sick feeling."[14] Initially, Heinz evades the orders. Despite his evasion, a year later, while the two wait to learn whether a last desperate attempt for a Mexican passport had succeeded, Neddermeyer, expelled from Luxembourg, is stopped by Gestapo agents just as the Belgian consulate in Trier, Germany, has granted him an emergency visa to reenter Belgium (*Christopher and His Kind* 279–80). Arrested May 12, 1937, Neddermeyer is, in turn, tried for draft evasion and homosexual acts, convicted, sentenced, and ultimately conscripted into the German army. Alone now, attachment and anguish mark Isherwood's diary entries. A month following his lover's arrest, he writes on July 26, 1937, "Oh, Heinz, don't forget me! Or do forget me, if it makes things easier, to forget. Now I am crying. How futile it all is. Sleep well tonight, my dear little brother. How am I to go on living and never see you again?" ("Diary, 1935–38"). As we subsequently learn, Neddermeyer did survive his imprisonment and miraculously survived the war, having fought on both Eastern and Western fronts. He would marry after the war and would meet Isherwood again in 1952.

The passage of some four decades affords the author of *Christopher and His Kind* an opportunity to reflect on his loss of Neddermeyer, as his camera persona in *Goodbye to Berlin* had not. His memoir not only chronicles their attachment but also makes clear that what had prevented

Neddermeyer's safe haven in 1930s England, where the pair had sought refuge, had as much to do with Heinz's working-class status as a German foreigner as it did his homosexuality. To be precise, the very circumstances that had liberated Isherwood's sexuality in Berlin, his class and nationality, are tragically what foreclosed Heinz's own liberation. His worker status and foreign birth foil his attempted immigration to England in 1934. The protections that the homosexual Isherwood enjoyed of class and citizenship entering Berlin in 1930 are exposed as exclusionary ones—exclusions that still persist, as Judith Butler's 2010 rejection of the Zivilcourage Prize attests. They are ones, too, that Puar and Duggan disclose in their work on homonationalism and homonormativity. These privileges, ones inaccessible to Neddermeyer, prevent this working-class German from entering England to be reunited with his lover.

The impact of this heavy loss appears in the novel Isherwood proposes to write in his diary for 1935–38. There, Isherwood plainly states that it is to be the story of Heinz and himself.[15] And contrary to his later stated embargo on straight narratives, the plot is blatantly heterosexual. It depicts an educated and politically active Englishwoman named Karin, who teaches English in Berlin, and her proletarian German lover, Erich, trapped together in the crosshairs of Hitler's rise to power, as had been Isherwood and Neddermeyer's plight. Similarly under duress, the fictional couple escapes Germany for England, where, first, immigration officials and, then, family members make it impossible for them to remain. Because Erich's passport says he is a *Tischler* (carpenter), immigration agents grant him only a month's stay. In that month, Karin's affluent family, offended by Erich's working-class status, rejects the couple. Shunned, the pair resolves to leave England for refuge in another country. When an activist friend of the couple is arrested in Berlin, Erich returns to Germany to lend assistance but is, instead, also arrested and detained. Isherwood's sketch of the novel ends with Karin's despair over their separation and Erich's incarceration. Isherwood concludes in his diary: "Gradually, [Karin] realizes that she must continue on with her life. There is no consolation. There is only hope. One day, perhaps. . . . She returns to England" ("Diary, 1935–38"). While same-sex love is dropped in the proposed narrative, entitlements of class and of national identity for the English Karin and the barriers of class and national identity for the German Erich remain and are decisive in separating the couple.[16]

This recognition of the privileges of class and of nation rehearsed in Isherwood's diary has, I suggest, a more public scrutiny than that of Isherwood's unpublished reckoning. It is the novel Isherwood set in 1933, the same year that Isherwood and Neddermeyer would begin their search for a safe haven. I refer to his novella *Prater Violet*, which was published in 1945. Its setting, significantly, is not Berlin but Isherwood's own London. In this work, too, contrary to *Goodbye to Berlin*, the role of tourist and guide is not an all-knowing Englishman. Instead, the foreign-interloper-cum-tour-guide is the leftist Austrian film director Friedrich Bergmann, a fictionalized depiction of Berthold Viertel. Although in *Prater Violet* the character Bergmann may not adopt the persona of a camera per se, he does have a certain familiarity with cameras, while the young local is portrayed by another of Isherwood's self-characterizations, appearing as a character named Christopher. In the role of the boyish native, albeit of imperial London, this Christopher is hired to assist Bergmann in translating the film's screenplay of a sentimental musical, that of the title *Prater Violet*.

This novella of moviemaking, situated as it is in the same moment of Hitler's seizure of power in Germany and his ambitious designs on Austria, sets the Austrian Bergmann and the English Christopher to do battle with England's imperial commercial forces in the form of a film studio. Given the aptly titled Imperial Bulldog Pictures (a stand-in for Gaumont-British), which is headed by its pugnacious and loutish chief, Mr. Chatsworth, the irony of the narrative becomes clear. There is the patent incongruity of the English Chatsworth retaining the Jewish avant-garde Bergmann to direct his pet project of a second-rate melodrama. Chatsworth, we are told, wanted the best for his picture and he could pay for the best. Once again as John Lehmann's novel had demonstrated, *monnaie fait tout*—money is everything. This time around we have the English setting of a London film studio, not the fraught nightlife of Berlin, and a materialistic studio chief intent on portraying a pre–Great War romance between a student prince with artistic ambitions and a Prater flower girl. And to satisfy Chatsworth's film fantasy of the past, it is the immigrant director Bergmann, fleeing from a city under siege, whom he procures to lend the film authenticity and status. If the tragic Bergmann represents, as the character Christopher observes in meeting him, "the face of Central Europe, the face of a political situation, an epoch," Chatsworth represents the face of the British Empire,[17] acquisitive, overreaching, and indifferent to any political ramifications, in short, the culmination of an imperial epoch.[18] Early on, the studio's arrogance becomes manifest in its heedlessness of the political tragedy unfolding in Europe. An oblivious studio assistant thoughtlessly observes of the two cities, Vienna and Berlin, that they are "pretty much the same kind of set-up" (4). For the studio, there is no difference between Vienna, the site of the screenplay and then under siege, and Berlin, the locus of Nazi rule. Imperial ignorance and disinterest set the tone that Isherwood's narrative deftly pursues.

What is most conspicuous in Isherwood's *Prater Violet*, then, is the tacit comparison the novella makes between imperial London and subjugated Berlin, a comparison that exposes the dominant and dominated relationship of England to Germany in the postwar period. If over the course of this essay I have been offering a reading of Isherwood's queer progress in the thirties in recognizing his entitlements of class and nation, I am here suggesting that, as a work, *Prater Violet* offers its denouement of the 1930s. Even more, I argue, *Prater Violet* serves as a coda to *Goodbye to Berlin*, and not merely because it is the first long piece of fiction Isherwood would write in the ten years since the Berlin stories. In the novella, the artist-interloper-tour-guide, the Austrian director Bergmann in London (and he specifically takes on the role of tour guide) replaces the artist-interloper-tour-guide that was the Christopher Isherwood of his Berlin stories.[19] The London sights Bergmann explores include "the slums and the scandal of unjust ownership [and] the jungle within which Jack the Ripper goes about the business of murder in the elegant overcoat of a member of the Stock Exchange," and "the Tower, where Bergmann lectured me on English history." Indeed, Christopher acknowledges, "He was always the guide, and I the tourist" (52). In this turnabout, Bergmann provides his local-boy apprentice the political education that Christopher's prerogatives of birth, education, class, and nationality had evidently denied him.

Especially noteworthy are the scenes in which Bergmann directly challenges the naive Christopher over his entitlements. In one, when Christopher attempts to dissuade Bergmann from returning to Vienna on news that his family might be victims of the violent turmoil spreading in the city, Bergmann counsels Christopher:

> You do not understand. How can I leave them alone at such a time? Already, they have endured so much. . . . You are very kind, Christopher.

You are my only friend in this country. But you cannot understand. You have always been safe and protected. Your home has never been threatened. You cannot know what it is like to be in exile, a perpetual stranger. . . . I am bitterly ashamed that I am here, in safety. (95–96)

Of course, the reality is that, by the time Isherwood is writing *Prater Violet* in 1943–44, he is residing in California, where he, too, would very likely know the complications of exile and the shame of safety to which the fictional Bergmann confesses. And Isherwood would have experienced exile and safety on at least two fronts: in terms of his own family living in England enduring the war with Germany and in terms of his lover in a German uniform fighting it, while he, by contrast, is living in proverbial sunny California.

In another exchange, it becomes clear that, under Bergmann's direction, the film has become more than Chatsworth's nostalgic fairy tale. It has become an allegory of the privileged artist in turbulent times. To an imperceptive Christopher, Bergmann explains that the film's prince-artist, accustomed to wealth and security, must decide which side he is on in the midst of his country's chaos. "He now has to make a choice. He is declassed, and he must find a new class. Does he really love Toni [the Prater flower girl]? Did his beautiful words mean anything? If so, he must prove that they did. Otherwise . . ." Bergmann chides Christopher over the symbolism of the screenplay: "'This symbolic fable,' [he] continued, with sadistic relish, 'is particularly disagreeable to you, because it represents your deepest fear, the nightmare of your own class'" (50).

Such a nightmare, however, is one that Isherwood can and does now imagine of himself, of his class and nation, and of Germany. Reported in his diary entry for April 3, 1944, the nightmare is dramatized in *Prater Violet*.[20] The character Christopher shudderingly recalls dreaming, montage fashion, of a German courtroom in which he helplessly watches as one of several Communists on trial is shot by a female state prosecutor as she leads the prisoner to the dock. Shift to another scene on a narrow street in which a Jew, hands pushed into his pockets, approaches Christopher, who shockingly realizes that the man's hands have been shot off and that he hides the bloody stumps in his pockets to avoid being seized and shot again. The final scene shows Christopher seeking shelter in the British Embassy, where he is welcomed by an officer who, surreally, points to the embassy walls decorated with the postimpressionist and cubist artwork favored by the ambassador (55–56). The trauma and symbolism are unmistakable. In his dream, Christopher witnesses the impersonal brutality of the German state and the vicious mutilation committed by its citizens. He is able to escape the bloodshed himself only by retreating to his country's embassy opulently ornamented with the avant-garde works of artists, most likely all under threat. The great irony, given his own experiences of loss, dislocation, and exile, is, of course, that the artist Christopher in his dream *chooses* the protection of his then nation, Britain. His dilemma and choice, indeed, are the very ones of class and nationhood that Bergmann unmasked. They are the artist-prince's nightmare.

Isherwood's progress that I have been tracing here from Berlin nightlife to nightmare is poignantly captured in the closing scene of *Prater Violet*. With the filming concluded, two solitary, nocturnal figures, Bergmann and Christopher, bid farewell on a deserted London street. Christopher thinks: "A traveler, a wanderer. I was aware of Bergmann, my fellow-traveler, pacing beside me: a separate, secret consciousness, locked away within itself, distant as Betelgeuse, yet for a short while, sharing my wanderings. . . . Like me, he had his journey to go" (122–23). There is, in this moment, mutuality, recognition, and respect: the Austrian Jew and his young English apprentice are fellow wanderers, caught in a tragic history that neither could avoid.[21]

This reading of the vignettes of *Goodbye to Berlin* in tandem with the novella *Prater Violet* allows us to imagine what must have been the writer Isherwood's own critical self-awareness, if not self-reproach, and not just his fictional stand-in's. Proof is suggested much later in the 1960s. In the notes Isherwood prepared for a talk about his books, he looks back on the camera-apparatus of "A Berlin Diary" that began this essay. He recalls "the various pieces which had appeared in *New Writing* brought together in *Goodbye to Berlin*; 1939" and observes: "The 'I' became Christopher Isherwood, the camera. *But the camera became a human being and got increasingly out of hand in my later novels*" (emphasis added).[22] This human being, who in Isherwood's words "got increasingly out of hand," is, in sum, what I have been describing on these pages—a pilgrim representing what I would call a queer progress.

NOTES

I wish to express my sincere gratitude to the Christopher Isherwood Foundation and to the Huntington Library for support of my research of the Christopher Isherwood Papers evident in this essay. To the University of Minnesota, I extend a sincere thank-you for its funding of Imagine Awards and a grant-in-aid and the leave to put these funds to good use. Finally, to Jim Berg and Chris Freeman for their unstintingly heroic efforts in bringing this scholarship into print—my profound thanks.

1. The sentence was deemed light, as Isherwood records. Neddermeyer could have been treated as a pariah and interned indefinitely in a concentration camp bearing the stigma of a pink triangle on his clothing. See Christopher Isherwood, *Christopher and His Kind* (New York: Farrar, Straus and Giroux, 1976), 286–87.

2. On homonationalism, see Jasbir K. Puar, *Terrorist Assemblages: Homonationalism in Queer Times* (Durham, N.C.: Duke University Press, 2007). On homonormativity, see Lisa Duggan, "The New Homonormativity: The Sexual Politics of Neoliberalism," in *Materializing Democracy: Toward a Revitalized Cultural Politics*, ed. R. Castronovo and D. Nelson (Durham, N.C.: Duke University Press, 2002), 175–94.

3. See Eve Kosofsky Sedgwick's *Tendencies*, Series Q (Durham: Duke University Press, 1993), 8; original emphasis.

4. Christopher Isherwood, "A Berlin Diary (Autumn 1930)," in *The Berlin Stories: The Last of Mr. Norris* [and] *Goodbye to Berlin* (New York: New Directions, 1963), 1.

5. See Stephen Melville's observation on "the automatism of the photograph" in "The Time of Exposure: Allegorical Self-Portraiture in Cindy Sherman," *Arts Magazine* 60, no. 5 (January 1986): 17–21.

6. Friedrich Kittler, *Discourse Networks, 1800/1900* (Stanford, Calif.: Stanford University Press, 1990), 351.

7. Impersonal technology augurs the collapse of the sexed economy of the Victorian century: "The typewriter," Kittler observes, "brought about (Foucault's *Order of Things* overlooks such trivialities) 'a completely new order of things'" (352).

8. See Norman Page, *Auden and Isherwood: The Berlin Years* (New York: St. Martin's Press, 1998), 34–35.

9. It is worth noting that Isherwood's full name was Christopher William Bradshaw-Isherwood. Lehmann would have known that.—Eds.

10. John Lehmann, *In the Purely Pagan Sense* (London: Blond and Briggs, 1976), 44.

11. Humphrey Carpenter, *W. H. Auden: A Biography* (Boston: Houghton Mifflin, 1981), 90.

12. Beachy records that, from the end of the Great War to the Nazis' rise to power, on the order of "twenty-five to thirty separate homosexual German-language journal titles appeared in Berlin." Robert Beachy, *Gay Berlin: Birthplace of a Modern Identity* (New York: Knopf, 2014), 189.

13. "Prologue," *Mr. Norris and I* (1956, 86–87), quoted in Anthony Shuttleworth, "In a Populous City: Isherwood in the Thirties," in *The Isherwood Century: Essays on the Life and Work of Christopher Isherwood*, ed. James Berg and Chris Freeman (Madison: University of Wisconsin Press, 2000), 151. Obviously, Isherwood here refers to *The Last of Mr. Norris*.

14. "Diary, 1935–38, 1947," A. MS. (1 vol.), Christopher Isherwood Papers, box 85, CI 2751, Huntington Library, San Marino, California.

15. "The story is really about Iris Wright—i.e. H and myself" (33). The plot becomes a heterosexual romance of his and Heinz's struggle to get away ("Diary 1935–38," July 24, 1938).

16. Glyn Salton-Cox has recently arrived at a different interpretation of Isherwood's sexual and political commitments of the 1930s that warrants remark. He quite brilliantly interprets the object status of Isherwood's camera-narrator as a refutation of normative bourgeois subjectivity that in turn allows a queer transcendence of class and national identities. Compelling as this reading is, in his projected novel at least, which appears to anticipate *Down There on a Visit*, Isherwood abandons the argued object status visibly assumed in *Goodbye to Berlin* to cope with the abject loss of Heinz. See Salton-Cox's *Queer Communism and the Ministry of Love: Sexual Revolution in British Writing of the 1930s* (Edinburgh: Edinburgh University Press, 2018).

17. Christopher Isherwood, *Prater Violet* (Minneapolis: University of Minnesota Press, 2001), 17.

18. Viertel, on reading the manuscript of *Prater Violet*, ironically comments that "the mastermind Chatsworth" is the hero of the novel and on English entitlements: "Oh, holy English system, Empire above all empires! God bless it!" Berthold Viertel to Christopher Isherwood, October 26, 1944, Christopher Isherwood Papers, 1864–1997, CI 2638, Huntington Library.

19. The tours Bergmann leads of London pointedly reference, among others, Charles Dickens and Bertolt Brecht (51–54).

20. See Christopher Isherwood, *Diaries*, vol. 1, *1939–60*, ed. Katherine Bucknell (New York: Harper, 1996), 342.

21. Viertel expressed similar sentiments: "Really I am worried about your going away, and if I were able to I would prohibit it. That would be wrong, probably. Because the freedom and the courage of a bird of passage belongs to the

characteristics of your generation in general and particularly to you [as a] person, as a writer. You are a bird of passage, and for that reason a born eye-witness, whose mission it is to testify." Berthold Viertel to Christopher Isherwood, January 13, 1937, Christopher Isherwood Papers, CI 2633, Huntington Library.

22. See "The Autobiography of My Books Lecture: Notes," Berkeley, May 1963 (1), Christopher Isherwood Papers, CI 1018, Huntington Library. It is published in *Isherwood on Writing*, ed. James Berg (Minneapolis: University of Minnesota Press, 2007), 143–216.

6. Fellow Travelers

Isherwood and Auden

Theirs was one of the most remarkable literary friendships of the twentieth century. It began in school and continued across decades and continents. There are so many words written by them, to them, and about them that it can be hard to discern what was important about the lifelong connections between the two writers, W. H. Auden and Christopher Isherwood.

After more than a half century of British and American scholarship on Auden and Isherwood, it is time to reconsider this complex relationship. Isherwood was central to Auden's life, before and after they left for America. Even into middle age, when they lived on opposite sides of the United States, they each felt their relationship integral to their identities as men and as writers. It seems apparent that the years 1938, 1939, and 1940 were critical for both men, together and apart, as writers and occasional lovers, so an examination of their lives and works in that context will perhaps offer a shift in perspective regarding what we thought we knew about them.

PRE-1938: ARRIVING

W. H. Auden first met Christopher Isherwood when they were boys at St. Edmund's School in 1915. They did not know each other well there, but they met again, ten years later, while Auden was at Oxford and after Isherwood had left Cambridge. By most accounts, Auden looked up to Isherwood, whom he saw as an already established writer, even though Isher-

Christopher Isherwood and W. H. Auden in New York City, 1952. Copyright Eve Arnold/Magnum Photos.

wood had not yet published his first novel. In those years, Auden showed many if not most of his poems to Isherwood in early drafts, and Isherwood acted as a mentor and editor to the younger poet.

Much of what is known about this part of their relationship comes from two books by Isherwood: the "not truly autobiographical" *Lions and Shadows: An Education in the Twenties,* which he suggests should be "read as if it were a novel," and his later recollection of the thirties, *Christopher and His Kind,* which he promises will be "as frank and factual as I can make it."[1] Isherwood's memoirs and diaries have often been seen as one-sided or as an attempt to put the best light on himself, sometimes to the detriment of his friends. However, many passages from both works are quoted by scholars and biographers without comment. Stephen Spender, who knew both men well, provides a retrospective insight into Isherwood's "autobiographical fiction" in a review of Isherwood's final book, *My Guru and His Disciple*. He suggests that for Isherwood, "By the process of self-criticism, fiction and non-fiction add up to a whole which is closer to the truth than the fiction alone."[2] Supplementing these works are Isherwood's published diaries, biographies of the two men, and letters exchanged between them and among their friends. Auden's letters to Isherwood (as well as those to Spender) provide some of his side of the story. Isherwood's letters to Auden, unfortunately, do not survive.

At the age of twenty-four, Isherwood published his first novel, *All the Conspirators*, in 1928. It was neither commercially nor critically successful. Nevertheless, he had begun to garner the respect of his peers. Within the small social world that was literary London, the two men became the center of what would soon be dubbed "the Auden circle." In 1929, showing early signs of frustration with life and expectations in England, Isherwood followed Auden to Berlin, first to visit and later to stay, encouraged by the sexual availability of foreign working-class boys.[3] This time spent traveling together was an early highlight in their relationship. Recalling a brief visit to Amsterdam with Auden, Isherwood wrote that he and his friend "were both in the highest spirits. It was such a relief and happiness to be alone with each other" (*Christopher and His Kind* 10).

The two were also sleeping together, at least occasionally. Auden's diary of that period records his feelings for Isherwood and the pleasure he got out of their collaborative relationship.[4] Isherwood disclosed in *Christopher and His Kind* that he and Auden had been lovers but downplayed the relationship: "they had been going to bed together, unromantically but with much pleasure, for the past ten years, whenever an opportunity offered itself. . . . They couldn't think of themselves as lovers, yet sex had given friendship an extra dimension" (264).

Auden's first book, *Poems*, was published by Faber in 1930, and it was received very well by readers and critics alike. A second edition was brought out in 1933. Isherwood's second novel, *The Memorial* (1932), was more popular than his first and was praised by E. M. Forster, whom Isherwood admired. In 1936, Auden published his acclaimed collection *Look, Stranger!* It was published in the United States in 1937 under his preferred title, *On This Island*, and, that same year, it was awarded the Gold Medal for Poetry by King George VI. By this time, it was hard to say who was the more accomplished writer, although Auden was perhaps more widely recognized.

Their literary collaboration began casually, when they read each other's work. Not surprisingly, they commented about each other's writing. In 1937, Isherwood wrote: "When Auden was younger, he was very lazy. He hated polishing and making corrections. If I didn't like a poem, he threw it away and wrote another. If I liked one line, he would keep it and work it into a new poem."[5] Auden credited Isherwood for the political consciousness of their group, as in the poem he wrote on the occasion of Christopher's birthday, "August for the people" (1935): "So in this hour of crisis and dismay, / What better than your strict and adult pen / Can warn us from the colours and the consolations, / The showy arid works, reveal / The squalid shadow of academy and garden, / Make action urgent and its nature clear?"[6] These accounts are roughly contemporaneous, but we should also recognize in them that self-deprecation and self-promotion are operating at the same time. And it is worth noting that for these two writers, especially at this time, "self-promotion" means promoting themselves and each other. As Auden wrote in his 1929 Berlin journal, "That is what friendship is. Fellow conspiracy" (Parker 153).

They began working together on stage plays, which drew on their different talents and strengths: Isherwood, a lifelong theater and film fan, provided the structure and the narrative of their plays, while Auden provided the poetry in speeches and song. Their first collaboration happened almost by accident in Berlin in 1929, when Auden was working on a play about a reformatory, which became "The Enemies of a Bishop." As Parker points out, this partnership provided benefits to both writers. For Isherwood, it recalled his youthful work with Edward Upward, and for Auden, it was "the marriage of true minds." In Isherwood, Auden had found the ideal writing partner. He later claimed, "In my own case, collaboration has brought me greater erotic joy—as distinct from sexual pleasure—than any sexual relation I have had" (153). Their play was not a success; it was rejected for publication and was not performed. Nevertheless, the two began another project, again instigated by Auden, which became their first produced play, *The Dog Beneath the Skin* (1935).

Two years later, when they were writing *The Ascent of F6*, Auden joined Isherwood in Portugal, "the first time for several years" that the two were together more than a few days.[7] According to Isherwood, Auden wrote quickly, producing nearly finished drafts, while Isherwood, concentrating on the dialogue, was much slower and needed many more revisions. An additional dimension of their difference would become important later: "Wystan writing indoors with the curtains drawn; Christopher writing out in the garden, with his shirt off in the sunshine" (*Christopher and His Kind* 239).

The Auden–Isherwood plays are essentially parables. Their final play together, *On the Frontier* (1938), is more overtly political in nature, consistent with the evolution of both men's work in this decade. Though they seemed to think of the plays as side projects, these collaborations mirror developments in their individual work, as, for example, in Auden's poem "Spain" and Isherwood's Berlin novels. The first performance of *The Ascent of F6* was in 1937; that year also saw the publication of Isherwood's *Sally Bowles*, Auden's *Letters from Iceland,* and the double issue of *New Verse* devoted to Auden. At the same time, their doubts about the efficacy of literature in the face of political reality surfaced in *On the Frontier,* which, according to scholar Christopher Innes, "explicitly dismisses humanistic poetry as a way of changing the situation."[8] World War II marked a "complete break with the ethos and literary modes of the 1930s": the Group Theater closed after a revival of *F6* starring Alec Guinness, marking "the end of symbolic Expressionism on the British stage" (Innes 90).

During this period of their collaboration, they rarely lived in the same place. Auden was working as a schoolteacher and writing. Isherwood was living in Berlin and traveling around the continent with his boyfriend, Heinz Neddermeyer. The young German, in flight from service in the Nazi army, was refused entry into England in 1934. In response, Isherwood "symbolically rejected [his mother's] England," which he continued to see as the land of "the Others" (*Christopher and His Kind* 172). Eventually, Isherwood rejected his financial inheritance as well as his citizenship.

1938–39: DEPARTING

The period from January 1938 to August 1939 was a key time for Auden and Isherwood, personally and professionally. Now in their early thirties, they were literary celebrities in London. As such, they were commissioned by Auden's publishers—Faber and Faber in England and Random House in the United States—to write a book together about the East, which meant, to their delight, months of travel, including a return trip through the United States. That journey would change their lives.

On January 19, 1938, they left for China en route to the Sino-Japanese War. Many writers had taken part in and written about the Spanish Civil War, and now, as Auden reportedly said, they would "have a war all of our very own" (*Christopher and His Kind* 289). They spent the next six months together, traveling by ship through the Suez Canal, stopping in Hong Kong and Shanghai. In Hong Kong they were welcomed by the British ambassador, Archibald Clark Kerr, who "turned out to know Auden's poetry and be a fan of *Sally Bowles*" (Parker 327). Auden had been in Spain the previous year and had seen the chaos of war; for Isherwood, it was a new experience. The plan was that Isherwood would be the observer, contributing a prose narrative, while Auden "would write about the war parabolically to provide a theory of human violence."[9] The resulting book, *Journey to a War* (1939), illustrates the same modernist assemblage they had used in their plays.[10]

On the voyage back to England, they landed in Vancouver and crossed the continent by train. They spent a short time in New York City, where they were welcomed by George Davis, literary editor of two influential American magazines, who had been holding their royalties for several American publications. Davis also introduced Auden and Isherwood to some handsome men—Isherwood took a liking to Harvey Young (he sometimes used the pseudonym "Vernon Old" when writing about him), who would later become his lover.[11] Auden and Isherwood thought New York seemed "immensely exciting, an outlier of Europe vitalized by America" (Carpenter 240)—perhaps it could be their new Berlin.

Back in London, Isherwood and Auden continued to experience the trappings of their fame. Their play *On the Frontier* was produced by John Maynard Keynes in Cambridge in November. By his own admission, Isherwood was "good at self-exposure; he knew all the tricks of modesty and never boasted except in private" (*Christopher and His Kind* 332). Auden, on the other hand, claimed to find literary life in England "particularly stultifying" (Carpenter 243). Talk of a return to the United States had begun while they were in New York. Conveniently, a special visa granted them in Shanghai would make it easy for them to enter the United States again.

There is some disagreement about whether a return visit was meant to be permanent or just the next of their voyages away from England. Auden seems to have been the more resolute about making New York his new home: "I felt the situation for me in England was becoming impossible. I couldn't grow up" (Carpenter 243). As scholar Alan Jacobs points out, his move "represented for Auden means of distancing himself from the expectations British intellectual culture had for him."[12] Years later, Isherwood wrote in his diary, "What surprises me is the unhesitating way that [Auden] declared, to the BBC interviewers, that he came to the U.S. not intending to return to England. Unless my memory deceives me altogether, he was very doubtful what he should do when the war broke out."[13] For Isherwood, those expectations may have been more personal, as he was breaking away from family perhaps as much as from country. In *Christopher and His Kind,* Isherwood describes the casual nature of their leaving: "He and Wystan exchanged grins, schoolboy grins which took them back to the earliest days of their friendship. 'Well,' said Christopher, 'we're off again.' 'Goody,' said Wystan" (332).

The transatlantic voyage allowed Isherwood and Auden an opportunity to contemplate their future. According to Isherwood, this was the first time they had been alone together in several months. Their extended conversations led them to reject the leftist political stances they had adopted publicly throughout the 1930s. No longer "repeating slogans created for them by others," the two men agreed that "they wanted to stop. . . . Their agreement made them happy. Now, more than ever, they were allied. Yet their positions were really quite different" (333). That Isherwood draws a contrast between their positions in this comment from a vantage point of more than thirty-five years later is instructive: they were doing similar things, but with significantly different reasoning and motivation. For him, his own more personal realization that he was a pacifist left him emotionally unsettled.

Upon their arrival in New York, Isherwood resumed his relationship with Harvey Young, and Auden soon met Chester Kallman, with whom he would fall in love. Auden took to New York very well—and New York took to him. For Auden, New York felt like a place where he could truly write in peace, but Isherwood did not experience the city in the same way. He found the dark, gloomy winter insufferable. Unlike Auden, the personal and professional notoriety he enjoyed in London had not followed Isherwood to New York. Although *Journey to a War* and *Goodbye to Berlin* were both published in the United States that year, the Berlin novel did not sell as well as he had hoped, making it necessary for him to find another way to earn a living. Life in America was more expensive than he'd expected, and Isherwood knew that his independence from family and home required him to pay his own way.

By April, Isherwood was longing to leave the city. As he wrote to E. M. Forster, "It's really not New York's fault, but mine, that I've got so little out of being here, except the feeling of pure despair, values dissolving, everything uncertain."[14] In the same letter, Isherwood discusses the possibility of returning to England if war breaks out and of joining the immigration quota system in America, which would allow him and Auden to work legally in the country. Auden had already been offered a teaching position. Isherwood hoped to find work in Hollywood.

Isherwood headed for Los Angeles with Young, taking a long Greyhound bus trip down the East Coast and through the southern United States. His goal was to talk to a friend and fellow expatriate, the noted philosopher and science writer Gerald Heard, who had been lecturing on pacifism. Once in California, Isherwood settled in Los Angeles, enjoying the sunshine and social atmosphere. Auden and Kallman visited in the summer of 1939, but they thoroughly disliked it. The stark contrast between the two men was clear to Isherwood's longtime partner Don Bachardy, who observed, "Chris was all sunshine and warmth. Wystan liked the dark and the cold."[15]

When war broke out in September 1939, both Isherwood and Auden strongly felt an obligation to return to England, but it was now much more dangerous to make the journey across the Atlantic, where German U-boats were lurking. Having declared himself a pacifist, Isherwood thought he could return only if there were a way for him to contribute to England's defense as a conscientious objector. He wrote to Forster at the end of September, "What shall I do? Stay here for the present. I am half an American citizen, anyway. Later, perhaps, an ambulance corps. Wystan is in New York. Whatever we do will probably be together" (Zeikowitz 88).

Rumblings in the press about English writers in the United States began in the summer of 1939 and continued through the next year. Particularly offensive to Isherwood and Auden were the remarks of other writers such as Spender and Cyril Connolly. Isherwood was particularly attacked for the joint sins of settling in Hollywood and adopting yoga. For a certain set in England, "Hollywood" stood for all of Southern California, and "yoga" was pejorative shorthand for anything related to Hinduism. He felt somewhat defensive but also defiant, perhaps even more so as a result of these personal attacks. Auden and Isherwood both wrote letters to Spender, accusing him of betraying their friendship. Auden wrote to his brother in June 1940, "I dont [sic] see the point of writing in a cottage waiting for the parachutists. . . . All that we can do, who are spared the horrors, is to be happy and not pretend out of a sense of guilt that we are not, to study as hard as we can, and to keep our feeble little lamps burning in the big wind" (Davenport-Hines 207). Infuriated over what he saw as petty and misguided criticism, Forster came to the defense of his friends, stating in a letter to the *Spectator* (July 5, 1940) that the attacks raise "the uneasy feeling that there must be something else behind them, namely, unconscious envy." He went on to say, "There is a further objection to this undignified nagging: it diverts public attention from certain Englishmen who really are a danger to the country."[16] According to Richard Canning, much of the criticism was "certainly informed by jingoism, homophobia and philistinism," but even Forster, "deep down," did "resent the flight to America."[17] Nevertheless, as reviews of works by and about the two writers continue to show, those attitudes toward the men persist in England to this day.

Auden and Isherwood independently began the process of becoming U.S. residents, if not citizens. They had entered the country on visas that did not allow them to work, so each left for brief periods in 1940 (Isherwood to Mexico in June, Auden to Canada in November) in order to reenter through the U.S. immigration system that set strict quotas for most nations. As Auden wrote, "Just got back from Canada where I had to go in order to start becoming American."[18] This process did not guarantee or even imply a successful citizenship application, and each man still considered returning to England a possibility.

"AMERICA PARTED US"

Crucial differences in the two writers' personalities can be seen in the geographical choices they made that turned out to be life changing. Isherwood was becoming committed to life in Southern California; Auden preferred to base himself in New York. The two saw each other frequently by the standards of the days before inexpensive air travel: Isherwood occasionally visited the East Coast, and Auden often stayed with Isherwood whenever he was on a lecture tour that included California. However, what they might have thought of as a temporary living situation became permanent as the years went by.

From all indications, it seems that Auden minded their separation more than Isherwood did. Nearly every letter Auden sent ended with a plea for Isherwood to visit, whether in New York, Austria, or England. Isherwood recognized Auden's devotion to him but did not return it fully. He also believed that Auden wanted him to be "properly domestic" and that Auden "had been in love with Christopher."[19] Throughout Auden and Isherwood's relationship, Auden seems to have been "the more loving one"; Isherwood, apparently, was never in love with Auden. Looking back on their relationships, Isherwood wrote in his diary, "He loved me very much and I behaved rather badly to him, a lot of the time" (*Liberation* 402). This dynamic haunted Auden and colored their relationship, especially in the forties and fifties, when Auden's partnership with Kallman was at its most problematic and when Isherwood realized that, in Bachardy, he had met the love of his life.

After Auden's death, Isherwood wrote to Spender, "We were so close to each other when we were young, and then America parted us—it's very strange to realize this, but it did. We never got together for long enough after that" (Parker 681). Auden very much wanted a relationship that mirrored a traditional marriage. His relationship with Kallman was therefore ultimately unsatisfactory, even though it was long lasting, because Kallman had no interest in a conventionally monogamous life. Their frequent separations left Auden lonely and disappointed throughout his later years. According to Isherwood, Auden "made a wall around himself, for most people, by his behavior and prejudices and demands" (*Liberation* 393). Bachardy spent time with both Kallman and Auden, together and separately, over a period of about two decades, and he believes Auden never gave up his love of Isherwood: "I think there would never have been a Chester if Chris had fulfilled Wystan's hopes. I think Wystan would have been perfectly happy to have settled down with Chris" (Bachardy interview).

The contrasts between the writers were, of course, much more than romantic differences. Auden was an intellectual, as is evident in his erudite writing—poetry and prose—from this period. Influenced by Carl Jung, in 1940 Auden described his "dominant faculties as intellect and intuition, [and his] weak ones feeling and sensation" (Bucknell and Jenkins 72). Isherwood, by contrast, was a sensualist. They often saw themselves this way and once joked that "poems are written with the head for the heart. Novels are written with the heart for the head" (Bucknell and Jenkins 71). Additionally, the two approached their roles as writers in the United States differently. Isherwood saw himself as the eternal outsider. Although he became an American citizen, he continued to see his role as that of someone off to the side, observing. The language of his writing became more Americanized, but slowly. Auden, on the other hand, came to "identify himself as unabashedly American," according to Peter E. Firchow.[20] Auden wished to immerse himself in American literary life, and his influence on American poetry—through teaching, lecturing, and editing—is widely recognized.

The postwar relationship between Auden and Isherwood was complicated by their increasing devotion to different religions. Auden began attending Anglican services almost as soon as he arrived in New York. In Los Angeles, Heard and Aldous Huxley introduced Isherwood to Vedanta, the philosophical branch of Hinduism. He began an enduring relationship with Swami Prabhavananda that would last the rest of his life. Relocating to the West Coast had not yet brought Isherwood domestic stability. His personal life was in some turmoil in the early forties. As he engaged more deeply with Vedanta, he lived for some time in the enclave of the Vedanta Society of Southern California and considered becoming a monk, but he was unwilling or unable to renounce his sexual life. Professionally, he had nearly stopped writing. His first American novel, *Prater Violet,* was not published until 1945. As early as the summer of 1939, writing to Forster from Los Angeles, Isherwood expressed anxiety over his lack of productivity—and praised Auden's: "Wystan's work is getting better and better—classic, really. In my little way, I think I am imitating your curve. The war-silence is moving in, before, I hardly dare to hope, the *Passage to India.* But alas, I'm not writing a *Maurice*" (Zeikowitz 84).[21]

Auden had various reactions to Isherwood's turn to Vedanta, including dismissing it as "heathen mumbo-jumbo" (*My Guru* 204). He also, however, mounted a strong defense of Isherwood's conversion. He wrote to Spender: "Christopher feels that he is called, and is certainly taking it very seriously. I think his friends should have enough faith in him to trust his judgment for himself" (Bucknell and Jenkins 77). Auden saw Isherwood's spiritual journey as similar to the one he himself was on: "You mustn't judge [Christopher] by rumours or even anything he writes to you, because in what is a period of re-organisation for him, he cant [sic] express himself properly . . . but deep down, I have a firm conviction that we are not apart but all engaged on the same thing" (80). Agreeing with this assessment much later, Spender argued that "Auden's and Isherwood's attitudes toward religion had a good deal in common. They both used religion as an external discipline modifying their behavior in their lives. . . . They both give a feeling of having a 'special relationship' with God" (Spender 14).

A final attempt at an Auden–Isherwood collaboration, during the American years, shows how their lives had diverged by the 1960s. They talked off and on for years, in person and through letters, about using Isherwood's Berlin material to write a musical. Auden had already written opera librettos for Benjamin Britten and Igor Stravinsky. The final attempt seems to have been when they were both in London in 1961. Isherwood was there to support Bachardy's first one-man show at the Redfern Gallery; Auden and Kallman were in London for the premiere of their opera *Elegy for Young Lovers* at Glyndebourne. Auden brought Kallman in on their project, to Isherwood's chagrin: "He's no use," he noted in his diary. Isherwood's heart was not in the project: "We've had another of these futile talks about the musical. I simply do not see one. . . . It is a sheer waste of time talking about it."[22] To his relief, Auden and Kallman's departure for Austria felt like a tacit abandonment of the idea. Clearly, given the astonishing success of John Kander and Fred Ebb's *Cabaret* toward the end of the decade, there was a musical to be found in that material. However, Isherwood's and Auden's sympathies had shifted, finally, to their new partners.

TOGETHER AND APART

In designating a loosely affiliated group of writers from the 1930s "the Auden generation," scholar Samuel Hynes established critical dogma— Auden was elevated to the pinnacle of his contemporaries. Among those of secondary importance—his supporting cast—were Isherwood, Spender, and a few others, notably Connolly, Upward, and Cecil Day-Lewis. Clearly, though, the fact that Auden and Isherwood departed England together inevitably paired them. According to Gore Vidal, emigration did lasting damage to *Isherwood's* career. Auden's was less affected, owing to the different ways that poets and novelists are viewed. Poets, Vidal claims, "are licensed to be mad, bad, and dangerous to read, while prose writers are expected to be, if not responsible, predictable."[23]

The postwar dominance of the New Criticism in literary scholarship devalued Isherwood. Because of the highly autobiographical nature of most of his writing, formalist analysis had little to say about his work. On the other hand, such criticism of poetry was tailor-made for the kind of work Auden was doing, and his poetry received much attention from scholars. Also, Auden had a caring and well-placed literary executor in Edward Mendelson, who has produced significant scholarship and has been helpful to others in their study of Auden's work. This presence in academia—and his ubiquity in anthologies—has firmly established Auden's place in the pantheon of twentieth-century poets in English.

Additionally, certain prejudices have had a detrimental effect on Isherwood's reputation. The general suspicion about California and his devotion to Hinduism have been a lingering problem. Significantly, too, it was easier to identify the homosexual elements of Isherwood's fiction, particularly the later, American work, than to fault Auden's work for that particular sin. Whereas for decades, readers could assume that the "sleeping head" in Auden's "Lullaby" was a woman's, overt homosexuality in Isherwood's American work resulted in numerous homophobic reviews.[24]

But, with the emergence of queer theory and gay studies, it has become more possible to evaluate Isherwood's work across his entire lifespan. In the past twenty years, the predominance of memoir as a form has also contributed to a resurgence of interest in Isherwood. Furthermore, the publication of his voluminous diaries adds to our understanding of his life and makes possible greater appreciation of his work. Much of the material in these volumes also sheds important light on Auden's life and work. Perhaps now it is again possible to see Auden and Isherwood as the peers that they were when they arrived together in New York in the winter of 1939.

NOTES

A different version of this essay was published as "Auden and Isherwood," in *W. H. Auden in Context,* ed. Tony Sharpe (Cambridge: Cambridge University Press, 2013), 316–25.

1. Christopher Isherwood, *Christopher and His Kind* (New York: Farrar, Straus and Giroux, 1976), 1.

2. Stephen Spender, "Isyyvoo's Conversion," *New York Review of Books,* August 14, 1980.

3. For more on this era, see Lois Cucullu's essay in this volume, chapter 5, "A Queer Progress: Christopher Isherwood, Sexual Exceptionalism, and Berlin in the Thirties."

4. Peter Parker, *Isherwood* (London: Picador, 2004), 150–57.

5. Christopher Isherwood, *Exhumations* (New York: Simon and Schuster, 1966), 19.

6. W. H. Auden, *The English Auden: Poems, Essays, and Dramatic Writings, 1927–1939,* ed. Edward Mendelson (London: Faber and Faber, 1977), 157.

7. Humphrey Carpenter, *W. H. Auden: A Biography* (Boston: Houghton Mifflin, 1981), 192.

8. Christopher Innes, "Auden's Plays and Dramatic Writings: Theatre, Film, and Opera," in *The Cambridge Companion to W. H. Auden,* ed. Stan Smith (Cambridge: Cambridge University Press, 2004), 90.

9. Richard Davenport-Hines, *Auden* (London: Pantheon, 1996), 170.

10. For more about *Journey to a War,* see Marsha Bryant, "Documentary Dilemmas," in *The Isherwood Century,* ed. James J. Berg and Chris Freeman (Madison: University of Wisconsin Press, 2000), 172–86.

11. As we point out in note 7 of Sara Hodson's essay in this volume, "Vernon Old" was the name Isherwood often used in print for Harvey Young.—Eds.

12. Alan Jacobs, *What Became of Wystan? Change and Continuity in Auden's Poetry* (Fayetteville: University of Arkansas Press, 1998), xiv.

13. Christopher Isherwood, *Liberation: Diaries,* vol. 3, *1970–1983,* ed. Katherine Bucknell (London: Chatto & Windus, 2012), 402.

14. Richard Zeikowitz, *Letters between Forster and Isherwood on Homosexuality and Literature* (New York: Palgrave Macmillan, 2008), 78.

15. Don Bachardy, interview with the authors, December 6, 2009.

16. Quoted in P. N. Furbank, *E. M. Forster: A Life,* vol. 2 (Oxford: Oxford University Press, 1979), 238.

17. Richard Canning, *Brief Lives: E. M. Forster* (London: Hesperus Press, 2009), 88–89.

18. Katherine Bucknell and Nicolas Jenkins, eds., *"The Map of All My Youth": Early Works, Friends, and Influences,* Auden Studies, vol. 1 (Oxford: Clarendon Press, 1990), 106–7.

19. Christopher Isherwood, *Lost Years: A Memoir, 1945–1951,* ed. Katherine Bucknell (New York: HarperCollins, 2000), 93n.

20. Peter E. Firchow, *W. H. Auden: Contexts for Poetry* (Newark: University of Delaware Press, 2002), 170.

21. For more about the importance of *Maurice* in the relationship between Forster and Isherwood, see the essays by Xenobe Purvis and Wendy Moffat in this volume.—Eds.

22. Christopher Isherwood, *The Sixties: Diaries,* vol. 2, *1960–1969,* ed. Katherine Bucknell (London: Chatto & Windus, 2010), 82.

23. Gore Vidal, "Art, Sex and Isherwood," *New York Review of Books,* December 9, 1976.

24. For more on the negative reviews of some of Isherwood's work in the 1950s and '60s, see essays by Dan Luckenbill and David Garnes in *The Isherwood Century.*

LISA COLLETTA

7. Isherwood as Travel Writer

Christopher Isherwood's early peripatetic life was for the most part chronicled in his diaries and letters, but nearly all his narratives are marked by a certain formal restlessness. Throughout his career, Isherwood played with generic boundaries, traveling beyond fixed ideas of fiction and memoir, essay, and travel book. Edward Mendelson once noted that Isherwood "writes about himself as if he were not a single person but a disconnected sequence of persons," adding that "to an editor who met him infrequently," he might seem like a "different person every time."[1] As Aaron Jaffe has noted with reference to Isherwood's autobiographical works such as *Christopher and His Kind* and *Lions and Shadows*, "To seek the true Isherwood . . . leaves one with a sense of tautology, shuttling from fictional representation to fictional representation."[2] Isherwood's literary performances have been well examined in his fiction and memoir, but his travel books remain somewhat critically less traveled territory.[3]

His two books overtly dedicated to travel are *Journey to a War*, written with W. H. Auden and published in 1939, and *The Condor and the Cows*, written ten years later and including photographs by his lover at the time, William Caskey. Isherwood frequently engages the idea of the journey in his writing, however, and even just the titles of his other works (both his own and those with Auden) convey the suggestion of movement: *Goodbye to Berlin, Mr Norris Changes Trains, The Ascent of F6, On the Frontier, Down There on a Visit, An Approach to Vedanta, A Meeting by the River.*

Given this topos of movement, one would expect Isherwood to have been a natural travel writer: he was in constant motion at many stages in his life, he was always a keen observer of subtle details, he was endlessly fascinated by the anomalies and inconsistencies of people and things that surrounded him, and he was always a gorgeously descriptive writer, using the freshest of metaphors. Isherwood's "classic" travel books, however, those that hew most closely to travel memoir, are rather awkward examples of the genre, and they are not the best examples of his trenchant eye, keen wit, or frank self-examination. The two travel books are engaging, but for reasons other than those that are generally thought to make travel books good.

In his Berlin stories Isherwood claimed, famously, to be a camera eye, but in his fiction he was never as objective as that metaphor suggests. There are strong elements of autobiography in nearly everything he wrote, and, as Jaffe notes, the reader is always wondering whether the fictional Isherwood carries "the traces of the true Isherwood, or [whether] the autobiographical subject began as a figment of the novelist's license" (46). Oddly enough, in his overt travel works, he is the distanced observer, embracing the use of objective facts and a journalistic narrative style in a genre that actually allows for—and is made interesting by—the filtering of experience through the mind of a quirky or eccentric traveler. Isherwood's literary performing self helped him explore the themes of personality and selfhood in his fiction, but in the travel works, his performance is rather narratively obvious and therefore, ironically, more limited and less truly revealing. He employs the standard types of traveling characters: the appreciative guest, the cranky traveler, the awkward foreigner, and the imparter of curious geographical and historical facts. These performances are part of the travel writing tradition—they are stock characters—and Isherwood's use of them seems to inhibit a more revealing literary performance where the "true" Isherwood can be glimpsed.

This essay is for the most part concerned with *The Condor and the Cows*, since the writing was not part of a collaborative effort. By contrast, in *Journey to a War*, Auden often takes center stage. There is, nonetheless, an interesting moment in the introduction of the 1973 reissue of *Journey to a War*, in which Isherwood, using third person, writes:

> *Journey to a War* was well received, on the whole, when it first appeared: but there were two or three critics, I seem to remember, who objected to Isherwood's narrative tone of voice. Isherwood is indeed all too con-

scious of being Little Me in China; his new riding-boots and his beret and his turtleneck sweater are symptoms of an amateur's stage-fright. So is his excessive use of similes. Disregarding these, however, one can pick up a surprisingly varied assortment of information from him about the country and the period. I therefore make no apology for the republication of his part of this book.[4]

Isherwood switches to first person in the last sentence to rebut the criticism and defend his parts of the book. His comments seem to suggest that criticism must have actually bothered him, or that the self performed in *Journey to a War* is not one of his favorite performances. Notably, in the introduction to *The Condor and the Cows*, Isherwood writes that he will not try "to forestall criticism by apologizing for the many absurdities, inaccuracies and errors of judgment which will probably be found in my work." Then, switching from first to third person, he writes, "A diarist ought to make a fool of himself, sometimes. He aims at being impressionistic and spontaneous, rather than authoritative."[5] So, *Journey to a War* is defensible because it offers the reader "a varied assortment of information . . . about the country and the period," while *The Condor and the Cows*, a decade later, is defensible for exactly the opposite reasons, because it reveals the absurdities of a diarist. Clearly, Isherwood had the earlier criticism in mind when writing *The Condor and the Cows*, and the paradoxical goal of being informative and absurd led to a certain narrative instability.

In his South American book he aimed at being spontaneous and therefore had done no research before leaving because, he tells us in the introduction, "increased knowledge could only have induced humility and an inferiority complex. Most likely, it would have stopped me writing altogether" (*Condor* 4). The book is written in diary form (as is *Journey to a War*), but, actually, it shares very little of the spontaneity or self-revelation evident in his actual diaries. It is very much, though, a "travel diary"—in the sense that it recounts schedules, events, lunches, people met, surly passport officials, and accommodations, pleasant and unpleasant, often with a gem-like clarity of observation. Isherwood is quick to reveal his dislike of discomfort and the boredom of travel, but those are hardly surprising revelations. They are part of the *travail* that accounts for the allure of travel. They are the material manifestation of the larger explorations in the journey. In *The Condor and the Cows*, we really do have an objective, camera-eye narrative, with Isherwood for the most part recording and describing what he does and where he goes, but it seems uncomfortably at odds with his desire to be spontaneous and impulsive. The reviews of the book were generally positive, but the range of responses reveals the narrative imbalance of the book. In one periodical, George Pendle wrote, "Mr. Isherwood is a detached and unemotional observer. Therefore, his slick and entertaining travel-book has documentary value."[6] In the *Hispanic American Historical Review*, an unnamed critic claims that "the book is so much a reflection of personality, that it is difficult to ask what it Means or Signifies."[7]

Just as South America itself seems impossible to understand (many American and British writers seem to go to pieces there, according to Paul Fussell), the narrative voice in *The Condor and the Cows* reflects Isherwood's struggle to be a revealing personality with judgments and prejudices, and the desire to acknowledge that "Christopher Isherwood" is an appearance or a projection, as he wrote just a couple of years earlier in his introduction to *Vedanta for the Western World* (1945). He wants one thing as a writer— to be clever and perspicacious—but he wants to be quite another thing as a human being, empathetic and nonjudgmental, his writerly narcissism tamed. He accepts his dual roles as keen observer and clever performer very early on, but he struggles throughout the book to balance them.

The first chapter, "The Voyage Out," is a direct reference to Virginia Woolf's novel of the same name in which the protagonist Rachel Vinrace travels to South America. Woolf, of course, uses the voyage as a metaphor of self-discovery. At the same time the mismatched collection of passengers on the ship provides her with ample opportunity to satirize Edwardian society. Isherwood wants to do the same, and his genius for observation is evident, but he resists the satirist's delight in attack. His description of his and Caskey's dining table companions on the ship sets the tone for the book, revealing the kinds of things he will observe, the conclusions he will draw, and his desire to be a polite guest so that others are at their ease.

With his characteristic perspicacity, Isherwood takes the couple's measure: the trip was, "almost certainly, her idea. He's a little unwilling. He can't quite relax. For him, as for so many Americans of his kind, a pleasure journey is just another sort of investment—a sound one, most likely, but he has got to watch it" (*Condor* 8). She is determined to enjoy herself— and to make him enjoy himself, too, and Isherwood notes that "the energy she brings to this task is really beautiful and touching." He muses on their relationship:

Perhaps even she isn't quite consciously aware of the significance of their trip. A holiday of this kind is the test, and may be the vindication, of an entire relationship. After years of accepted routine—office work, raising children, shopping, cooking—you take your marriage out of its little suburban frame and set it against a tremendous classic background of ocean, mountains, and stars. How does it stand up? Is it self-sufficient, deep, brilliant and compact like a Vermeer? Or a messy amateur sketch which doesn't compose? (8)

He doesn't speculate any further. Rather, he refrains from satirizing them, and by extension the American values, the traditional gender roles, and commodity culture the couple could represent, and he resists connecting their suburban values with the American and British oil business and imperialism in South America. Instead, Isherwood wonders:

What can we do to help them? We have our place, of course, in the scheme of travel values. We belong to that necessary class of Some Interesting People We Met on the Boat. We are like The Ruins and The Little Restaurant with Atmosphere. No journey is complete without us. (8)

Aware that they will be discussed and described to friends and relatives once the couple's journey is over and they are back in suburbia, Isherwood helps them in the test and in the vindication of their relationship:

Our duty, therefore, is to be strange. Not alarmingly odd; that would scare them. Not enviably independent; that might make them feel somehow dissatisfied with the limitations of their own lives. I must tell stories about China, England, Germany, Hollywood, Nazis, missionaries and movie stars. I must appear bohemian, lively, happy-go-lucky. But I must also drop reassuring hints of wander-weariness, of a longing to settle down in a home of my own. . . . And I must make it very clear, especially to him, that I really earn and respect money. (8–9)

Why he thinks he needs to do this is never made clear, but evidently, he feels the same burden to be pleasant and perform well as a travel writer, too, for he plays a similar role for his reader. His descriptions are lush, his metaphors are fresh, his confessions of boredom, disgust, and wonder ring true, but he resists taking the reader beyond these observations. He generally refrains from making judgments about the people he meets, nor does he inquire about the background of the number of German "refugees" he runs into in post–World War II South America, and he leaves unexplored the bare-knuckled, capitalist escapades of British and American business and political interests.

The travel memoir is clearly a form that Isherwood is not comfortable with. In fact, Brian Finney noted in his biography of Isherwood that while writing *The Condor and the Cows,* Isherwood felt constrained by his inherent good manners. "I should really have approached it in the spirit of *The Air-Conditioned Nightmare* [Henry Miller's 1945 satire on America], but my fatal politeness gripped my pen, and anyhow one cannot insult all kinds of people who sincerely tried to please us and probably thought us as dreary as we thought them" (quoted in Jeffrey Meyers's foreword to *Condor* xv–xvi). One feels he wants to spare his reader this same kind of anxiety. He seems to feel the need to divert us from the more sinister aspects of South America and to entertain us with a clever performance and vivid descriptions of exotic locales.

There is little evidence that those he encountered were bored with him at all, as he is invited to parties and lunches, introduced to politicians, poets, and bullfighters, given tours of everything from the Manicomio (mad house) in Quito to the Shell Oil compound in the Ecuadoran jungle. In fact, everywhere he goes he is celebrated and welcomed into cultural and artistic circles, and this is often the source of his boredom and insecurity, prompting him to unfailing politeness. He writes, "I have tried to show my gratitude in the only way I can, by playing my part as a minor cultural object" (55). He is showered with gifts and books, and constantly embarrassed that he has brought nothing to give his hosts in return. In Colombia, finding himself once again in this situation, he muses, "As usual, I was humiliated—having nothing to give in return. Auden could have sat down and dashed them off a couple of sonnets" (71).

The fact is, Isherwood had no reason to be in South America other than to write a book, which is the worst motivation for a work of travel literature. He admits in a letter to John Lehmann that South America bored him; he is ashamed that it bored him, and he hates it for making him feel ashamed (Meyers, Foreword xvi). He admits, in his diary, that the book lacks a goal, the impetus behind any journey or travel account: "The ideal travel book should be perhaps a little like a crime story in which you're in search of something, and then either find it or find out that it doesn't exist in the end" (xv). The goal of this journey is Buenos Aires and the return home to write a book. In his diaries he refers to "grinding out the

Bogotá chapter,"[8] and Peter Parker claims that Isherwood felt the book was "hackwork."[9] Perhaps Isherwood had a hard time with what he called the "straight journalism" of travel writing because, for the most part, he was no longer anxiously searching for something. He didn't really have a wanderlust, and he had found, to a certain extent, what he was looking for in Los Angeles and in Vedanta, so his complaining about the discomforts of travel sounds very much like mere complaint: dirty hotels, missed trains, rude passport officials.

In his foreword to the 2003 edition of *The Condor and the Cows,* Jeffrey Meyers compares Isherwood's travel work to that of D. H. Lawrence, but this seems a very odd comparison to me. Lawrence was constantly in search of something and someplace. On his deathbed in Italy he wrote, "This place is no good," and as Paul Fussell noted, Lawrence's signature characteristic is his "acute, almost neurotic, sense of place."[10] Lawrence's fascinating and exasperating travel works are marked by the anxious need to get going, as in the fabulous first line of *Sea and Sardinia,* which abandons the subject pronoun in order to hurry on to the verb, to hurry into motion: "Comes over one an absolute necessity to move."[11] Lawrence, like Isherwood, is full of complaint, but each dirty inn, rough journey, and arrogant passport agent is steeped in mythic meaning. The incidents of travel reveal some deep vein of truth about a culture, about the deep eternal struggle for power, or Manichaean opposites. We can only imagine what Lawrence might have done with that poor couple on the boat with Isherwood! They would have sent him into febrile deliberations about how the overly self-conscious modern world has infected the deep unconscious meeting of masculine and feminine power, about how the need for intellectual power militates against the sensual, etc. But it never, certainly, would have prompted him to wonder how he could help put the couple at ease or reassure them in their middle-class fantasy. More likely, it would have led him to the political situation, for Lawrence was a keen though extraordinarily eccentric political observer, and he saw most forms of modern politics—fascism, communism, global capitalism—as forms of neutered, self-conscious, intellectual power subjugating the primal, the sensual, and the individual.

Of course, this is the fundamental difference between Lawrence, the antitourist and modernist traveler, and Isherwood, the postmodern tourist. Lawrence's encounters with government officials, tourist touts, and unscrupulous innkeepers are a struggle between the individual and the gray intellectual power of political systems. Isherwood, who by 1949 is already spiritually skeptical that the individual even exists beyond an "apparition" or a "projection," knows that being a tourist has replaced being a traveler. Lawrence's travel writing is deeply personal, balancing internal feelings with external observations, to create idiosyncratic accounts of interwar Europe that are critical of all overarching ideologies that diminish the individual. As Jeffrey Meyers notes, "Though Lawrence criticized democracy, he did not support Fascism, which was absolutely opposed to his profound belief in spontaneity and individuality."[12] In this way, Lawrence epitomizes what James Buzard defines as the post-Romantic, anti-tourist persona, who in defiance of the "tired classical associations of the Grand Tour" cultivated the "need to demonstrate uniqueness."[13] Lawrence declares forthrightly in *Sea and Sardinia*, for instance, "Happy is the town that has nothing to show. . . . I am sick of gaping at *things*, even Peruginos. I have had my thrills from Carpaccio and Botticelli. But now I've had enough" (141). Though he had had his fill of the great masters, Lawrence's travel writing is written in response to the grand touring tradition.

Isherwood, on the other hand, reveals little need to respond to the inherited European tradition of travel and the Grand Tour. He had shed most of his European baggage upon his arrival in Los Angeles, where, under that "great eye of the sunshine," he finally felt free to be Chris and live "openly . . . and if you appear dressed in red velvet, leading a baby puma nobody bats an eyelid."[14] The acceptance Isherwood found in Southern California is actually more conducive to his famous objectivity than the paranoid culture of prewar Berlin. Judgment is suspended in Hollywood, and the environment, shaped by the movies, the substance of which is in fact a projection, coupled with his dedication to Vedanta and yoga actually encourage an objective observation of life. In his travel book, Isherwood is often disinclined to extrapolate from his own subjective experience a larger meaning. Alan White, his British publisher at Methuen, who was for the most part pleased with the book, admitted that he preferred the parts that were more subjective and "noticed that when called upon to generalize Isherwood did it reluctantly" (Parker 584). *The Condor and the Cows* is fascinating as Isherwood oscillates between recording impressions and then distancing himself from them, but the narrative doesn't fully form a unified whole, a result of his struggle to be a subjective writer and an objective observer.

Isherwood's travel books do not fit neatly into most modern categories. He is not the Grand Tourist, carrying European values to the outermost regions of the globe; he is not the Romantic antitourist who seeks to define himself against mere touristic vacationers; and he is not defined by the tourist gaze, that all-consuming view so typical of contemporary tourist practices. Instead, what he is most thoroughly in *The Condor and the Cows* is a paid tourist. He is there to write a book, and he is far too good natured and well mannered to write something unpleasant. But South America in 1949 is full of historical and political unpleasantness. It was obvious to a writer of Isherwood's perspicacity, but he avoids thoroughly engaging it, lapsing into clever descriptions of people and places, and into the occasional humorous whining when the going gets uncomfortable.

South America is varied and complicated, with its remnants of European colonial past and its politically volatile present. Isherwood knows that we can only know parts of things, and his unsettled narrative reflects the throes of historical and political change in South America. He is deeply aware that he is and can only be a tourist, a word that, in the modern world, is nearly always pejorative. He tries very hard to be a good visitor, but he often pays for it at the expense of being a perspicacious writer. In his fiction, being called a tourist is a shortcut for being unconscious or unaware of some complicated, harsh truth. In *Down There on a Visit*, for instance, Paul accuses the Isherwood character, "You know, you really are a tourist, to your bones," and in *Prater Violet* a film editor essentially accuses the literary types in Hollywood of being tourists, "bloody romantics" who mistake the movies for literature.

Isherwood's position as a tourist, that is, traveling without much of goal or without looking to solve a crime—a crime of history, of place, of passion—or a mystery about himself, is at the root of much of the restlessness, anxiety, and boredom he feels in South America. Meyers notes in the foreword that Isherwood's persona is in "striking contrast to the grim experiences he describes" (*Condor* xvii), and also to the haunting black-and-white photographs by Caskey. Meyers describes his style as "spontaneous, breathless and sketchy," but it is also rather superficial. He mentions the poverty he sees, the American and British exploitation of the people and the land, but his desire to be an engaging visitor frequently prevents him from writing ambivalently, or even ironically, about government officials or business executives who took time out of their busy days to escort him to prisons and oil refineries deep in the jungle.

As Isherwood himself said, he had trouble writing *The Condor and the Cows* because his "fatal politeness" hindered him in writing more honestly about what he saw, and this could account for the numerous references to feeling guilty, ashamed, and humiliated. It could also account for some of the dark metaphors that abound in the book, which frequently involve crime and punishment. He describes a political leader he is introduced to as "capable" and "impassive. . . . Not a man to be friends with, but one you might temporarily rely on to get you out of an emergency, such as a rape charge" (24). He and Caskey stay at the Hotel Departmental in Bogotá and have a room "rather like a prison cell" (41). Their Colombian guide, who knows all the painters, writers, and composers in town, is so conscientious about answering their questions that "you would think he was testifying on oath at a murder trial" (49). The intellectuals he meets want to talk politics, but Isherwood refuses the "trap" for fear his responses will be printed (51), and when Isherwood is asked to read an excerpt from one of his books, Caskey looks on "with the expression of one who is forced by circumstances to be present at an abortion but is determined to see, hear and know nothing of what takes place" (59). Once, as Isherwood was leaving a church in Bogotá, an Indian shouted at him "Aleman, Nuremberg, Truman!" Isherwood's reaction was, "No doubt these were just words someone had read to him, but to my chronically guilty conscience they sounded like an accusation. From the Indian point of view, no doubt, all whites are equally responsible for all the trouble in the world. However, everybody laughed pleasantly—so I laughed too" (69). That pleasant laughter—the kind we do to put others and ourselves at ease—is often born from a feeling of anxiety.

Isherwood was always aware of the ways politics and ideology constrain the individual, but he was never much interested in writing about those things, per se. He was more at ease writing about the complications and anomalies of the human personality. South America, however, demanded a different kind of narrative response than his autobiographical fiction did.

When visiting Quito, Isherwood's observational and breathless style can't seem to reconcile with what he is seeing. He describes the fifty-seven churches, the public statues, which are "good, bad and incredible," and the bustling sidewalks filled with all classes of people, all of whom suffer from low wages and a rising cost of living. Isherwood notes that it is only an "obstinate barrier of pride" that separates the striving middle-class workers, who wear their only suit every day to work, from the manual laborers, dressed in "unashamed rags and patches" and marked by lowered eyes, their heavy burdens held on their backs by leather straps across their foreheads, and dirty barefooted poverty (82).

Isherwood refrains from drawing any connections between the lives of the inhabitants of Quito and the fact that the people he has met so far "have been mostly Americans and British," whom he describes throughout the rest of the Quito chapter. The U.S. ambassador, the British cultural attaché, and the manager of the Shell Oil Company of Ecuador are all there to forward the "angular realities of business and politics." In "Oil in the Jungle," we see Isherwood in one of his politest performances in the travelogue, and he loses much of his distinctive voice and clever similes. In some ways, it forms the symbolic center of the book, as it lays bare in a rather detached way the global economic, political, and environmental issues at stake for South America in the latter half of the twentieth century. The run-up to his and Caskey's visit to the Shell-Mera Oil compound that stretches from outside Quito, deep into the Amazon rainforest, to the borders with Colombia and Brazil, includes a visit to Quito's Manicomio, arranged by the British cultural attaché, and to the local prison. In Freudian terms, I cannot imagine a more symbolically overdetermined itinerary. Within the metaphorical web of discipline and punish, and Isherwood's own preoccupation with guilt in the text, prisons, madhouses, and big business create a disturbing symmetry. He records his visits to the Manicomio, with its four hundred patients and lack of proper facilities, and the prison with a precise camera eye. It is not clear who is running these institutions, and Isherwood has nothing but praise for the small staff who work with the patients. The experience, however, seems to have had a powerful effect on him, as evinced by his retreat into detachment and straight description. He mentions only two patients, an Indian boy who laughed hysterically with "a kind of cosmic mirth" and a Czech immigrant who mumbled incoherently in German about "a pain in his heart" (86). Isherwood remains at a distance from the narrative, only briefly revealing himself in a humorous aside about his fear of being grabbed by the throat as he knelt down to better translate the man's rambling German.

The prison housed 350 men, most of them murderers, which Isherwood puts down to the tropical climate, "where killing is very seldom premeditated" (87). The premeditated violence, those of the armies and the business interests that help pay for them, are hinted at in the following entry as they make their way to the Shell Oil compound. Perhaps in a telescoped way, Isherwood wants his reader to make a connection between big business, corrupt politics, and exploitation of the local population, as the British attaché's Ecuadoran assistant laments the poor sanitation, bad food, and inadequate accommodation, while all the government's money goes to the army. This becomes clearer, though a direct connection is never made, when Isherwood remarks on the positively military efficiency and orderliness of the oil compounds. As they travel by bus to Ambato, a pleasant town that houses many of the oil company's workers and their families, and a number of German immigrants who run restaurants and chocolate shops. The presence of so many Germans raises no narrative eyebrows, only a clever note about seeing *Mein Kampf* in the rectory of a church, even as Isherwood noticed that the names of several of the buses they passed en route to Ambato are named "Lenin" and occasionally "Hitler" (apparently most Ecuadoran buses have names). He relays this information as a humorous oddity, a quirk of Ecuadoran fancy, but it is telling. As intellectual and literary classes in Ecuador, Peru, Colombia, and Argentina argue using increasingly worn-out ideological language, American and British interests are piercing the interior of the jungle and creating a new kind of economic world order, happy to exploit former fascists and indigenous workers. Up in the camp, with its "military order and tidiness," Isherwood marvels that only a few short years ago, "the site was a swampy virgin jungle" (92). As they fly out over the Amazon, Isherwood performs his nervous traveler self, too preoccupied with his own fear of flying to question what he is seeing. The oil fields below look like "neat rectangular pieces cut out of a very thick rug," and the huge irony of the camp being named for a Jibaro Indian chief passes without comment. As they go farther into the jungle by jeep, Isherwood notes that the Aucas Indians are a real danger to the workers, with their long blowpipes and small featherless spears, the tips dipped in poison. The hatred of whites, he journalistically explains, probably goes back "to the period of rubber raids, when prospectors murdered and tortured hundreds of forest Indians" (95, 93). As he describes the derricks, bulldozed tracks of land and twisted trees, and rows of Indians watching from the sidelines, it is hard to feel empathy with Isherwood complaining about mosquito bites and the humidity. His only truly spontaneous comment is that despite the "good-humored bitchery" among the drillers and engineers, he found something "sinister about the place, even in the daylight. All around the clearing, the dark, living tangle of the forest stands up like a prison wall" (96).

The rest of the narrative describes more cultural entertainments, visits with artists with leftist sympathies, rich families who are "pro-Shell," and local leaders who are in favor of "letting American business interests run" things (136). Isherwood astutely avoids political arguments and discussions, retreating to the safety of a clever remark when pressed by an artist or writer. He saves his commentary for the last entry of the book, but it is somewhat noncommittal. He writes that South America is a land of contrasts, a rare clichéd misstep from Isherwood, revealing just how uncomfortable he is drawing conclusions about the various forces at work in the places he visited. Wisely, Isherwood admits that he hasn't seen South America "as a whole" because there were many countries they did not visit, and he writes that the metaphor of the condor and cows is the most apposite. The condor is the emblem of the Andes and the mountain republics, while the cows represent the great cattle-bearing plains, specifically Argentina. As Meyers suggests, the title seems to point to the internecine warfare of the continent, the appalling prospects for the immediate future of much of South America. The condors peck out the eyes of the cows and then drive them off the edge of a cliff, where they later feast on them. Isherwood writes that this sad state of affairs is a result of the colonial past: "In order for the countries to be nations, they must cease to be colonies" (213). He seems more comfortable writing about the past, not the present, and the legacy of colonialism and corruption left by Spain and the Catholic Church, from which countries must free themselves in order to move into the future. Indeed, the church's legacy of exploitation and superstition is one of the few areas in which he readily makes a judgment. He claims that he and Caskey are not "good tourists" when, in Quito, they "tire easily of" seeing "so much splendor—of golden altars, carved choir stalls, intricately molded ceilings, murals painted on marble, crucifixes of silver and ivory, monstrances flashing with jewels" (83). Isherwood's reaction again seems almost clichéd, an antitourist, antiromantic admission that he perhaps felt free to express because he and Caskey were not hosted by any church officials.

The rise of modern tourism occasioned numerous reflections and much humor about the tendency of tourists to invade or occupy foreign places. More sophisticated "travelers" sought ways of demonstrating that they could be, as Lord Byron put it, "Among them, but not of them" (quoted in Buzard 80). Disavowals of transformative power went hand in hand with claims to a special kind of ownership of the visited place, and this attitude can be seen in some of Isherwood's summing-up statements at the end of the book. Isherwood is not a travel writer in either of these senses, however; he readily admits that South America bored him, and mostly he just felt guilty and uncomfortable. More postmodern than modern, his literary traveling performance rejected any transformative power of place, and he harbors no romantic desire to be "among them but not of them." He comments only once on the seductive appeal of dropping out and living as a tropical expat, "Known all over the Caribbean. They call him Curacao Chris" (12). He knows full well, though, that if American business interests pull out, civil unrest will follow:

> The single brutal word SHELL, painted black on the silver storage tanks in the harbor, should be enough to recall the tourist from his daydreams. . . . [The place] depends on Venezuela for its crude oil and its food, and on the world's shipping lines for its trade. It is at the mercy of every economic crisis, not to mention local political disturbances and global wars. It has little agriculture and hardly any rainfall. If its lifelines are ever cut, or interrupted even for a comparatively short period, most of the inhabitants will have to quit or starve. This is no place for beachcombers. The romantic tourist had better leave it to its extremely businesslike tradespeople, pay for his beer and get back on board his ship. (12)

This is postmodern antitourism—mocking the self-conscious, modernist romantic traveler who longs for exotic authenticity—and it is Isherwood at his best. But ironic postmodern detachment is a tough performance to sustain in travel writing. A witty, distanced observation of people in the grip of political, economic, and environmental exploitation can seem merely superficial or glib. Isherwood's well-mannered performance in *The Condor and the Cows*—focused on a destination off the beaten track, indeed on the very edge where the first and the developing worlds collide, in a period in which the West's international political agenda seems to be laying down pipe for a global cycle of economic boom and crisis, war and revolution—

demonstrates both a wise postmodern detachment and a superficial narcissism. Most notably, it dramatizes—in quite engaging prose—the attempt to reconcile a posture of aesthetic detachment with a politically implicated one that attaches to one side or the other in a relationship of unequal power between host and guest. Isherwood's South American book looks back on tourist and antitourist practices, implicitly calling all such performances into question by displaying its own uncomfortable negotiation between good manners and low politics.

NOTES

1. Edward Mendelson, "The Myths of Christopher Isherwood," *New York Review of Books,* December 19, 2013, 79.

2. Aaron Jaffe, *Modernism and the Culture of Celebrity* (Cambridge: Cambridge University Press, 2005), 45–46.

3. On this, see Lisa Colletta, "The Celebrity Effect: Isherwood, Hollywood, and the Performance of Self," in *The American Isherwood,* ed. James J. Berg and Chris Freeman (Minneapolis: University of Minnesota Press, 2015), 227–42.

4. W. H. Auden and Christopher Isherwood, *Journey to a War* (London: Faber and Faber, 1973), 8.

5. Christopher Isherwood, *The Condor and the Cows: A South American Travel Diary* (Minneapolis: University of Minnesota Press, 2003), 4.

6. George Pendle, *International Affairs* (Royal Institute of International Affairs 1944–) 26, no. 2 (1950): 295.

7. A. M., *Hispanic American Historical Review* 30, no. 2 (1950): 220.

8. Christopher Isherwood, *Diaries,* vol. 1, *1939–1960,* ed. Katherine Bucknell (New York: HarperCollins, 1996), 408.

9. Peter Parker, *Isherwood* (London: Picador, 2004), 584.

10. Paul Fussell, *Abroad: British Literary Traveling between the Wars* (New York: Oxford University Press, 1980), 145, 147.

11. D. H. Lawrence, *Sea and Sardinia* [1921], in *D. H. Lawrence and Italy* (New York: Penguin, 1986), 11.

12. Jeffrey Meyers, *Lawrence: A Biography* (New York: Knopf, 1990), 135.

13. James Buzard, *The Beaten Track: European Tourism, Literature, and the Ways to "Culture," 1800–1918* (Oxford: Oxford University Press, 1993), 110.

14. Christopher Isherwood, *Kathleen and Christopher: Isherwood's Letters to His Mother,* ed. Lisa Colletta (Minneapolis: University of Minnesota Press, 2005), 136 (letter of May 23, 1939).

8. *The World in the Evening*

Character in Transit

> He sees only what we all ought to see, and can't: ... the throbbing
> self that formed this covering shell and then slipped out of it.
> —ELIZABETH RYDAL, *A GARDEN WITH ANIMALS*

Christopher Isherwood, who is best known for his Berlin stories from
the 1930s and for his novel *A Single Man* from the 1960s, produced in
1954 *The World in the Evening*, a work of fiction that ever since its appearance has been the object of derogation. Isherwood himself approved the
hostility in his public talks, given between 1963 and 1965, at the University
of California, Berkeley, and the University of California, Los Angeles.[1] He
planned a detailed explanation in an unfinished memoir, *Lost Years*, which
he began in 1971 (and which was posthumously published in 2000). Isherwood based *Lost Years* on his memory and on his diaries of 1945–51,
the period the book aims to recover. "With a scholarly precision he might
have mocked when [he was a Cambridge undergraduate] studying history in the 1920s," Katherine Bucknell writes, "he sharply criticized and
questioned his memories, trying to establish exactly what happened and to
understand why."[2] Confusing transitions in his life appear to have caused
his novel's alleged inferiority. Religious doubts (he had thought of becoming a Vedantic monk) troubled him. And he was assailed by eros-inspired
conflicts. Isherwood notes that "neither [he] nor [his lover at the time Wil-
liam] Caskey was wicked enough or desperate enough to create an authentic Hell around himself. Their guilt and their suffering was miserably half-

assed. Which is why ... it was ... commemorated by a miserably half-assed novel, *The World in the Evening*" (*Lost Years* 182).

It's an evaluation that critics and biographers have fixedly maintained, not least because they have been bent on pursuing matters that are, so to speak, whole-assed. Isherwood, sharing the pursuit, lays the blame for the novel above all on his not being true to himself (*Lost Years* xxv). He thought he needed to identify with his I-narrator protagonist, but the character of the narrator escaped him. I want to propose the unintended irony of his lament. Despite Isherwood's complaints, the novel forcefully demonstrates that character of an integrated, fixed kind, the very sort Isherwood claims to have missed, is elusive and illusory. That transition is a never-ending fate. *The World in the Evening* argues, in effect, that when a novelist, or a literary critic, or a biographer-historian, attempts to grasp a person's or an era's essential definite character, the effort is not likely to succeed. Fiction ought to admit the difficulty, especially if real-life norms of representing character and history suggest otherwise.

Without such admission, however, the recovery of integrity has become the established story of Isherwood's emergence from his postwar uncertainty. Surely neither the author nor his critics can be wrong, especially when the author and his critics agree! Queer cultural historians have signed on to the standard "authorized" dismissal of *The World in the Evening*. They explain the novel's aesthetic flaws, or posit them, as a result of Isherwood's being cagily closeted, compromised not by Vedanta or Caskey but by his submission to his pre-Stonewall era. The novel therefore is Isherwood's alibi for a lack of candor, for merely tepid gay partisanship. Such claims are surprising, if only because the novel is narrated by a bisexual protagonist, and includes three gay men: one who seduces the narrator before going off to fight against fascism in Spain, and the other two a gay couple, one of whom is a navy man and gay militant (no global conflict seems to matter, he says, "compared with this business of being queer and the laws against us" [*World* 281]). Even more, a seminal discussion of high and low camp is one of the text's prominent components. For queer commentators the book was bad, and remains so, it seems, because history got better, and Isherwood was late in catching up.[3]

Lost Years was his attempt to catch up. Bucknell rightly recalls Isherwood's Cambridge curriculum: with *Lost Years*, the novelist returns to the study of history, in an effort to establish the truth of his wartime and postwar past. *Lost Years,* I want to suggest, appears to conform to the notion of history advanced in Isherwood's era by the English historian R. G. Collingwood. For Collingwood in *The Idea of History* (1946), history is what results when historians approach the mind of the past with deliberated questions and reflections about it, and when they assume that past minds are also purposeful, reflective ones. The meeting of past and present minds—the integration of like aspects of differing identities or characters—amounts to a historian's reenactment of the past. It reveals new meanings about the relationship between two historical moments. The disparities between those times, or between earlier and later selves, is recalibrated in the meeting of past and present. Accordingly, a trustworthy retrospection, and a fixed and authentic identity, can be saved from misleading, merely transitory appearances.

But does *Lost Years* really exemplify such careful historiography? Inasmuch as Isherwood knew in the past what he felt but frequently did not know what he wanted, he therefore did not know what he planned on. His "history" is partly impaired by his object: himself, or the self that he was. The impairment might show when Isherwood, who historicizes himself by writing in the third person, makes notes such as "Christopher had supper with Tony Hyndman and this was most likely the night . . . when they had sex together. The sex was as enjoyable as it had been in the old days, only now it was Tony who fucked Christopher" (145). That note probably does not amount to what Collingwood calls history. What history is made, and what reflection is achieved, by "now it was Tony who," et cetera? It records a fact of immediate experience, to be sure; but for Collingwood "the immediate, as such, cannot be re-enacted" by the historian, because its immediacy, fleeting and unstable, escapes the self-conscious reflection of the past actor and the present archivist.[4]

The immediacy of sex might throw real history for a loop. But whether or not Isherwood's historical writing evokes sex, it is liable to become less than history (or more than it) because it is attached to what Collingwood recognized as a difference between history and art. The difference is formulated in one of Collingwood's "Epilegomena" to *The Idea of History*: "The artist is a great deal less reflective" than other thinkers, Collingwood says; the artist "seems to be working in a world of pure imagination . . . never in any sense knowing what he is going to do until he has done it." His resulting achievement "is grafted on the body of his unreflective experience" (314). Stephen, the bisexual narrator of *The World in the Evening*, is legible as the novelist's own "body of unreflective experience." "I don't think I knew clearly *what* I wanted" (261) is the narrator's refrain as he reflects on the course of two marriages and one homosexual affair. His plaint can be assessed as the symptom of Isherwood's insufficient graft of his reflective capacity as a novelist onto unreflective experience. Unsatisfied as he and we are with such an impairment, what if the insufficiency, and its impact on Isherwood's characterization of unstable Stephen, is a symptom of a perennial divide between history and fiction, is a counterhistorical element that our research into fiction will always confront?

Rather than be impatient with what T. S. Eliot in "The Dry Salvages" calls "Something that is probably quite ineffable: / The backward look behind the assurance / Of recorded history," we might adopt an alternative attitude toward fiction's uneasy relation to historical reflection and documentation. More in tune with that uneasy relation, Kenneth Burke defines history differently from Collingwood. In the 1955 introduction to *Attitudes toward History* (1937), Burke writes, "By history is meant primarily man's life in political communities"; and political communities, he says, are composed of "characteristic responses of people in their forming and reforming of congregations." Those congregational responses are attitudes whereby "some pure aim or vision" is translated into a "corresponding material embodiment . . . necessarily involving elements alien to the original, 'spiritual' ('imaginative') motive." Burke calls such material translation of pure aims the "bureaucratization of the imaginative."[5] Any utilitarian routine bureaucratizes imaginative possibilities and involves elements alien to the original. Scholarship—in the forms, for example, of history or literary criticism or queer studies—is surely one of the utilitarian routines. We professional critics and literary historians are, for better or worse, bureaucrats of vision. Perhaps Isherwood, in looking back at his characterization of Stephen as well as at Stephen's story, was bureaucratizing his vision of his own transitions, and of his character's.

If and when bureaucratization might absorb imaginative motives, it might betray them. In the name of the value of post-Stonewall progress (another story of triumphant issue from an insufficiently whole past), an inevitable bureaucratization has not betrayed, but perhaps has missed—or misprised—a postwar wave of queer fictions, amid which Isherwood's novel and his characterization of Stephen emerged. Constituting a virtual gay liberation *avant la lettre,* the prominence of gay lives in novels published between 1946 and 1953 marks a significant literary- historical transition of its own. A partial list of period authors for whom homosexuality and bisexuality are imaginative motives must name James Baldwin, James Barr, John Horne Burns, Isabel Bolton, Paul Goodman, William Goyen, Patricia Highsmith, Chester Himes, Charles Jackson, Willard Motley, Thomas Hal Phillips, Gore Vidal, and Donald Windham. Those names do not include authors like Norman Mailer, Tennessee Williams, and Calder Willingham, whose novels represent homosexuality less centrally. English novels must be reckoned as part of the wave—William Cooper's *Scenes from Provincial Life* (1950), Mary Renault's *The Charioteer* (1953)—as must novels in translation, Thomas Mann's *Dr. Faustus* (1948) for one. The awarding of the Nobel Prize in 1947 to André Gide canonized a subject matter and experiences that in the history outside of fiction remained bureaucratized as illegal. Yet Gide's career summed up a previous half century of queer literary presence. The postwar surge of gay novels (complete with happy endings in Highsmith and Renault) can be interpreted as itself already a further step in the congregational normalizing—by novelists—of the pure imaginative aims inspiring it. Did the suddenly refreshed field of gay fiction thereby pressure Isherwood to characterize Stephen as bisexual because gay men were already becoming less original material? The influence of other gay novels on Isherwood's controversial compositional choices for *The World in the Evening*—the sexually labile narrator is only one such choice—has scarcely been addressed, although *Lost Years* gives us hints of the influence via Isherwood's lists of the books he read each year. And hints are an essential medium of literary history—by which I mean the history of fictions in relation to each other, a business that goes on ineffably, behind the assurance of history recorded outside of novels.

Although I have cited a group of queer fictions that exhibit the character of homosexuality in transition, and that underwrite, or cowrite, Isherwood's work, I don't claim it as an all-defining matter. Fictions intermingle with each other, as do the diverse times of their production. Their character, and their meanings, remain transitory. Isherwood's reading suggests his disconnection from the daily situations to which his diary and his history are affixed. Enabled by absorption in others' imaginations, the medium of his detachment is an unmoored temporality—and a transitive identity. On rereading Cyril Connolly's 1936 novel *The Rock Pool* in 1947, Christopher "loved it, and has loved it ever since" (i.e., into the 1970s), even though originally he had hated it because it seemed not "socially conscious" (*Lost Years* 141). In 1947 its lack of social consciousness, embodied in its drifting protagonist and in the lesbians he becomes obsessed with in a Riviera watering hole, appears to be part of its new appeal. Indeed, in *The World in the Evening* the bohemian Riviera setting where, in 1935, Stephen meets his second wife-to-be, and where his mortally ill first wife, Elizabeth, who is a novelist, describes her visits to magical rock pools, seems lifted from Connolly.

The point of recounting this "theft" is the support it might give to an assessment of Stephen's characterization that resists Isherwood's later censorship of his own creation. Connolly's anti-hero scraps his plans to write a historical monograph and devolves into aimlessness. The devolution is valuable, as Connolly points out in an introduction to his novel, because the aimlessness of *The Rock Pool's* characters models an escape from their historical time. They embody what Connolly discovered in his belatedly realized love for Horace and other Roman poets: that literary history is not the same as history, and that one could have one's being in the former, in a state of mind "not without elevation and melancholy, but unsuitable . . . for the place which it was hoped [one] would take in a democratic and modestly industrious world."[6]

The unsuitable place evades historical consequence. Isherwood's Stephen might be said to cling to this ahistorical attitude, even if it means that at the novel's end he seems only on the brink of a story of his own. In relation to story or history, Stephen indeed is a monster, which is why neither his Frankenstein nor his readers feel easy about him: a fully formed character at the novel's start and one still awaiting invention (and even nativity) at the end. Ever in a transitional state, he is at once an adult and a fetus. His characterization remains a permanent crux. Its crossing of opposites, along with Stephen's never quite knowing what he wants, resists the reflective address that a historian—including Isherwood as his own historian—would look for in a real person or real events. Fiction becomes history only when its imaginative extravagances are made more useful to demanding congregations. The characterization of Stephen belongs more to something like Connolly's transhistorical state of mind than to situated circumstance. It belongs as well to the split and inchoate identities in whose terms

Isherwood always represents himself in his novels, even though he objects to this particular example of his practice.

The contemporary gay-related novels that Isherwood read and liked—Willingham's *End as a Man* (1947) and Barr's *Quatrefoil,* published in 1950—might have contributed more than the history of Isherwood's life in 1947–50 to the making of Stephen, who, as Bob Wood in the novel characterizes him, is a "hermaphroditic mermaid" (*World* 116).[7] And so in a way is Isherwood. If his reading of fiction unmoors him from a determinate historical time, similarly, in his appreciation of the novels by Willingham and Barr, he straddles diametrically opposed attitudes toward dissident sexualities. The military cadet hero in *End as a Man* engineers the flight from the academy of a classmate who is aggressively queer. The cadet's action marks an advance in his assumption of worldly manhood. In contrast to Willingham's cadet, the young naval officer hero in *Quatrefoil* finds his manly end by yielding to his desire for an older male and retreating from his worldly responsibilities. Juxtaposed with those other protagonists, Stephen is in transit between them, an intermediate type, determined so by a self-splitting in Isherwood's imaginative engagements with antithetical visions. The putative unevenness or irregularity of Isherwood's treatment of his hermaphrodite might have been also influenced by Willingham's and Barr's novels. Both give the impression of their authors resisting a unity of form and content, of their wanting off-kilter, unresolved visions of their protagonists.

The gap between imaginative vision and its bureaucratizing or normalizing containment might be indicated in fiction by any novel's poetics of character. Does a novel offer its readers characters whose hearts and minds can be read in the same disparity-leveling way that fits the historian's mind to the mind of the past? Implicitly probing the question, *The World in the Evening* adventures a metafictional drama about characters and characterization. Isherwood projects himself into the novel as a transitional, transgendered alter ego: as the novelist who is Stephen's first wife, Elizabeth, and whose surname—Rydal—suggests that novels are written riddles rather than reflective histories. Elizabeth formulates "the Original Sin of novelists": their persuasion of readers that human beings are in reality "characters" and "that you can treat human beings as characters; that you can know them fully and possess them." But in life you can't do either, Rydal says. In conventional fiction characters are well-rounded; in life, she explains, "they're full of contradictions; and they have no shape . . . only a general direction" (236–37). The general direction itself dissolves in the medium of time, whose destabilizing effect, I would add, is the bane—as well as the impetus—of historical research.

The need to imagine character seems necessary for history (and literary history) because historical reflections cannot form themselves in the face of character-less phenomena. Even if the past is above all a matter of impersonal facts, we expect those facts to be given a shaping face, a stable figuration. But is Rydal's account of novelistic character necessary for fiction? If she appears to answer affirmatively, Isherwood disagrees with his female alter ego. Behind that alter ego is a male, E. M. Forster, whose *Aspects of the Novel* (1927) famously distinguishes "round" characters in fiction from "flat" ones—in fiction and in life. Elizabeth's version of "well-rounded" borrows from Forster. Much as Isherwood loved Forster (perhaps necessitating, to hide disagreement with *Aspects,* a hermaphroditical disguise), Isherwood makes Stephen's character move from rounded to flat and back again; and this means Stephen's character is both and neither. *The World in the Evening* experiments with character, allowing its slippery narrator to be a character and to be character-less, resistant to possession, simultaneously outside fictional conventions as well as inside them.

Isherwood's experiment in characterization is made possible by a notable device. Early on, Stephen is involved in an accident that leaves him in a body cast for the whole of his narration, largely a retrospective view of his loves and failures. The plaster cast, one might suggest, is by turns Isherwood's metaphor for history and his metaphor for a character who is stuck. By stabilizing Stephen temporarily, the cast makes historical reflections possible for him. They bring his mind back in touch with his late novelist wife through the documents—the letters and books—that are her life's traces. Stephen thereby prepares to become Elizabeth's literary executor, and her editor and biographer, as well as his own autobiographer. It requires a break with immediate life, however, to reenact the past—and to cast it into form.

The break and the cast are also metaphors for fiction. The break gives Stephen the opportunity to turn Elizabeth the novelist into a well-rounded character in a novel. Stephen sought that transformation when she was alive, in part resentfully, in order to get back his own. "You invented me," he complains to Elizabeth's ghost; "I was the most lifelike of all your characters"

(*World* 18). "Lifelike" on conventional fiction's terms, but somehow not living. When in the future Stephen will publish Elizabeth's correspondence, she will become the one character, the one likeness of "life," he has engendered—and yet he will remain inscribed as her creation. How will he free himself? When the reader first meets him, slamming the door on his doll's-house-like second marriage, Stephen is not a pure possibility, but the variant of an Ibsenite invention. Moreover, inside the doll's house is another version of Stephen's identity: the movie star pursuing Stephen's wife, Jane, also desires her husband, hence mirrors her husband's bisexual indefiniteness. Stephen has been here before, in the previous stages of his "novelized" life: in the triangle constituted, earlier in time but later in the narrative, by Stephen, Elizabeth, and Stephen's would-be adoptive son and then would-be lover, Michael Drummond. At Jane and Stephen's divorce celebration, Jane tells him that she and her newest husband are reading Elizabeth Rydal—including Rydal's novel *The World in the Evening*—and are feeling that Stephen and Elizabeth have taken on the glamour of fictional beings. Stephen cannot escape his lifelike but unliving fictive cast. Yet Stephen wants to escape the character traits that are continually being assigned to him. To the annoyance of commentators, Isherwood, queering Stephen's characterization in the form of the protagonist's desire to escape from the rigidifying effects of novelization, suggests a form of being that is neither a property of conventional fiction nor an intelligible historical entity. Such a being is between both, in transit.

The novelist's Original Sin tempts those to whom it is offered: it promises a cast-like stability of personhood, an equivalent of regulation. Stephen and Michael have both wanted to be interesting enough, and stable enough, for Elizabeth to put them in her books. She does. But clearly the novelist's Original Sin also constrains Isherwood's figures, who begin in search of an author and end in flight from one. Eros deregulates holistic, rounded, and "authentic" characterization. Stephen has a Quaker aunt whose associates have invented a rigid identity for her. When they discover that she has a withdrawn secret side—she has been in love with Stephen's father—they are shocked. Charles, a physician, is one member of the novel's featured gay couple. He notes that it's a drawback for a beloved to be fixedly legible. In effect, Charles can't read his partner, Bob. But "if I did," he says fearfully, "that'd be another kind of relationship" (111). The fact that one lover does not add up for the other one is not a promise of living happily ever after, however. There is a deep, melancholic logic to the surprising separation that the gay lovers undergo at the novel's end. Almost all Isherwood's pairings of lovers—I count up to twelve—break down.[8] The broken relations underline the war between fiction's Original Sin and the sin's potential redemption. The redemptive aspect or medium is escape from the eros that encloses lovers in plaster casts. The escape is downright painful, if only because it means an inchoate transition, a "passing back and forth," as Stephen says, "between . . . two utterly dissimilar halves of . . . life" (233); and a passing back and forth not only between being in love and out of it, but also between character and dissolution of character, or between history and dissolution of history.

The organization of *The World in the Evening* concentrates its emotional power in chapters 4 through 7 of the novel's second part. Stephen's marriage to Elizabeth, her miscarriage of their child, the whole of Stephen's affair with Michael, the resumption of Stephen's premarital promiscuity and his drift toward Jane, the death of Elizabeth, the death of Michael's lover Henri in the Spanish Civil War, and the final appearance and final loss to the narrative of Michael: all of it is compacted into the central 125 of the novel's 300 pages. E. M. Forster, in a letter to Isherwood, expressed bafflement at Isherwood's having interrupted the story of Elizabeth's failing heart in 1935 with a proleptic leap to 1937 when Stephen by chance meets Michael, and when Michael, on his way to inform Henri's mother of Henri's death in Spain, informs the reader—ahead of Stephen—of the death of Elizabeth.[9] Shouldn't that episode do better elsewhere? Forster asked. No, one might argue (pursuing, if not meeting, the mind of the author): the piling up of shocks consolidates the breakdown of the characters as characters. Michael first appeared as a young double of Stephen, wanting lifelike enlistment in Elizabeth's fiction; then he wanted to be given the character of a son to Stephen and Elizabeth; when he next reappeared, he had made himself into a queer political hero fit for fiction in the age of Auden and Isherwood. But his last appearance shows him fatigued, neutralized, out of character. Ironically, Stephen's jealous response to Michael's widowhood shows Stephen wanting to be what he complains about: he imagines that Henri has been for Michael the perfectly legible partner, fully integrated and fully alive, hence a character fit for a conventional novel—and for a history. Later, after his marriage to Jane, Stephen jealously assumes an authorial function and invents the character—as Elizabeth might have—of a rival father for the child Jane is carrying. His invention causes Jane to deliberately abort the child. It is a grim echo of Elizabeth's miscarriage. If we count Stephen's rejection of Michael as a son (before his rejection of him as a lover) the novel comprehends three stillborn beings. The attempts to produce characters that are fitting for conventional fiction make the conjuring of "character" in the novel deathly.

When at the end of *The World in the Evening* the failed couplings dominate the characters' histories, Stephen is about to be a single man. His singleness perhaps is a sign of a singularity that novels can't bureaucratize or make intelligible by means of stabilizing characterization. The singularity, another example of Kenneth Burke's pure aim or vision, drives the invention of character onward, even as it subverts it. Superficially, *The World in the Evening* is a comic narrative, ending with Stephen's release from his past novelist-endowed identity. His transitions have given his identity a clean slate, so that he can begin again, can join up with the historical future. Alas, history gives him a global war to identify with. Clearly, underlying what seems at first glance to be a comic vision is a grotesquerie of fate, a perspective by incongruity, as Burke would say, and not a perspective by congruity—by the integral, supposedly reparative, fitting together of things—as Isherwood the autobiographer or Collingwood the historian might argue or desire.

Isherwood's career-long reach of experimentation with the novelist's Original Sin finds a summary illustration in *Kathleen and Frank*, his 1971 history of his parents. Implicitly recapitulating the metafictional reflections on character and history in Stephen's story, *Kathleen and Frank* tells how Isherwood in his youth invented, as a substitute for his real father, Frank, a character he called the Hero Father; and then, having discovered the real Frank, Isherwood reinvented the Hero Father as a character he named the Anti-Heroic Hero. The Anti-Heroic Hero engendered in turn another character, whom Christopher—or is it Isherwood?—called the Anti-Son. In the character of the Anti-Son, Isherwood adopted flouting the Others as his life's project, as an intention to disrupt all the bureaucratizers, including the historical-political ones, that depend upon the fiction of character to steady their political hopes.

Hence, even when writing history, Isherwood utilizes novelistic character—raised to allegorical status and intensity—and, by virtue of being an Anti-Character, undoes characterization. The Anti-Son exemplifies constructive goodness, but, flouting the Others, he also is an all-dissolving force. Literary critics and historians alike exemplify a countermovement. We seek to overcome resistance to characterizations and thereby to overcome resistance to constructive explanation of history's characters. If we affirm that *The World in the Evening* expresses Isherwood as a virtual personification of pre-Stonewall repression and compromise, we are rounding out his character and taking possession of its transitional history, as if both were elements in a less than experimental fiction. History has every right not to be a fiction, experimental or otherwise. Fiction has every right to ally itself with dissolutions of history and character. And because art does not always answer to the demands of historicizing congregations, it might well be that critical tradition, including Isherwood himself, is unreliable about *The World in the Evening*.

NOTES

1. The texts of Isherwood's lectures about his novels can be found in *Isherwood on Writing*, ed. James J. Berg (Minneapolis: University of Minnesota Press, 2007). The epigraph of the present essay is drawn from a text Isherwood invented: an autobiographical novel by his female protagonist, Elizabeth Rydal, in *The World in the Evening* (New York: Farrar, Straus and Giroux, 1988), 128–29.

2. Katherine Bucknell, introduction to Christopher Isherwood, *Lost Years: A Memoir 1945–1951*, ed. Katherine Bucknell (New York: HarperCollins, 2000), viii. At the beginning of her introductory essay, Bucknell carefully describes the status of *Lost Years*: it is a reconstruction, first by Isherwood in 1971 of his date books and diaries from 1945 to 1951, and then by Bucknell herself. She has, in effect, constructed this "memoir."

3. Jaime Harker, in *Middlebrow Queer: Christopher Isherwood in America* (Minneapolis: University of Minnesota Press, 2013), hypothesizes that Isherwood internalized a Cold War homophobia and therefore "largely degayed the novel" (43). Harker judges the novel's protagonist, Stephen, to be "a down-low monster, manipulative and destructive" (28). The standard older evaluations, intermixing aesthetics and psychological analysis, are represented in Alan Wilde, *Christopher Isherwood* (New York: Twayne, 1971), and Lisa M. Schwerdt, *Isherwood's Fiction: The Self and Technique* (London: Macmillan, 1989). Wilde argues that Isherwood fails his intention, which "is clear enough. . . . Stephen is obviously meant to undergo . . . something in the nature of therapy or exorcism"; hence, "with a ruthless tidiness the novel contrives in its final section to . . . sweep away all Stephen's problems" (110). Schwerdt's psychological extension of the aesthetic assessment notes

that "Isherwood's own understanding of his behavior [projected onto Stephen] did not occur until he met [his lover Don] Bachardy and felt true commitment" (133). In *Isherwood: A Life Revealed* (New York: Random House, 2004), Peter Parker claims that "making Stephen . . . bisexual may have seemed like a breakthrough, but it also made him a character that Isherwood found basically unsympathetic, with disastrous consequences for the novel" (519).

4. R. G. Collingwood, "History as Re-enactment of Past Experience" [lectures delivered in 1936; first published in 1946], in *The Idea of History*, rev. ed., ed. Jan van der Dussen (Oxford: Oxford University Press, 1994), 297.

5. Kenneth Burke, *Attitudes toward History*, 3rd ed. (Berkeley and Los Angeles: University of California Press, 1984). The 1955 introduction in this edition is not paginated.

6. Cyril Connolly, *The Rock Pool* [1936], Direction 12 (New York: New Directions, 1946), 9.

7. In *Lost Years*, Isherwood says that *Quatrefoil* "is at least honest fag-trash" (275n).

8. The inventory of broken or separated pairings—ten out of twelve love relationships—would include Stephen and Jane, Stephen and Elizabeth, Stephen and Michael, Stephen and Gerda (when they go their separate ways, they acknowledge their potential as lovers), Michael and Henri, Bob and Charles (Bob's decision to join the navy separates them), Jane and Roy Griffin, Aunt Sarah and Stephen's father, Elizabeth and Mariano Galdos (whom she loved before Stephen), Jane and Martin Gates (a boyfriend whose initials rhyme with Mariano Galdos's, and whom Stephen treats as a rival). The two successful couples are happy only in prospect: Gerda is to be reunited with her prisoner-of-war husband; Jane is to marry Roger, a businessman who shares Jane's passion for Rydal's fiction, which includes *The World in the Evening*. Stephen, alone at the end, is headed for North Africa, where he will drive an ambulance.

9. Richard E. Zeikowitz, ed., *Letters between Forster and Isherwood on Homosexuality and Literature* (New York: Palgrave Macmillan, 2008), letter of July 2, 1954, 156–57.

9. Pacific Rimming

Queer Expatriatism and Transpacific Los Angeles

Christopher Isherwood was long invested in queer expatriatism. His preference for living outside England was intimately connected to his erotic interest in men. This connection of foreignness and queerness—and expatriate living as a long-term solution—was shared by a number of Isherwood's friends: Somerset Maugham in France, Gore Vidal in Italy, W. H. Auden in Austria (and the United States), and Paul Bowles in Morocco.

Isherwood's queer expatriatism in Europe has received critical attention, but his relationship to the Pacific Rim, in terms of queer desire, has been less explored. His move to Los Angeles in 1939 oriented him toward the Pacific and enmeshed him in a multicultural mix in which Asian culture figured prominently. And in the 1950s, his queer network of friends became increasingly interested in the Pacific Rim as a site of erotic encounters. In this essay, using Japan as a case study, I consider Isherwood's direct and voyeuristic queer adventures in Pacific Rimming, which includes sex tourism, rice queens, and ongoing cross-racial queer relationships that eroticize the Pacific Rim. I end by suggesting the limitations of Isherwood's transpacific imaginary.

Isherwood first visited Japan in 1938 with W. H. Auden. His memory of that trip centers on one image, one he recalled during his 1963–64 trip to India (with a stop at the Imperial Hotel in Tokyo): "Wystan and I first saw it in 1938, and my memory clings to an improbably symbolic tableau: under the chandelier . . . stand two figures in uniform, a Japanese officer and a Nazi gauleiter; in fact, The Axis. As I regard them the chandelier begins to sway—and this is my very first earthquake!"[1]

It is hardly a subtle image—in a hotel called the "Imperial," with the symbols of World War II aggression causing an earthquake through their collaboration. This connection of Japan and Germany would continue to inform Isherwood's understanding of Japan and his own relationship to it, however.

This association is particularly noticeable in Isherwood's unpublished account of his 1957 grand tour of Asia with Don Bachardy. The trip included stops in Hawaii, Japan, Hong Kong, China, Thailand, and (the ostensible purpose of the trip) India, where Isherwood planned to research his biography of Ramakrishna and visit key sites. Isherwood kept an extensive handwritten journal about the trip. He never completed this journal (and may have intended it as a publication), but he did complete a typescript of the journal, drawing from his own handwritten notes and from Bachardy's diary. It is not included in Katherine Bucknell's published diaries but exists as a fascinating artifact in Isherwood's archives at the Huntington Library, both in its handwritten original version and as a prepared written typescript.[2]

What one notices first about his Asia diary is that the journey was more about transpacific queer tourism than spiritual enlightenment. Isherwood's most repeated insight—that one can tell the difference between America and Japan based on the names of the gay bars (the Honolulu bar was named the Clouds and the Japanese gay bar was named Ibsen)—says a lot about how he and Don spent their time on this vacation. Isherwood's journal marks a number of these outings. A bar called the Sire featured "a few exaggeratedly graceful Japanese boys with spit-curls or high fluffy pompadours," called "Sister-boys." Isherwood explains, "Tokyo's night-life offers every kind of boy-lover, from boy-geishas in full drag rice-powder and black wigs to U.S. style tough guys with leather jackets and motorcyclist's boots in the manner of James Dean" ("Trip to Asia" [TS] 12–13). Trips to bathhouses also were on the itinerary, and while these bathhouses weren't predominantly gay (the way they were in the United States), they did have sexualized areas on the upper floors, and all-male enclaves in the basements, which served as places for sexual encounters for many American visitors and expatriates.

Despite the promise of an exotic, erotic Asian fantasy, Berlin was con-

Christopher Isherwood (far right) in India, 1957. Courtesy of Don Bachardy.

stantly on Isherwood's mind during this visit. At a coffee bar known for "gangsters," Isherwood noticed "a lot of quiet crafty-looking Japanese juveniles sitting sullenly around. The bar reminded me of Berlin in the twenties" ("Trip to Asia" [TS] 11). Another bar in Tokyo—the Shirobasha—was reminiscent "of Berlin; it was a sort of department-store-type establishment like the Haus Vaterland" ("Trip to Asia" [TS] 16). And "a handsome muscular boy named Takata" brought another Berlin memory: "He has a vain grin, very good-humored; he is perhaps just a shade too masculine to be quite natural; he hits walls with his fist as he walks along the street. In appearance and general personality, he reminds me very much of Walter Wolff (the original of Otto Nowak)" ("Trip to Asia" [TS] 11). Just why Isherwood is so eager to read Berlin into Tokyo—a city with a dramatically different language and culture—is an interesting question. One reason might be the prevalence of hustlers in postwar Japan. Like hustlers in pre-war Berlin, Japanese hustlers in postwar Japan were omnipresent because of economic despair. So common was sex work in postwar Japan that the U.S. Army set up an official brothel for its soldiers during the occupation of Japan. Young men in Japan found their own way through American soldiers and, later, tourists.

Japanese sex partners—both hustlers and younger Japanese men—were common in Isherwood's queer networks in the late 1950s through the 1960s. Stephen Spender enjoyed his contacts with Japanese boys during his visit to Japan, guided by the writer Yukio Mishima. Lincoln Kirstein would have his own Japanese "friend" on a visit to Japan in the late 1960s. Novelist John Goodwin, a wealthy friend of Denny Fouts, lived in Japan in the 1950s and wrote Isherwood in detail about gay life there. Jim Charlton, who had himself been Isherwood's fantasy of the American boy, moved to Hawaii. In part and as a result of his involvement with a young man whom he called "Mutsuo"—they met in 1961 in Kyoto—Charlton became one of the most enthusiastic advocates of Japanese boys in Isherwood's orbit.

Charlton's description of Mutsuo was lyric: "You are right to be interested in the character of Mutsuo. He seems to exist in a natural state of grace, with rare and disturbing gifts of intuition. In short, this is the friendship I have been longing for, and we are often very happy together. . . . I don't know what will happen when I leave. I think it will be all right."[3] Charlton was all in on the "cult of Japan," as Isherwood termed it. He wrote in his diary, "Jim is very vague and grand and treats everybody and everything here as so much non-Japanese trash" (*The Sixties* 199). Charlton's claim that Mutsuo is in a "state of grace" suggests the ways that Japan lovers saw the country as an erotic paradise, embracing sexuality as a natural part of life, before the "fall" of Christian repression. As Isherwood recounted in his diary about the same conversation:

> I forgot to note one of Jim Charlton's theories about Japan, namely that one of the chief differences between Japanese and Americans arises from their attitude to masturbation. The Japanese have no shame whatever about this, and Jim believes this is because they are capable of loving their own bodies and don't think it's shameful to do so. He theorizes that all this masturbation makes the Japanese incapable of aggression in their sexual attitudes. An English (or American) guest professor noticed that his students went to the bathroom regularly, almost every hour. He

asked, did they have stomach upsets? No, they explained quite calmly, they had to masturbate, in order to relieve their nervous tension. (208)

Isherwood very carefully doesn't comment on this theory in his journal, though his tone suggests some skepticism. He had already heard a number of theories about the Japanese and sex during his trip to Japan. Don Richie, an American expatriate, was full of similar notions, claiming that "most compliance in sexual relationships is motivated by a sense of obligation and consideration for the foreigner's dignity and feelings. Even if the Japanese doesn't like it, he feels it is his duty to be friendly and agreeable." Further ruminations on the "sex-life of the Japanese" included their "poverty of spirit which matches their economic poverty, and a very limited emotional capacity. They have learned to make do with very little love. If too much demand is made on their emotions or if they are offered too much affection, it confuses them." Homosexuality was accepted, but "there is no secure place for the homosexual in the Japanese social structure, any more than there is in the social structures of the West" ("Trip to Asia" [TS] 15).

These essentialist pronouncements about the Japanese character, and its implied inferiority to Western consciousness, are strangely traditional in their eroticization of Japan. Japan, from the earliest days of *Japonisme*, was seen as an exotic, erotic playground, with cultured and sexually available women who put their own repressed Victorian counterparts to shame.[4] Japanese culture was figured as feminine, submissive, and pleasure granting—a kind of wet dream for heterosexual European men. After World War II, Japan continued to be eroticized through geisha stereotypes. While most of this public Japonisme was heterosexual (James Michener's *Sayonara* is the prototype), American gay men participated in this mystification with great pleasure, and with all the ethical problems of cross-cultural gay sex tourism, which contemporary queer theorists have discussed at length in the last decade.[5]

Isherwood found this queer cult of Japan disturbing. In his Asia journal, he critiques it in ways that echo recent criticism of sex tourism. After describing a "sinister little New Zealander who boasted suggestively of his conquests in bath-houses," Isherwood burst out in his diary, "Ah, how disgusting this sexual colonialism is! And how guilty of it I have been, myself, when young! On the one hand, there is a quite vehement cult of the Japanese; it is regarded as tasteless and almost perverse if you dream of any non-Japanese sex-partner. And yet, how these people despise the Japanese in their sex-relations with them!" ("Trip to Asia" [TS] 12). And that was not the only time he commented on the unethical behavior of "American sex-colonists," as he termed them.

After dinner with a group of expatriates, Isherwood writes, "How indecently they boast, these middle-aged lotharios, of their conquests! What conquests? They herd boys in from the street, half bewildered, half embarrassed and anxious to please." Later, visiting some art dealers in Kyoto, Isherwood goes further in his identification with Japanese hustlers: "The three American art dealers. Sentimental over their human acquisitions and indignant at this lack of gratitude. But why should a boughten boy be expected to feel more of it than a lacquerbox, containing 200 year old dildoes?"[6] Treating the Japanese as objects, American "sex colonists" had no right to complain about their treatment by these hustlers. That this anecdote about "boughten boys" and "dildoes" appears in his handwritten journal, and not (as the rest of the diary) in the typescript journal, suggests that Isherwood was already realizing his insights about queer sexual colonialism could not find an audience during the Cold War—at least not outside his queer circle.

Isherwood saves his most satiric vitriol, however, for "Bruce R.," who, Isherwood writes,

> bitches his fellow sex-colonists for
> (1) not being able to speak Japanese as well as he does
> (2) having a "butch" boyfriend who is secretly queer—one would be ashamed of having a queer boyfriend because one loathes one's own queerness—
> (3) believing in love.
> (4) He admits frankly that he likes living here because he is "a big frog in a small pond." He talks about "extra-curricular activities." He speaks of the boys with hostility and contempt. They are angrily dismissed as being not so young as they were—maybe all of seventeen! Boys are not allowed in his home. He keeps a "playroom" for sex. ("Trip to Asia" [TS] 18)

Isherwood is struck, repeatedly, by the superiority complex and loathing exuded by these American "sex-colonists." But significantly, he includes himself in this indictment, again comparing his own youthful behavior in Berlin with the queer Americans in Japan.

This newfound awareness of the colonial inequities of Pacific Rimming emerges in Isherwood's early 1960s writing. His decision to have a Japanese-American character in *A Single Man* (Kenny's girlfriend, Lois Yamaguchi) was intentional, as he explained in his diary: "Today a Japanese girl character whom I'd introduced for no reason apparent to myself, just as a friend of Colin's (an early incarnation of George), suddenly acquired symbolic status as another Foreigner, stuck midway between being a Nisei in an America she despises and the alternative of going west and being a Japanese in a Japan she doesn't know" (*The Sixties* 186). Isherwood imagines Lois as a heroic counterpart to George, a foreigner whose distance from mainstream culture marks him as superior to the commodified American culture in which they both find themselves. She, like George, cannot return to the place of "origin" and yet will never accept the "America she despises." Though Isherwood doesn't end up doing as much with Lois in the final version of the novel, the fact that he sets up a Japanese character as sympathetic is significant. Isherwood is identifying with the Japanese character, resolutely not exoticizing or eroticizing her, unlike the American sex colonists he so mistrusted. As small as this detail is, it is notable in that it is the only transpacific cross-racial relationship he depicts in his fiction, despite his immersion in Pacific Rimming in Los Angeles. That omission is telling. Was Isherwood so traumatized by the American sex colonists in Japan that he couldn't figure out how to depict such relationships in ethical ways? Was he so worried about enmeshing his Hinduism (another transpacific exchange) with explicit queer sexuality that he couldn't embrace Pacific Rimming in his fiction? Or was it simply that he wasn't attracted to Asian men, and so couldn't depict such relationships sympathetically?

Isherwood's experiences in Japan seem to have prompted him to reflect on his own sometimes unethical relationships with male hustlers in Berlin. In *Down There on a Visit,* which he began writing shortly after he returned to the United States from Asia, he depicts somewhat sanitized, "de-queered" hustlers in all their cheerful, amoral, sometimes campy glory. In particular, the characters Waldemar and Paul get extensive treatment. But perhaps the most direct analogue to the sexual colonialism of Japan is Ambrose's island, populated by young Greek boys. Ambrose sets up an anarchistic kingdom in which the "natives" run the show, blowing up his buildings, serving just-fucked chicken, and otherwise horrifying the white sexual colonialists who would subsume their identities into some kind of colonial fantasy. Geoffrey's priggish English disgust stands in for the white sexual colonialists of Isherwood's Japanese sojourn. Isherwood indicts himself in this sexual colonialism when he and Maria commiserate as monsters, who liked to watch and occasionally to cause drama on the island. "We monsters," explains Maria, in her heavily accented English, "we feel only curiosity. . . . Monsters are heartless, *mon vieux.* You know this—do not be so hypocrite! You cannot hold a monster by his emotion, only by puzzling him. As long as the monster is puzzled, he is yours."[7]

This indictment of voyeuristic, heartless pleasure is important, I think, because despite his horror at the American sex colonists, Isherwood was not immune to the attractions of Pacific Rimming. Some of this appreciation of Japanese "natural physicality" can be seen in his description of going to a bathhouse during his trip to Japan in 1957. The "small groups of naked men squatting around pools of hot water" was "pleasingly animal," Isherwood explained. "You feel like a baboon in a Japanese print. A nice baboon—good-humored, grotesque, quite shameless" ("Trip to Asia" [TS] 15). Isherwood described the initial scene of sex in Waldemar's apartment in similar terms in *Down There on a Visit,* as an "unforgettable, happy, shameless afternoon—an afternoon of closed Venetian blinds, of gramophone music and the slippery sounds of nakedness, of Turkish cigarettes, cushion dust, crude perfume and healthy sweat, of abruptly exploding laughter and wheezing sofa springs" (54). Isherwood translated his transpacific sex tourism into European sex tourism in this novel, showing it as tantalizing and attractive. Even though he recognized the problems of sexual colonialism, his disapproval didn't prevent him from going to bars, baths, and "playrooms" in Tokyo, as well as enjoying the accounts of his friends' affairs with Japanese boys and keeping photographs of them.

Isherwood's epiphany about the exploitative nature of American sex colonists in Japan didn't seem to cause him to reconsider his own relationships, as an English expatriate, with younger American men—relationships not in the past but concurrent with his friends' sexual fascination with Japan. In the early 1970s, when Isherwood was constructing his sexual myth, he talks about his first American relationship with "Vernon Old," and how he "he fell in love with Vernon as the embodiment of The American Boy."[8] That equation of a lover with a nation and a culture continued in his affair with Bill Harris while ostensibly living a celibate life in a Hindu monastery. Bill, he writes, "represented The Forbidden. Also, he was The Blond, an important myth figure in Christopher's life—Christopher had a strong belief that he was, or ought to be, automatically attracted to spectacular blonds. (No reason for this occurs to me at the moment; if I think of one, later, I'll insert it as a footnote.)" (*Lost Years* 18–19). Isherwood's later "insight" about his attraction to blonds (which he did, indeed, insert as a footnote in his diary), is a bombshell of speculation and sexual colonialism, perhaps best described as the "cult of the Viking":

> May 14, 1973. An explanation *has* just occurred to me. It sounds ridiculous, but then psychological insights often do, according to psychologists. . . . Is The Blond maybe an archetype peculiar to the British Collective Unconscious? . . . The Blond, in relation to a primitive Briton, would be the blond Norseman or Saxon invader of his homeland. The Blond conquers, plunders, rapes. He is the masculine yang to Britain's feminine yin. As an individual Briton, you are free to deny that you are feminine, to fight him and get killed—but that's your own affair. The Blond is unalterably yang. As for Christopher, he was quite ready to be yin.
>
> So much for the archetype theory. It may account for Christopher's feelings about blonds as a group. But the fact remains that many of the blonds in Christopher's life were definitely un-yang—pretty, feminine boys who wanted to be fucked. This compels me to theorize further: maybe Christopher unconsciously took over the role of Invader when he went to live in Germany and later in the States? He couldn't become The Blond (though he did, occasionally, dip his forelock in the peroxide bottle) but, as The Invader, he could fuck yin boys even if they happened to be blonds. If the blond boy was yang, Christopher merely had to stop being an invader and think of himself as a yin Briton! (*Lost Years* 19)

This obsession with the conquering Norseman, a rape fantasy, becomes Isherwood's trope for his sexual interest in younger men, both in Germany and in the United States. He is describing his own conduct as similar to that of the "aging Lotharios" in Japan, but by 1970, Isherwood isn't horrified by sexual colonialism. Partly, as I discuss below, this is because gay liberation had provided another way to understand such relationships, but it is also because he ascribes to himself more positive motives than he allows the Americans he meets in Japan. He concludes his exploration of his sexual myth with a different interpretation:

> Still, I can't believe that Christopher literally thought of himself as an
> invader—that is such a Jewish fantasy. Certainly, he wanted to "possess"
> Germany and the United States; not by conquering them, however, but
> by exploring them and learning to love them. He tried to do this by look-
> ing for an ideal German and later an ideal American Boy, through whom
> he could explore and love these countries. (*Lost Years* 19)

Leaving aside (for the moment) the casual anti-Semitism of Isherwood's
absolution of himself, he reclaims his own relationships through pure
motives. Using ideal German boys and American boys to learn to love his
adopted countries makes his relationships with younger men an act of love,
rather than an act of exploitation.

At the time of Isherwood's visit to Japan, he was three years into his
relationship with blond Don Bachardy, a young man thirty years his junior,
who was financially dependent and who would remain his partner until
Isherwood's death. Yet Americans' relationships with Japanese men strike
him as entirely different from his relationship with Bachardy. The complex-
ity of his understanding of his relationship with Bachardy does not seem
to extend to the Japanese hustlers he met, for whom he felt sympathy but,
it seems, no real sense of identification or empathy. Isherwood's unfortunate metaphor of invasion as a "Jewish fantasy" suggests a lack of empathy
with racial others such as Jews and Asians. He could not understand being
attracted to the Japanese boys he met, and he couldn't frame those relationships as being anything but exploitative. The possibility that they could be
at once loving and exploitative doesn't seem to have occurred to him.

This unexpected schizophrenia in Isherwood comes into sharp relief
when one considers his friendship with the Japanese writer Yukio Mishima
in the late 1950s. Isherwood met Mishima in 1957, when he came to the
United States after Alfred A. Knopf published a translation of his 1954
novel *The Sound of the Waves.* Isherwood was already planning a visit to
Asia when he met Mishima—one letter from Mishima ends, "Have a
nice trip with your charming and beautiful young friend!"[9] Mishima was
a literary Golden Boy of the Cold War era, benefiting from an interest in
Japanese literature in translation in the United States—a larger trend of
"world literature" in an America eager to prepare for its central role on the
world stage. Unlike Junichiro Tanizaki and Yasunari Kawabata, however,
Mishima was known not just for his literary talent but also for his cosmo-
politanism and his open homoerotics. In *Confessions of a Mask* (which

Isherwood blurbed on the cover of the American translation), Mishima used a recurring trope of Saint Sebastian to describe the masochistic queer desires of his narrator, who desired both men and death, and fixated on multiple penetrations (by arrows) that resulted in orgasm/expiration of a martyred saint. While the connection of sickness, neurosis, and homoerotics made this fictional exploration safe in a homophobic 1950s environment, Mishima also described explicit desire for men openly. American gay men fascinated Mishima; many of Isherwood's correspondents discussed Mishima with him in letters. And Mishima himself seemed happy to meet as many of them as he could. Faubion Bowers, who had served during the Allied occupation of Japan as General Douglas MacArthur's interpreter and aide-de-camp, claimed, in a rather homophobic essay published in the *Village Voice* in 1970, that Mishima took advantage of the American occupation to meet as many handsome gay men in the army as he could: "Mishima first caught the eye of the faggot contingent of the Occupation of Japan in 1945. He was only 20, then quite good-looking . . . and he had hair on his chest (and this too, then, was most unusual and a matter of much banter and display among the whites of the Occupation and their brown-skinned brother, Mishima)."[10] Bowers maintained that Mishima's erotic interest in white men continued: "One night Mishima flew over to America just for sex." Furthermore, Bowers denied helping Mishima find what he wanted. With the help of Isherwood, however, Mishima had better luck in San Francisco and Los Angeles.

Mishima visited Isherwood and Bachardy in Santa Monica—before the American publication of *Confessions of a Mask* queered him for American readers—and he seems to have had a gay time with Isherwood. As he wrote to Isherwood in July 1957, "I am in Ann Arbor I spent a very puritanic time. Your friendship in Los Angeles is really unforgettable. I enjoyed very much that bright afternoon. . . . CAUTION: your sweetheart is very very attractive to me. I can't forget his youthful smile and voice. Please give my greetings to Mr. Druten and your attractive friend."[11] Mishima's open lust for Don Bachardy—and willingness to express it to Isherwood—is notable, as is his casual acceptance of a queer community, one that Isherwood provided in the United States. Isherwood connected Mishima with the bisexual Frank Taylor (one of the models for Stephen in *The World in the Evening*) for an edited collection of stories he wanted published. In a thank-you letter, Mishima told Isherwood, "I wrote about you today to two friends of mine, (I am sorry to say, both of them are *not* gay)."[12] Mishima's easy use of queer terminology and jokes about gay men suggest an easy transpacific camaraderie of gay men, Pacific Rimming, that was equally successful in Los Angeles and Tokyo.

This transpacific queer exchange continued with a number of Isherwood's queer artistic community. Mishima writes Isherwood about meeting Tennessee Williams:

> I've forgotten to write about Tennessee Williams. On the last October, I could meet him finally. My preoccupation about him which tells he is a sort of difficult person, was destroyed at first meeting. He was so sweet and talked frankly from first time. I was invited to his weekly party several times which entertained me very much. . . . I like Tennessee so much. When you'll write to Tennessee, please write that I never stop to like him.[13]

Mishima's distinctive English diction makes him seem both charming and childlike, and that seems to be how Isherwood understood him. Mishima's gay adventures were not limited to the United States. In 1958, he wrote Isherwood about Stephen Spender's trip to Japan: "we had a very open enjoyable party with him one evening, after then I took him over [to] several gay-bars, which are quite famous tourists' places [in] contemporary Tokyo."[14] Spender's delighted trip to gay hotspots gave him his own transpacific erotic adventure, one that Isherwood had already enjoyed during his own visit at the end of 1957.

Mishima shared something else with Spender, besides a love of gay bars: a simultaneous interest in heterosexual marriage. His roundabout way of announcing this to Isherwood, right after describing their gay outing, suggests the Cold War bisexuality that often infuriated Isherwood:

> We talked about you much, and he described your happiest life with Don at California. He talked me that you were changed very much compared with your life in Berlin. It was his point of view that Don made you so happy and changed you into most happy figure. I thought I was lucky to meet you at your happiest circumstances.
>
> On the contrary I could not get any perfect happiness from my long gay-life and now hope to get it (or its elaborate counterfeit) with my heterosexual marriage. Strangely it seems to me that I might get it with not so much difficulty. Do you think it is my wishful thinking? (Mishima to Isherwood, September 2, 1958, CI 1814)

Mishima's praise of Isherwood's relationship with Bachardy seems intended to soften the blow of Mishima's marriage to a woman. Like Spender, Mishima married, perhaps to pass as heterosexual. For Mishima, public recognition in Japan seemed dependent upon such a union; no novels after *Confessions of a Mask* deal with homoerotics so openly. Yet his hopes for happiness betray doubt when he quickly follows up happiness with "its elaborate counterfeit," and ends with a plaintive question, "Do you think it is my wishful thinking?" There is no record at the Huntington of Isherwood's reply. Although one more letter arrived from Mishima (roughly three months later), the friendship seems to have ended with Mishima's marriage, suggesting that Isherwood wasn't sympathetic to Mishima's desire for an "elaborate counterfeit" of happiness outside a transpacific queer network.

Mishima's subsequent literary career complicates his persona in the Isherwood archive as a cheerful, somewhat childlike Japanese trick—a Western tourist fantasy of a gay geisha. Mishima may have first gained acclaim for a masochistic association of gay desire and martyrdom, but his own gay martyrdom took on a decidedly more fascistic, martial air. After forming his own private army in the 1960s and calling for a return to Japan's warrior spirit and pre–World War II emperor-centered militarism, Mishima put his ideology into action in 1970. He and a band of his soldiers took the general of a Japanese military base hostage (with only samurai swords, because the terms of Japan's surrender did not allow its military to bear arms). Mishima addressed the troops and called on them to mount a coup, reject the American-written constitution, and return the emperor to power. He insisted they stand up for Japan and its traditions and prove they were men. The troops shouted insults at him and heckled him. He went inside, as he had planned, and committed hara-kiri, after which his younger male lover cut off Mishima's head, then disemboweled himself.[15]

The Japanese were horrified at this return of the repressed ritual; no one in Japan had committed hara-kiri since the end of World War II. Isherwood wrote in his diary, "I suppose he had become completely crazy. I just cannot relate this to the Mishima we met."[16] In this, Isherwood repeats the common response to Mishima at the time. But given his experience and insight, Isherwood might have made much better sense of Mishima's end, because Mishima was a product of the sexual colonialism Isherwood denounced in Japan. Mishima was one of the "boughten boys" who grew up to create an indigenous fascistic alternative to such sexual colonialism.

Before that dramatic suicide, Mishima argued that Western culture had a skewed sense of Japan, seeing it as cultured and feminine and willfully ignoring its violent, militaristic streak. Using Ruth Benedict's famous anthropological study of the binaries of Japanese culture (which he admired), Mishima argued that Westerners wanted to embrace the chrysanthemum and ignore the sword (Stokes 17). Isherwood had this same insight about Japan during his second visit: "At the end of long avenues, you see mighty square wooden arches, which have a kind of barbarian brutality about them, the very reverse of Japanese daintiness and indeed, perhaps, a symbol of Japan's other face" ("Trip to Asia" [TS] 10). Isherwood seems familiar with Benedict's thesis in this offhand comment.

Mishima's fascistic reinvention—his public embrace of the sword and the samurai—provided a way for him to continue his same-sex liaisons after his marriage, through the militaristic friendships he constructed in his private army. Rather than being a handsome, desperate twenty-year-old hustler in an asymmetrical relationship with Western soldiers, he was the man in charge, with energetic young recruits for whom loyalty, patriotism, and desire made for a potent and deadly combination. These critiques of the suppressed homoerotics that animated fascist ideology were common in the 1930s. Underneath the explicit persecution of homosexual behavior was a necessary linkage of violence and same-sex longing.

Indeed, Isherwood had made a similar argument in his 1938 memoir *Lions and Shadows*, when he explained that had he met the right (or wrong) homoerotic fascist leader, he would have fallen under his spell in a heartbeat. "'War,' which could never under any circumstances be allowed to appear in its own shape, needed a symbol," and his was "a cult of the public-school system," which combined idealism and homoerotics into a grand fantasy of adolescent triumph:

> I built up the daydream of an heroic school career, in which the central figure, the dream I, was an austere young prefect, called upon unexpectedly to captain a "bad" house, surrounded by sneering critics and open enemies, fighting slackness, moral rottenness, grimly repressing his own romantic feelings towards a younger boy, and finally triumphing over all his obstacles, passing the test, emerging—a Man. Need I confess any

more? How, in dark corners of bookshops, I furtively turned the pages of adventure stories designed for boys of twelve years old?[17]

"It is so very easy," Isherwood warns, "in the mature calm of a library, to sneer at all this homosexual romanticism. But the rulers of Fascist states do not sneer—they profoundly understand and make use of just these phantasies and longings." An "English Fascist leader," he concludes, "clever enough to serve up his 'message' in a suitably disguised and palatable form . . . would have converted me, I think, inside half an hour" (78–79).

Who could have understood the peculiar pressures, pleasures, and authoritarian fantasies Mishima embodied more than Isherwood? I can't think of another queer writer of the time with more insight into the homoerotics of Fascism—who had seen Japan in the 1930s and noted parallels between German and Japanese systems, and who had, in the 1950s, seen the sexual colonialism that had marked Mishima and against which he rebelled as he constructed himself as the master to doting younger men. What is uncanny about Isherwood's description of English Fascism is how accurately it describes what would happen with Mishima in Japan more than three decades later. Mishima translated his homoerotic desire for younger men into tradition and honor, nationalism and manhood, and he drew young men to him through his "homosexual romanticism"—in fact, one would die with him and the others would stay to take the blame. Isherwood understood that dynamic very well in the 1930s; he identified the parallels between Japanese and German fascism in the late 1950s, so much so that his Japanese sojourn inspired critiques of it, and identification with the Japanese, in the 1960s.

Reading the best account of Mishima in the period right before his suicide—*The Life and Death of Yukio Mishima,* by his friend Henry Scott Stokes, especially his unedited diary of encounters with Mishima—I am struck by how much Stokes notices but cannot comprehend. Describing Mishima's private army, he writes, "Fantastic uniforms, Mishima's kitsch taste, that's about all. Color is sort of yellow-brown and rows of brass buttons down front which give wasp waists to Mishima's young men. Is this a homosexual club? No evidence of that. . . . Met Morita, student leader of the 'private army,' and found him to be a dull boy, about twenty-three, not very bright; seemed devoted to Mishima and to confuse him with the Emperor."[18] Stokes notes Mishima's "kitsch" taste repeatedly, his campy love of excess, his sense of clowning and performance—a camp sensibility that Isherwood famously articulated in *The World in the Evening*. Stokes also notices the focus on physique and beautiful bodies, in both Mishima and the young men who follow him, yet quickly runs away from the notion of the army as a "homosexual club." This willful blindness regarding Mishima's sexuality haunts most of the journal, but never so much as when Stokes tells Mishima the "amusing" story of male soldiers dancing together:

> The Korean base had been full of virile, healthy young men; and they had no women. . . . After the karate exercises the Korean soldiers had danced for us. In Western style. Tall men danced as men and the short men were the women; they had clutched one another and rotated slowly on the parade ground before our eyes, while others sang and clapped their hands in time. Some of the men blushed deeply. I myself had not known which way to look, but Bernie had taken pictures with great sang-froid. As I finished this story I saw that Yukio did not think it funny. Not at all amused. Stony-faced, in fact. (Stokes [1974] 20)

Why Mishima was "stony-faced" is obvious to the queer reader. Displays of homosexual desire were seen as laughable and shocking for straight observers, and the desire of Mishima to construct a Japanese public space—one linked to Japanese nationalism—for his homoerotic desire must have seemed hopeless in the face of such disdain. Stokes cannot understand Mishima's camping or his despair. One of the most poignant moments of Stokes's diary, in retrospect, was when Mishima "talked in melancholy fashion about heroes in the Japanese tradition. He insisted that 'all our heroes have failed, they have all been miserable failures.' I can't imagine what he was trying to say. What are heroes to him or me? Usually he is so cheerful but today he was really depressed. . . . There were all manner of curses in Japan, he said; curses had played a great part in Japanese history" (Stokes [1974] 22). His sense of failure may have inspired his most Japanese attempt of "honorable" suicide, which had the opposite effect, placing him outside Japanese literary tradition and imperiling his place in world literature.

Isherwood could have made sense of Mishima's fall, and the desperation and myth that made it seem the only solution. He is perhaps the only writer at the time who could have. That he did not do so is a surprising failure in a writer noted for his empathy with criminals, spies, even collaborators, as long as they were "his kind." Indeed, so strong was Isherwood's sense of connection with a queer tribe that he was able to identify with the closeted gay man who denied Heinz Neddermeyer's entry into England. After the customs agent refused Heinz entry, Auden told Isherwood, "As soon as I saw that bright-eyed little rat, I knew we were done for. He understood the whole situation at a glance—because he's *one of us*."[19] Despite this betrayal, Isherwood insisted that all "of his fellow tribesmen . . . were his brothers—yes, even those who denied their brotherhood and betrayed it—even that man at Harwich" (*Christopher and His Kind* 163).

It is sad to realize that Isherwood was able to embrace the humanity of the man who sent Heinz into a German prison and the German army, while being unable to embrace the humanity of Mishima, a man he knew who had succumbed to the lure of bigotry and Fascism on the other side of the world. By 1970, Isherwood seems to have forgotten his horror of sexual colonialism and the complex roots and homoeroticism and nationalism. He was inventing a new, gay liberation Christopher Isherwood, in which emphasizing gay solidarity became a priority, and in which he, as a gay rights grandfather, could take an honorary role. That Mishima could not be included in this gay universalism suggests that such "universalism" oversimplified power relations within gay communities and was implicitly white. Isherwood's gay liberation narrative of queer identity in *Christopher and His Kind* is less attuned to the colonial implications of gay sex tourism. The critique of sexual colonialism, which Isherwood saw so clearly in his 1957 journal, would wait until the "queer of color" critique in queer studies made such complexities visible again. His retreat from such insights in the 1970s is disappointing, but only highlights how remarkable his critique was during the Cold War. Remembering how Pacific Rimming once inspired Isherwood's multicultural queer fifties and sixties helps us to appreciate the prescience and insight in his writings from that period.

NOTES

1. Christopher Isherwood, *The Sixties: Diaries,* vol. 2, *1960–1969,* ed. Katherine Bucknell (New York: Harper Perennial, 2011), 302.

2. Christopher Isherwood, "Journal of a Trip to Asia," Christopher Isherwood Papers, CI 1076, typescript (hereafter cited in text as "Trip to Asia" [TS]), Huntington Library, San Marino, California.

3. James Charlton to Christopher Isherwood, April 3, 1961, Isherwood Papers, CI 721.

4. For more, see Earl Roy Miner, *The Japanese Tradition in British and American Literature* (Princeton, N.J.: Princeton University Press, 1958).

5. For a few examples, see Jasbir K. Puar, "Circuits of Queer Mobility: Tourism, Travel, and Globalization," *GLQ: A Journal of Lesbian and Gay Studies* 8, no. 1–2 (2002): 101–37; Kevin Markwell, "Mardi Gras Tourism and the Construction of Sydney as an International Gay and Lesbian City," *GLQ: A Journal of Lesbian and Gay Studies* 8, no. 1–2 (2002): 81–99; Dereka Rushbrook, "Cities, Queer Space, and the Cosmopolitan Tourist," *GLQ: A Journal of Lesbian and Gay Studies* 8, no. 1–2 (2002): 183–206.

6. Christopher Isherwood, "Journal of a Trip to Asia," Isherwood Papers, CI 1074, handwritten.

7. Christopher Isherwood, *Down There on a Visit* (New York: Simon and Schuster, 1962), 125.

8. Christopher Isherwood, *Lost Years: A Memoir, 1945–1951* (New York: HarperCollins, 2000), 13. [Isherwood used the pseudonym "Vernon Olds" or "Vernon Old" to refer to his boyfriend at the time. For more information, see note 7 in Sara Hodson, chapter 1, this volume.—Eds.]

9. Yukio Mishima to Christopher Isherwood, August 13, 1957, Isherwood Papers, CI 1811.

10. Faubion Bowers, "A Memory of Mishima," *Village Voice*, December 3, 1970.

11. Mishima to Isherwood, July 21, 1957, Isherwood Papers, CI 1810; emphasis in original. By "Mr. Durten," Mishima is referring to John van Druten, who wrote *I Am a Camera* for the stage in 1951 based on Isherwood's *Goodbye to Berlin*.

12. Mishima to Isherwood, June 10, 1958, Isherwood Papers, CI 1813.

13. Mishima to Isherwood, February 14, 1958, Isherwood Papers, CI 1812.

14. Mishima to Isherwood, September 2, 1958, Isherwood Papers, CI 1814.

15. For more on this incident, see Henry Scott Stokes, *The Life and Death of Yukio Mishima* (New York: Farrar, Straus and Giroux, 1974). The 1974 edition of Stokes's book contains more material on Mishima's sexuality than do later editions.

16. Christopher Isherwood, *Liberation: Diaries*, vol. 3, *1970–1983*, ed. Kathleen Bucknell (New York: HarperCollins, 2012), 119.

17. Christopher Isherwood, *Lions and Shadows: An Education in the Twenties* (Norfolk, Conn.: New Directions, 1947), 77–78.

18. Henry Scott Stokes, *The Life and Death of Yukio Mishima* (New York: Cooper Square Press, 2000), 10.

19. Christopher Isherwood, *Christopher and His Kind* (New York: Farrar, Straus and Giroux, 1976), 162.

10. Rereading *Down There on a Visit*

The Christopher Who Was Encounters the
Christopher Who Might Have Been

In *Down There on a Visit,* Christopher Isherwood sets out to capture or
rather to compose, with an older man's hindsight and a novelist's height-
ened sensibilities, scenes that illustrate who he was at four key points in
his life. A retrospective of Isherwood's development as a man and as a
writer, these vignettes function as a bridge between the European and the
American Isherwood. They illustrate, through these crucial episodes, Isherwood's development from very young, newly published author; to British sojourner in Berlin; to British exile seeking a new home; to émigré in
America and recent convert to Vedanta.

But these vignettes not only reconsider the life Isherwood in fact led.
They also contemplate the life that Isherwood might have led, the paths
he might have taken but did not. In this sense, the semiautobiographical
Isherwood character resembles the Henry James protagonist in his short
story "The Jolly Corner," an expatriate who returns to his long-deserted
New York home to find it inhabited by the ghost of the man he would have
been had he stayed.[1]

As the episodes in *Down There on a Visit* reveal, what prevented Isherwood from pursuing alternative life possibilities was his relationship with
the four figures who served as extreme alter egos, who were able in their radical positions to reveal to Christopher a fundamental truth about himself.
In his dealings with Mr. Lancaster the dogmatist, Ambrose the anarchist,

143

Waldemar the hedonist, and Paul the cynic, Christopher encounters himself or a grotesque version of himself in a series of fun-house mirrors, in each of which he gets to view, engage with, and ultimately reject one of his own most extreme possibilities. All of these episodes, parts of a larger project Isherwood envisioned, titled "The Lost," present answers to that most crucial of life's questions, the one Joseph Conrad poses in *Lord Jim* through the German-born adventurer, Stein. Stein repeatedly asks, "How to be?" At one point he elaborates: "Adapting the words of your great poet: That is the question. . . . How to be! *Ach!* How to be."[2]

But Isherwood poses his answer only in negative terms, in the form of alternatives he rejects. Why only negative responses? Because Christopher Isherwood, the perennial rebel, refuses any ready-made, prepackaged answer to this fundamental question. In particular, he rejects the constricting heteronormative narrative of male heroism offered by a writer whom Isherwood otherwise much admired, Ernest Hemingway, in his novel that Isherwood most appreciated, *The Sun Also Rises*. It was this book specifically that preoccupied Isherwood at the time he was writing drafts of *Down There on a Visit*.[3]

On the one hand, Isherwood was taken with the lost characters of Hemingway's novel—and in his diary he cites them as precursors of the characters he wishes to present in his own new novel, which he had started to work on. As he describes his early idea for the novel, he imagines "something quite unlike me—Kafkaesque—about a journey. A journey that is meticulously described and yet unreal: the reality being the relationships between the characters. Maybe they are all dead—as, in a sense, the characters are in Hemingway's *The Sun Also Rises*" (*Diaries* 475). Not only does Isherwood cite Hemingway's novel in his diary, but he also contemplates writing a screenplay in which the heroine resembles Brett (742). And, while drafting "Ambrose," his account of an anarchic homosexual fiefdom, Isherwood reads an excerpt from *The Sun Also Rises* on a television program dedicated to Hemingway's novel (835). Further, *Down There on a Visit* resembles *The Sun Also Rises* in its loose, episodic structure and in the despair of Isherwood's four main characters.

Clearly, Isherwood was greatly taken with Hemingway's work but not with the psychosexual perspective it presents with such insistence. In response, Isherwood counters Hemingway's notion of the "code hero," who can show the male protagonist how to be a man, with a series of anti-code heroes, each of whom personifies what Isherwood called "the anti-heroic hero."[4] In *Down There on a Visit,* they present the fictional Chris with four different scenarios of "how not to be." Each is an extreme version of rebellion against Hemingway's stereotypical version of manhood—taciturn, conventionally courageous, and invariably heterosexual. Isherwood's diverse versions of life, refracted through multiple characters, suggests that there is no pattern for the life of a gay man, no set of guidelines. For this reason, these anti-heroic episodes are anticlimactic and open-ended. They are, in fact, deliberate rejections of the conventions of that familiar literary narrative, the heroic journey.

The fictional Christopher as well as the author Isherwood will have to fashion his own unique life course. Unlike Hemingway's code hero, Robert Wilson, in "The Short Happy Life of Francis Macomber," this Christopher will not be a self-proclaimed role model.[5] Rather, he will be a renegade explorer—a prospect that is both terrifying and radically liberating. He will be "affronting" his destiny (as Henry James puts it, in the preface to *The Portrait of a Lady*) as a myriad of possibilities.[6] And in his ongoing exploration he will reveal himself to be not a single consistent self but a composite of selves, mutable and ever evolving.

Interestingly, Isherwood, as much as Hemingway, was preoccupied with the question of what it means to be a man. For both writers, the answer was connected with the Great War. For Isherwood, as he admits in his autobiography *Lions and Shadows,* the War "meant The Test. The test of your courage, of your maturity, of your sexual prowess." Because he had been too young to fight, the War continued to pose an unanswerable question: "'Are you really a Man?'"[7] As Isherwood admits, "Subconsciously, I believe, I longed to be subjected to this test; but I also dreaded failure. I dreaded failure so much—indeed, I was so certain that I *should* fail—that, consciously, I denied my longing to be tested, altogether" (*Lions* 76).

Significantly, Isherwood, the son of an English hero killed in the Great War, looked to Hemingway for an answer. Not only had Hemingway experienced the War, but also, as an American, his impressions did not evoke for Isherwood either invidious comparisons or patriarchal reproach. Reassuringly for Isherwood, while several of Hemingway's characters in *The Sun Also Rises* have fought in the War, they have not been able to prove themselves as men by means of fighting. Indeed, the War has had the reverse effect on the life of Hemingway's protagonist, Jake Barnes, who has been unmanned by the War—quite literally: his war wound has rendered him impotent.

Hemingway's disaffected characters in *The Sun Also Rises*, whether they have served in the War or not, are equally lost. Thus, they reinforce a jaundiced view of heroism that Isherwood adopted early on—perhaps in self-defense. As Isherwood writes in *Lions and Shadows*:

> The Test exists only for the Truly Weak Man; no matter whether he passes it or whether he fails, he cannot alter his essential nature. The Truly Strong Man travels straight across the broad America of normal life, taking always the direct, reasonable route. But "America" is just what the truly weak man, the neurotic hero, dreads. (207–8)

Notably, Hemingway and Isherwood responded to their postwar malaise in diametrically opposed ways. Hemingway answered his early disillusionment by looking for other Manhood Tests—hunting, boxing, bullfighting. Isherwood, on the other hand, turned away from these public displays of courage and self-imposed tests of manhood to seek inner meaning and ultimate truth in a quest that continued for many years.

Down There on a Visit describes four way stations along Isherwood's protracted path. The first episode, "Mr. Lancaster," presents, through the figure of Christopher's pseudorelative, Alexander Lancaster, a personification of the late Victorian world against which the young Christopher must rebel if he is ever to fashion a life for himself. An embodiment of Victorian smugness, conformity, prudery, and self-righteousness, and a veteran of the First World War who reproaches Christopher for his lack of wartime experience (although Christopher had been too young to serve), Mr. Lancaster represents everything the young Christopher must leave behind if he is to make a life for himself.

Poor Alexander Lancaster! He is the victim as well as the mouthpiece of his domineering Victorian father, whose portrait hangs prominently over his mantel, a paterfamilias whom Christopher fittingly dubs "The Beard." All that Mr. Lancaster is, is dead, a hollow echo of the past. Small wonder, then, that at the end of the episode we learn that, shortly after Christopher's visit to him in Germany, Mr. Lancaster commits suicide:

> He had lived too long inside his sounding box, listening to his own reverberations, his epic song of himself. . . . Then suddenly, I suppose, he ceased to believe in the epic any more. Despair is something horribly

simple. And though Mr. Lancaster had been so fond of talking about it, he probably found it absolutely unlike anything he had ever imagined. But, in his case, I hope and believe, it was short-lived. Few of us can bear much pain of this kind and remain conscious.[8]

Thus Mr. Lancaster serves as an object lesson in helping Christopher to kick over the traces of his forebears, to repudiate the earnestness, piety, and conformity of the late-Victorian world. At the same time, his experience with Mr. Lancaster helps Christopher recognize that he must leave England behind, for as long as he remains there, he can see Mr. Lancaster only as a cardboard figure of the Enemy, rather than the pathetic human being that he is.

But the question arises: if Mr. Lancaster serves as a negative role model in helping Christopher to rebel against his forebears, what is Christopher rebelling toward? Toward Berlin, of course, which immediately became Christopher's destination the moment Mr. Lancaster condemned it as a den of iniquity.

By the opening of the second section, "Ambrose," however, the freedom and sexual openness of Christopher's life in Berlin are threatened by the rise of fascism. From a Berlin grown alien and ominous after Hitler's rise to power, Christopher gladly escapes with his friend Waldemar (a disguised portrait of his lover Heinz, with touches of other German boys he had known) to a remote Greek island, presided over by a former acquaintance at Cambridge, an anarchist and outspoken homosexual, Ambrose. Ambrose, Christopher observes, reminds him "of one of Shakespeare's exiled kings; exiled, but by no means without hope" (100), for he plans to fashion an alternative kingdom on his tiny strip of land, a homosexual preserve and refuge. In Ambrose's provocatively sly words:

Of course, when we do get into power, we shall have to begin by reassuring everybody. We must make it clear that there'll be absolutely no reprisals. Actually, they'll be amazed to find how tolerant we are. . . . I'm afraid we shan't be able to make heterosexuality actually legal, at first—there'd be too much of an outcry. One'll have to let at least twenty years go by, until all the resentment has died down. But meanwhile it'll be winked at, of course, as long as it's practiced in decent privacy. I think we shall even allow a few bars to be opened for people with those unfortunate tendencies, in certain quarters of the larger cities. They'll have to be clearly marked, with police at the doors to warn foreigners what kind of

places these are—just so that no one shall find himself there by mistake
and see something which might upset him. Naturally, from time to time,
some tourist with weak nerves may have to be rushed to hospital, suffering from shock. We'll have a psychologist on hand to explain to him that
people like that do exist, through no fault of their own, and that we must
feel sympathy for them, and try to find scientific ways of reconditioning
them. (100)

For the young Christopher, there is delicious revenge in the prospect of
turning the tables on a tyrannically heterosexual and heteronormative
world. But there is a fly in the ointment. On Ambrose's island, there are
no laws, no duties, no obligations. Everyone lives for himself. And yet, as
Christopher observes, this laissez-faire situation does not foster harmony
or justice. In fact, what happens is that people realize their worst selves:

Consciously or unconsciously, Ambrose encourages jealousy. He has
the coquetry of the benevolent despot. His coquetry consists in a display of impartiality whenever a quarrel arises. Since one person in the
quarrel is usually in the wrong and the other in the right, his impartiality
amounts to favoring the one who's in the wrong. (95)

In fact, Christopher considers himself "wronged" by Ambrose's so-called
impartiality. Over time, without structure or discipline, Christopher stops
working, thinking, or planning. He is unable to write or to make the sim-
plest decisions. He is actually unable to leave—until Ambrose in effect
kicks him out, telling him there is no reason for him to stay. Even his loyalty
to Ambrose is inadequate, as Ambrose himself rejects it as insufficient. The
episode makes clear that Christopher needs to find his own way to express
his sexual identity without entirely eschewing the heterosexual world.

"Waldemar" is the third and, in my view, least successful section of
the book. It is a transposition of Christopher Isherwood's actual plight in
the years leading up to World War II, as he frantically attempted to rescue
his lover, Heinz, from extradition and conscription. In this episode, the
writer displaces his own dilemma onto Dorothy, an earnest, upper-class
English woman who is a devout Communist. Like Christopher in actual
life, Dorothy is hell-bent on defying her upper-class parents in England by
bringing her working-class lover, Waldemar, home and by attempting to
get him work in England so as to avoid his inevitable draft into Hitler's
army. By the end of the episode, Dorothy is defeated by her parents and by

her futile efforts to save Waldemar, and Waldemar has deserted Dorothy. He then turns to Christopher, asking him to take him to America, which Christopher has no way of doing.

What gets obfuscated in this episode by transposing Christopher's plight onto the story of a young woman is the peculiar set of circumstances that prompted Isherwood to leave England, preferring exile to a life that he was destined for, even before birth. Born in 1904 into a family of landed gentry that could trace its pedigree back before the beheading of Charles I (in fact, one of Isherwood's ancestors was judge at King Charles's trial), Isherwood as firstborn son was expected to perpetuate the family name by marrying appropriately and producing heirs; to inhabit and maintain the ancestral hall; and to join the communicants of the Church of England. Although to many such a position would seem advantageous, indeed highly desirable, for Christopher Isherwood, it was an unbearable burden that would require him to lead a life of hypocrisy, avowing publicly a sexual and religious identity at odds with his true self. By displacing his youthful rebellion onto a generically rebellious upper-class young woman, in the third episode of the book, Isherwood empties his peculiar dilemma of the personal and narrative urgency that in fact energized and directed his odyssey.

In the final episode, "Paul," Christopher is a newcomer to Los Angeles and a neophyte to Vedanta. As such, he invites Paul, a notorious gigolo who is going through a crisis, to accompany him in his daily spiritual practice. He and Paul embark on a successful period of cohabitation as new practitioners of Vedanta in devotion to a spiritual ideal until Christopher's unconscious rebellion and unfounded suspicion of Paul combine with Paul's aggression and intransigence to capsize their efforts. Later, when Christopher offers to smoke opium with Paul, so that he can understand his addiction, Paul, true to his all-or-nothing character, accuses Christopher of being a dilettante:

> "Oh, darling Chrissikins! If you only knew how funny you are! So you want to try it? *Once! One pipe!* Or a dozen pipes, for that matter! You're exactly like a tourist who thinks he can take in the whole of Rome in one day. You know, you really are a tourist, to your bones. I bet you're always sending post cards with 'Down here on a visit' on them. That's the story of your life." (315–16)

Paul and Christopher then go off to alternative war service as conscientious objectors. Later, Christopher is offered a new temptation when he revisits Germany and encounters a middle-aged Waldemar, now married and a father, who broadly hints that he would like Christopher to adopt him and his family. As clearly as Christopher turned his back on the monastic existence he attempted with Paul, so too, just as firmly, he rejects this offer of life with a ready-made family. Incidentally, in rejecting this option, Christopher is rejecting the life course chosen by Isherwood's good friend E. M. Forster, who adopted and was adopted by the working-class family of his policeman lover, Bob Buckingham.

In each of these episodes, Christopher pits himself against a person who is an absolutist, who acts as a litmus test of his sincerity and commitment. Apart from these apparently discrete and disparate encounters with a series of extreme characters, there is one apparently slight connecting thread that ties these episodes together—the figure of Waldemar, the only character who appears in all four episodes.

But is this connection really so slight? It is Waldemar, after all, who reminds us that Christopher is getting older, as he himself ages. Thus, Waldemar changes from the mischievous boy with a deceptively cherubic face to the hedonistic inhabitant of Ambrose's island to the opportunistic young man attempting by any means to escape his oppressive homeland to a somewhat fatuous middle-aged family man. He shows us, as if in a mirror, time passing and a man aging. We are asked to consider what analogous changes we see in Christopher over the same time period.

On closer scrutiny, we see that not only does Waldemar have an important role in binding together these apparently disconnected periods of Christopher's life, but he also brings with him the ghost of another story, one that has not yet been told and that will not get written until Isherwood undertakes to tell it fully in his candid 1976 autobiography, *Christopher and His Kind*. In that later work, Isherwood will tell Waldemar's real story: the story of Christopher's long relationship with his German lover Heinz—its evolution from casual to serious affair and then to long-term commitment, a love affair that ended abruptly when, after a great many efforts to obtain new citizenship for him, Christopher was unable to find a place where they could live together permanently or even to save Heinz from extradition and conscription.

That Waldemar is the only link connecting the four different settings and time periods of the book's episodes serves to underline Christopher's restlessness. Christopher is a wanderer. He does not have a home although, by the fourth episode, it is clear that he is searching for one. The figure of Waldemar is a constant in this world of flux, a kind of narrative arrow pointing toward an ultimate destination. Whether Christopher finds one remains an unanswered question—one that cannot be answered until, having revisited in fictional form these past selves and their temptations, Isherwood can at last tell the true story of his herculean efforts to make a home for himself and Heinz, an undertaking that, had it been successful, would have drastically changed the course of—and perhaps have limited unduly—his efforts to fashion a new life for himself by moving to America. Only after dealing forthrightly with that episode in his life will Christopher be able to tell the story of how he finally made a home for himself in America with the young American Don Bachardy.

If, to Paul, Christopher's restlessness is a character flaw, the four episodes, taken together, suggest that being a tourist is for Isherwood a saving grace and ultimately a path to salvation. He is a tourist in the same sense that Dante is a tourist in *The Divine Comedy*: a spiritual seeker, a pilgrim. Indeed, one of Isherwood's early ideas for the novel was that it would be a modern-day religious comedy based on Dante's. Like Dante, he would write a first-person account of a spiritual journey. Initially, Isherwood's treatment of the material was quite literal. As in *The Divine Comedy*, the journey would begin in Hell in the guise of Mexico—or "Mexico in the likeness of Hell."[9] In one version, he planned to center the novel on a friend who gets a long-distance call from his London editor, asking him to write a series of articles on Hell. He does indeed go there, has a series of encounters, then awakes to find that these experiences have all been a dream.[10]

Over time, the novel's treatment of Hell became not literal but metaphorical. In the final version, Hell is not theological but psychological—not so much a place as a state of mind—or, rather, four extreme states of mind embodied in four extreme figures. All that remained of the original conception was the title. And the title makes clear that the narrator is a visitor to Hell, not an inhabitant. For him, Hell is "down there," not "over here." Hell is the first, not the last, stop in Christopher's spiritual journey.

The principal characters in the four episodes of the book are not visitors but inhabitants. They are stuck in their own respective circles of Isherwood's Inferno: The worst part of being in Hell—what makes it Hell—is the sinner's immobility within it, his inability to escape. Where there can be no movement, there is no hope. The four extreme figures Christopher encounters, whether they are discrete people or merely extreme aspects of Christopher himself, are fixed, stuck, unable to move. Only Christopher is on his way somewhere.

But it is also important to remember that Isherwood's Hell is not as dire as Dante's, for Isherwood's spiritual perspective is not that of dualistic Christianity but that of monistic Vedanta, a perspective in which there are no moral absolutes—only choices that are relatively worse or better. All of Isherwood's figures, himself included, blunder on within the veils of Maya or illusion. For this reason, Christopher's restless searching is no guarantee of future happiness, and, indeed, the end of his quest will not be the sudden revelation of Christian parable. When Christopher at last finds himself at home in Southern California, he will simply observe, "the wandering stopped."[11] It's not that he has lost either the skepticism or the sardonic sensibility that energized his earlier narratives. Rather, his life has taken on enough ballast—through his pleasure in screen writing, his enjoyment of his adopted country, his nurturing relationship with his guru, his satisfaction with domestic life, and his love for Don—to persuade him to remain.

NOTES

1. Henry James, "The Jolly Corner," *Tales of Henry James,* ed. Christof Wegelin (New York: Norton, 1984), 313–40.

2. Joseph Conrad, *Lord Jim,* ed. J. H. Stape and Ernest W. Sullivan II, Cambridge Edition of the Works of Joseph Conrad (Cambridge: Cambridge University Press, 2012), 161.

3. Christopher Isherwood, *Diaries,* vol. 1, *1939–1960,* ed. Katherine Bucknell (New York: HarperCollins, 1996), 475, 742.

4. Christopher Isherwood, *Isherwood on Writing,* ed. James J. Berg (Minneapolis: University of Minnesota Press, 2007), 133.

5. Ernest Hemingway, "The Short Happy Life of Francis Macomber," in *The Short Stories of Ernest Hemingway,* ed. Sean Hemingway (New York: Simon and Schuster, 2017), 425–62.

6. Henry James, *The Portrait of a Lady,* ed. Robert D. Bamberg (New York: Norton, 1995), 8.

7. Christopher Isherwood, *Lions and Shadows: An Education in the Twenties* (Norfolk, Conn.: New Directions, 1947), 76.

8. Christopher Isherwood, *Down There on a Visit* (New York: Simon and Schuster, 1962), 57.

9. Edward Upward, quoted in Peter Parker, *Isherwood: A Life Revealed* (New York: Random House, 2004), 564.

10. For an extended analysis of *Down There on a Visit* and its relationship to *The Divine Comedy,* see Rebecca Gordon Stewart's essay "Down Where on a Visit? Isherwood's Mythology of Self," in *The American Isherwood,* ed. James J. Berg and Chris Freeman (Minneapolis: University of Minnesota Press, 2015), 139–53.—Eds.

11. See Carola M. Kaplan, "'The Wandering Stopped': An Interview with Christopher Isherwood," in *The Isherwood Century,* ed. James J. Berg and Chris Freeman (Madison: University of Wisconsin Press, 2000), 259–81.

11. Grumbling in Eldorado

A Single Man in the American Utopia

In 1947, one year after becoming a naturalized citizen of the United States, Isherwood published the autobiographical essay "Los Angeles" in *Horizon,* Cyril Connolly's London-based literary magazine. This short piece conveys some sense of the wonder still felt by the ex-pat Englishman in the midst of the Hollywood Hills: "At dusk, or in the first light of dawn, the coyotes can be mistaken for dogs as they come trotting along the trail in single file, and it is strange and disconcerting to see them suddenly turn and plunge into the undergrowth with the long, easy leap of the wild animal."[1] Two decades later, Isherwood returned to this description in the novel *A Single Man* (1964), when the protagonist recalls his first impressions of the same hills: "It was the wildness of this range, largely uninhabited yet rising right up out of the city, that fascinated him. He felt the thrill of being a foreigner, a trespasser there, of venturing into the midst of a primitive, alien nature."[2] His mood has changed considerably in the intervening years, as has the now-bustling metropolis of Los Angeles. Now, he feels "nothing of that long-ago excitement and awe.... He is oppressed by awareness of the city below" (*A Single Man* 111). Whereas in 1947 Isherwood can quip that "emigrants to Eldorado have really no right to grumble" (*Exhumations* 159), in 1964 his literary alter ego feels he has plenty of cause to complain.

Isherwood scholar Carola M. Kaplan, in an essay titled "Working through Grief in the Drafts of *A Single Man,*" in *The American Isherwood,* considers how Isherwood experienced a period of difficulty in his relationship with Don Bachardy and "worked through" the possibility of losing his

life partner in the drafts and in the final version of the novel. My essay picks
up on Kaplan's claim that Isherwood addresses multiple other losses, such
as "loss of innocence, of homeland, of youth [and] the ultimate loss, that
of life itself," as well as several questions posed by him in his notebook:
"Do you regret having come to America? Is life in America tolerable? Do
you want to go back to England to die? How are you going to bear the rest
of your life?"[3] Kaplan argues that Isherwood's protagonist, through various encounters, manages to relinquish his complaints and to "embrace the
larger grievances—and thus the community—he shares with the minority to which he is happiest to belong, the minority of the living" (45). I
reach to a different conclusion, arguing that the protagonist passes through
a series of missed opportunities to connect with other characters. In
either case, the drafts and final version of *A Single Man* provide a revealing
reflection on the experience of a seasoned immigrant in the United States
and his responses to the mainstreaming of minority identity politics in
the 1960s.

Isherwood's first working title for *A Single Man* was "The Englishwoman." In his planning notes of March 1962, he writes that what
interested him was to "show America through British eyes" and that his
intention was to do this "bifocally—showing how America seems to the
Englishwoman and how it seems to me."[4] By September 1962, he realized
that all of his objectives were better approached through his own character,
so he changed his working title to "The Englishman." As "a sort of Virginia
Woolf poem about life" ("The Englishwoman" 136), the novel has much in
common with *Mrs. Dalloway* (1925), Woolf's representation of a day in the
life of a high-society hostess in London, a key difference being the transna-
tional status of Isherwood's alter ego, who is an Anglo-American professor
at a state college in Los Angeles. In the first complete draft of "The Englishman," the protagonist is aware of "all the Americans around him, with their
American children and their American dogs, their American food and
their American cars and newspapers and gadgets and hopes and fears—all,
all American."[5] This is an awareness not of being surrounded but of being
in the "very midst of them," and he regards his role as "a kind of missionary,
self-doomed and self-dedicated to work amongst them for the rest of his
life" ("The Englishman" 7). Although he will fight against "commercials,
billboards, presidential addresses to the nation, gossip columns, books of
the month, radio sermons and professional sincerity," he considers that

this is his life now, that he accepts it, and that he is "even prepared to enjoy himself" (6–7).

Appropriately, the final version of the novel opens: "Waking up begins with saying . . . *I am now. Here* comes next, and is at least negatively reassuring; because *here*, this morning, is where it has expected to find itself: what's called *at home*" (*A Single Man* 9). Earlier drafts open with the protagonist's driving to work, in a passage substantially unaltered in the novel, when George feels a "kind of patriotism" for the freeways, which feed into the Interstate Highway System authorized by President Dwight D. Eisenhower in 1956 as a means of connecting and defending the nation in case of invasion (33). As a symbol of the nation, the freeway might be added to such metaphors as the quilt, the mosaic, and the rainbow, which, according to the anthropologist Arjun Appadurai, balance centripetal and centrifugal forces of identity in American life.[6] The merging traffic of this particular freeway consists of the Ford driven by Jewish-American Tom Kugelman, the MG driven by Swedish-American Buddy Sorensen, and the Pontiac driven by Chinese-Hawaiian Alexander Mong, each of which appears with its distinguishing marks and characteristics (43–44). The freeway leads to the college campus, where all around George are various "Negroes, Mexicans, Jews, Japanese, Chinese, Latins, Slavs, Nordics," who are fed continuously into this factory, to be "processed, packaged and placed on the market" (47). It is tempting to read the description of his arrival as an illustration of Appadurai's thesis that the hyphenation of American identity, in the sense of African-American, Italian-American, and so on, has reached a point of extremity and that "the right-hand side of the hyphen can barely contain the unruliness of the left-hand side" (Appadurai 172). From George's perspective, however, what might appear to observers to be a "mad chariot race" is more akin to the flow of a river, which contains "nothing to fear, as long as you let yourself go with it" (*A Single Man* 35).

Like the "melting pot" of old, this mixed metaphor of river and processing plant appears to imply an assimilation of diversity. This is also suggested by the sense that George is both an individual and a number. For instance, he navigates into the parking lot and "slips his parking card into the slot (thereby offering a piece of circumstantial evidence that he *is* George)." Then, when he checks into the office, "the three secretaries . . . recognize him instantly, without even a flicker of doubt, and reply 'Good morning!' to him." Finally, another card, "ciphered by an IBM machine expresses some poor bastard of a student's academic identity. Indeed, this card *is* his identity" (43, 45). This paradox is again implied by yet another image, which is introduced during an argument between George and Cynthia Leach in the faculty cafeteria. In earlier drafts of the novel, Cynthia is another immigrant from England, who complains that, in Southern California, "the families are exactly alike, the houses are identical, the meals are out of the deep freeze, the conversation is out of the national magazines" ("The Englishman" 34). When, in the published novel, she complains of the lack of character of tourist accommodations in the area, George immediately comes to the defense of "our motels," arguing that they do not provide *a* room but *the* room, "definitively, period." This room is based on a specific building code, which provides "certain measurements, certain utilities and the use of certain apt materials; no more and no less," with the expectation that "everything else you've got to supply for yourself." George's point is that the room is "a symbol—an advertisement in three dimensions, if you like—for our way of life" (*A Single Man* 90–91). As such, it stands not only for convenience, as George proposes, nor for utility and pragmatism, as might be implied, but also for the basis of citizenship that is provided by the nation and which newcomers are expected to supplement with the identities of their countries of origin.

Appadurai reminds us that such symbols are less than adequate where there is a contradiction between group identities and individual identities, which remain the "nonnegotiable principle behind American ideas of achievement, mobility, and justice" (173). A handwritten note to the final typescript of the novel records Isherwood's realization that "The Englishman" was ultimately unsuitable as a title because "the fact that George is English is not the most important thing about him."[7] Isherwood's intention was to bring out the "varied and to some extent paradoxical factors" in the constitution of his character. The change of title to *A Single Man* anticipates a sense of his being assembled and "made into a recognizable person."[8] In the opening sequence of the published novel, the awakening body contains "many faces within its face" (10). It is a male, strong, and middle-aged body that must be dressed before it enters the "world of the other people; and these others must be able to identify it." In the process of getting dressed, "it has become *he*," although this is not yet the whole George whom the others are prepared to recognize (11). To the identities of age, sex, gender, and ability are added signs of class and national origin in the memory of a nursery rhyme taught him by his nanny in England (14); signs of social status in his books, which he talks about in public (16); and, in the volume he takes from the shelf, John Ruskin "scolding the English" (17), signs of race, ethnicity, and diasporic identification.

The figure who takes Ruskin to read on the toilet is effectively a single, white, upper-class, able-bodied male of English ethnicity and British nationality. The change of title to *A Single Man* reflects another change of focus, however, for it is at this point that George realizes, with a "sick newness, almost as though it were for the first time: Jim is dead" (12).[9] The untimely death of his companion has exposed him to a sense of vulnerability in regard to his age and sexuality. Whereas George's property, which is surrounded by cliffs and trees and is accessible only by a small wooden bridge, might as well be on its "own island" (20), the houses of his neighbors face the street "frontally, wide-openly, in apt contrast to the sidewise privacy of George's lair" (22). In the "breeding-ground" which surrounds him, everything is directed toward procreation and the maintenance of a system of binary gender roles (18). A typical day is divided into morning, when the mothers supervise their younger children; midafternoon, when the older children return from school, the boys to take part in "the masculine hour of the ball-playing," the girls to "sit out on the porches, giggling together"; and evening, when the fathers return to rest and recuperate before their next working day (24–25). On weekends, there are parties for the adults, when the wives prepare salads and the husbands prepare the barbecue. Later, while "The Girls" tend to the washing-up, the men can be heard laughing on the porch, where they are "proud and glad. For even the least among them is a co-owner of the American utopia, the kingdom of the good life upon earth" (25–26).

Jim's death has exposed George to the suspicion that he is not a co-owner of this peculiarly heteronormative utopia, which extends from the suburbs to the campus, where his students are preparing for life in order to "raise children to prepare themselves for life" (47). He worries he will soon be dispatched to a nursery community and imagines himself to be already an outcast in terms of "the unspeakable that insists, despite all their shushing, on speaking its name" (27). George is a victim of anticipated homophobia and gerontophobia. His neighbor, Mr. Strunk, George imagines, tries to "nail him down with a word. *Queer*, he doubtless growls" (27), while, to his own mind, the designation "old" has become almost "as dirty a word as 'kike' or 'nigger'" (34). The prejudice and discrimination that result from such phobias are restrained by a new tolerance, or a "technique of annihilation by blandness" (27). While the senior citizen is encouraged into modes of "passive recreation" (34), the male homosexual might expect Mr. Strunk not to care "just as long as he stays away," and Mrs. Strunk to be trained in contemporary psychology to accept that it is glands, heredity, and/or early environment that have produced "a misfit, debarred forever from the best things of life, to be pitied, not blamed" (27–28). George chafes at this assimilation to heteronormativity, condemning Mrs. Strunk's book for implying that Jim is a substitute for a real son, a real spouse, or a real sibling. "Jim wasn't a substitute for anything. And there is no substitute for Jim," he counters, "Your exorcism has failed, dear Mrs. Strunk. . . . The unspeakable is still here—right in your very midst" (29).

George holds "three quarters of the population of America" accountable for Jim's death, in that "their whole way of life willed it, even though they never knew he existed" (40). Among the remaining quarter, he includes the African-Americans and Mexican-Americans who live in downtown and East L.A.; these people are not "The Enemy" and, if they ever accept George for what he is, "might even be allies" (42). Nevertheless, George's thoughts are remarkable for their iteration of contemporary stereotypes and prejudices: "Mexicans live here, so there are lots of flowers. Negroes live here, so it is cheerful. George would not care to live here, because they all blast all day long with their radios and television sets" (41). Likewise unexpected in its rhetoric is the impassioned speech he delivers in class, when he expands on his notion of a three-quarters majority which is opposed by a quarter of minorities. Defining "a minority" as such only insofar as it constitutes "some kind of a threat to the majority, real or imaginary," George dismisses the "liberal hysteria" of the new tolerance and its suggestion that a minority is "just people, like us" (70–71). "Sure, they're like us—but not *exactly* like us," he argues, maintaining that minorities "are people who probably look and act and think differently from us and have faults we don't have" (71). Admitting that we "may dislike the way they look and act, and we may hate their faults," he offers an alternative and defiantly unfashionable solution to the problem of persecution: "If we're frank about our feelings, we have a safety valve; and if we have a safety valve, we're actually less likely to start persecuting" (71).

George's speech is aimed in particular at Wally Bryant, who, he assumes, is a fellow homosexual and to whom he directs a "deep shining look that says, I am with you, little minority-sister" (70). Myron Hirsch and Estelle Oxford are representatives of two of the more obviously "tolerated" minorities of the civil rights era: Jewish- and African-Americans. If George expects them to admit to their faults and to accept prejudice and discrimination as lesser impositions than persecution, he goes even further: "A minority has its own kind of aggression. . . . It even hates the other minorities, because all minorities are in competition: each one proclaims that its sufferings are the worst and its wrongs are the blackest. And the more they all hate, and the more they're all persecuted, the nastier they become!" (72). George's own performance is exemplary of this logic. He dismisses Myron, "that indefatigable heckler of the *goyim,*" with an impatience to "leave the Jews out of this" (69–70). Estelle he finds to be exceptionally conscious, to the point of hypersensitivity, "of being a Negro"; he suspects her of suspecting him of all kinds of subtle discrimination and not only feels intimidated but also resentful of how she makes him feel (62–63). By the end of his speech, George is no longer sure what he has proved or disproved, or "whose side, if any, he is arguing on" (72–73). Indeed, it is difficult to see how Wally might have recognized his look of solidarity, when, all the while, George has been speaking from the position of The Enemy, in terms of the "we," "us," and "our" of the majority as opposed to the "they," "them," and "their" of the minority.

In the first draft of "The Englishwoman," the protagonist acknowledges his desire to "function as an Average Man, a Taxpayer, A Gallup Poll voter, a member of The Enemy" ("The Englishman" 2). The implication of "passing" among the majority is maintained in George, who has decided that "George will have to be George—the George they have named and will recognize" (*A Single Man* 41). The consequence of this is that he is "on-stage every second" (54), conducting himself with "a subtly contrived, outrageously theatrical effect" (56). A major factor in what mitigates this constant need to perform is his ability to rely on the privileges of his class and national origins. George speaks "boldly, clearly, with the subtly modulated British intonation which his public demands of him" (44). After class, he regards with "extra benevolence" the student who stays behind to compliment him on his accent and, in the office, he notes how the thought of Oxford, "towering up in all its majesty," utterly overawes one of his colleagues, who was born in one of the wrong parts of Chicago (74–75).

George's preference to "pass" among the Enemy is all the more pronounced in the context of his exchange with his colleague Grant Lefanu, who treats George as a fellow subverter even though, with "his license to play the British eccentric, and, in the last resort, his little private income, he can afford to say pretty much anything he likes" (86). In fact, George remains "all actor" on campus (55), and, although he regularly declines Grant's invitations to step among the countercultures of the city, "it simply does not occur to him that George might be scared" to do so (87).

George is much more comfortable in the "quasi-military relationship" he enjoys with Russ Dreyer, a top scholar and ex-marine, whose charming stories of manly bravado are, to his mind, reminiscent of ancient Greece (50). During the day, George favors such "man-to-man stuff" to the extent that his movements constitute something of an androcentric progress (51), in the course of which he derives sustenance from a secretive homoeroticism. Walking with Russ by the campus tennis court, George feels "a thrill of pleasure to find the senses so eager in their response" to the sight of two young male players (53). Later, while driving along the boulevard, he claims a kinship with the scowling youths who loiter on the corners, any one of whom he might persuade to take part, "a naked, sullen young athlete, in the wrestling bout of his pleasure" (104). Inspired "to rejoice in his own body—the tough triumphant old body of a survivor," he decides to stop by the gym, where he is able to compare and contrast himself favorably with the "fatalistic acceptance of middle age" of his age-mates (104–5). Buoyed by the confidence that he is "still a contender" (106), George is joined by the adolescent Webster, whose youth seems to take possession and instill in him the renewed energy to go far beyond his regular tally of sit-ups. George overstays his usual time at the gym, wishing that he could spend his entire life in this "state of easygoing physical democracy," where the young sit naked and innocent beside sixty- and seventy-year-olds, and where "surely everyone is nicer . . . than he is outside" (109).

George's appreciation of young men is offset by a denigration of mature women to the extent that, in the course of the day, his androcentric progress alternates with something of a misogynistic one. This begins in the canyon, which was transformed when war veterans came westward with their new wives, in search of "new and better breeding grounds." To George's mind, the veterans would have adjusted well to the original character of the canyon had their wives not insisted that "breeding and bohemianism do not mix" (18). In the first complete draft of "The Englishman," the protagonist explicitly qualifies his misogyny and misopedia: "As a matter of fact, he does not really dislike children—or even mothers, for that matter—only their symbolic status in our culture" ("The Englishman" 5). In keeping with the symbolic status he implicitly attributes to her, George assumes that Mrs. Strunk's attitude toward him is one of condescension. This impression is contradicted when the focalization of the narrative switches briefly to indicate that her status as a wife and a mother is not incompatible with sympathy toward George's difference. Mrs. Strunk "watches him back his car out across the bridge. (It is sagging badly nowadays. She hopes he will have it fixed; one of the children might get hurt.) As he makes the half-turn onto the street, she waves to him. He waves to her. Poor man, she thinks, living there all alone" (32). Mrs. Strunk's wave is an obvious invitation to connect, but when she calls on him later, George immediately assumes the worst: "Obviously she's nervous, self-conscious; very much aware, no doubt, of having crossed the frontier-bridge and being on enemy territory" (116).

When George stops by the hospital to visit Doris, he reduces her in his memory to "that body which sprawled stark naked" under Jim and, even further, to a more specifically female body part: "Gross insucking vulva, sly ruthless greedy flesh" (95). This outrageous synecdochic reduction assigns an explicit symbolic status to Doris, an old rival for Jim's sexual attention, who was "infinitely more than Doris, [she] was Woman the Enemy." Invoking the dominion of heteronormativity in order to claim her "biological rights," George imagines that she declares, "I am Woman. I am Bitch-Mother Nature. The Church and the Law and the State exist to support me," and demands that George "step aside, bow down and yield to the female prerogative, [and] hide his unnatural head in shame" (96). That the only bond between George and Doris is precisely his resentment toward Woman the Enemy suggests that he experiences little sympathy for the woman who is dying before him. Although Doris clearly wants his hand and grips it with "astonishing strength," George finds "no affection in it, no communication" (100). Implicitly, he attributes another symbolic status to her. As Isherwood suggests in his notes (Writing Notes 135), she is now also a *memento mori*, a shriveled female body (part) that refers to senescence, mortality, and death. Once outside, George is gleeful to be counted in "the ranks of that marvelous minority, The Living." Having passed among "the icy presence of The Majority, which Doris is about to join," he feels a "life-energy [surging] hotly through him" that, not unexpectedly, is peculiarly male: "How good to be in a body . . . that still has warm blood and live semen and rich marrow and wholesome flesh!" (103–4).

George indulges and celebrates his body at the gym, but, on the way home, is unable to sustain his mood and decides to call on his old friend, Charlotte, in anticipation of a kind of domestic contentment, which, according to Spanish usage, he terms *felicidad,* since it is "usually feminine, that's to say, woman-created." Freely acknowledging its "sublimely selfish" character, George enjoys the evening unperturbed by Charlotte's obvious distress concerning her estranged son. Seen through George's perspective, Charlotte gives the impression of a doubled woman. There is a certain catty jealousy in her explanation that Fred is now with "that girl" in Palo Alto; at the same time, she admits to smothering him in a "mother and son thing" (123–25). In this doubling lies a hint that Fred has succeeded in breaking free of the seductive and smothering femininity of Oedipus. Now, "slowly, thoughtfully, as though this were a mere bit of irrelevant feminine musing" (129), Charlotte hints that she would like George to move into Fred's room and, when she receives a lukewarm response, tries to persuade him to return with her to England. Pressing him with a "teasing, coquettish reproachfulness," she seizes on her favorite story, the one in which George and Jim considered buying a pub in jolly old England. Charlotte's nostalgia and her romanticization of this anecdote invoke the blessing of Jim as his substitute or successor, in her attempt to drag George into the oedipal past of the Bitch-Mother Country (134). George responds by humoring her, even when she kisses him "full on the mouth [and] suddenly sticks her tongue right in." As he did in the case of Doris, he defeats Woman the Enemy by yielding, wondering only if actual women "ever stop trying" (145).

Freeing himself from Charlotte's embrace, George indulges his own nostalgia by paying a visit to his old haunt, the Starboard Side, but soon realizes that the past is "just something that's over" and cannot be found in England nor "anywhere else" (141). He joins his young student, Kenny, who explains, mysteriously, that he was driven to the area by his girlfriend, Lois, and decided to walk around for a while. After several drinks, George imagines that they are engaged in a kind of Platonic dialogue, the point of which is not so much the topic as their "being together in this particular relationship," which is, by its nature, impersonal, in that the partners are somehow opposite and symbolic figures, being, in this case, "Youth and Age" (154). George wants to believe that Kenny understands this too and is delighted when the young man recalls his speech on minorities, arguing that "what's so phony nowadays is all this familiarity. Pretending there isn't any difference between people" and reasoning that if they are no different, "what do we have to give each other?" (158). Through this dialogue, the younger man attains maturity; reciprocally, the older derives youthful energy to the extent that, when Kenny challenges George to a swim in the ocean, they are able to escape their surroundings, becoming "refugees from dryness" (163). This escape takes the place of memory, returning George to the hedonistic beach culture of his early years in the canyon and giving him the illusion of a rebirth, which "washes away thought, speech, mood, desire, whole selves, entire lifetimes" (162–63).

Ultimately disappointed by Kenny, who repeatedly declines his invitation to spend the night, George insists that he has committed the "inexcusable triviality" of turning their encounter into a meaningless flirtation (176). Although George has essentially accused Kenny of a failure to connect, it is he who has failed to connect, for he has chosen to ignore Kenny's simple explanation of his motive to visit the bar, which is to ask George about the value of experience (160). Earlier in the day, in George's encounter with Kenny and Lois after class, there is a suggestion of the possibility of a real connection. At that moment, Lois could well be the one who "seems to know what he is, for she waves gaily to him" (76). In an earlier draft of the novel, her gesture conveys "such a charming intimation of friendship—not of *alikeness* but of the recognition of *difference*—that the whole day seemed to brighten."[10] Although Kenny seeks him out that evening, it is likely that Lois has prompted him to do so, for she is the one who suggests that George is "cagey," with the implication that he should not be (79). George's reply to Kenny, that he is longing to tell things, "absolutely frankly," in some context outside of class (80), not only anticipates their later dialogue of symbolic opposites but also suggests that it is not Kenny but Lois who would have been a suitable partner. As has been evident, George is willing to attribute only a nondialogic symbolic status to women and, in any case, he cannot imagine having such a dialogue with a woman, because "women can only talk in terms of the personal" (154).

If George's androcentric progress culminates in his flirtation with

Kenny, his misogynistic progress terminates in his failure to recognize Lois. His misogyny, which prevents him from registering Mrs. Strunk's wave, Doris's hand grasp, and Charlotte's desperate attempts to communicate through his indifference, also prevents him from making connections with other differences. In his diary, Isherwood writes that the character of Lois had acquired "symbolic status as another Foreigner, stuck midway between being a Nisei in an America she despises and . . . a Japanese[-American] in a Japan she doesn't know."[11] George empathizes neither with the consequence of her experience of minority that she cannot "take people in this country seriously" nor with Kenny's understanding from his experience of majority that she "certainly has the right to hate our guts" for how she and her family were treated during the war. Neither does he appreciate the contradiction of his idea of mutually hostile minorities by her admission to Kenny that "the Negroes were the only ones who acted decently to them" (168). Lois's wave remains an unspoken invitation to George to connect with her as a potential ally. Blinded by his misogyny, he fails to perceive this and, as was the case when he considered ethnic Angelenos as he drove to campus, he registers Lois's presence in stereotypes, wondering "who can be sure of anything with these enigmatic Asians?" (61). Later, in the evening, he dismisses Lois as a feeble rival: "I'm not saying one word against her. . . . But you can't fool a dirty old man; he isn't sentimental about Young Love; he knows just how much it's worth—a great deal, but not everything" (175).

At the end of the novel, George is back where he started, an "old" and "queer" man whom Kenny and Lois might be forgiven for dismissing as "a dirty old man" as he imagines them together for the purposes of masturbation. Smiling to himself with "entire self-satisfaction," he begins to fall asleep (180). It is here, Kaplan argues, that Isherwood's protagonist is "able at last to answer" those questions posed in his notebook, by deciding to stay in America and to look to the future in the belief that he will find another Jim (46). These unconscious decisions are known only through the intervention of an omniscient narrator, who proceeds to present a vision of some rock pools located a few miles up the coast, each of which is "separate and different, and you can, if you are fanciful, give them names, such as George, Charlotte, Kenny, Mrs. Strunk" (183). Wondering how such a variety of creatures can possibly coexist, the narrator suggests that the rocks "hold their world together" (184). Like the freeway, with its merging traffic, or the motel, with its multiple occupancy of *the* room, the rock pools suggest another of Appadurai's metaphors of diversity in American life. This is also a mystic vision, for, just as the ocean comes flooding over the rock pools at high tide, "so over George and the others in sleep come the waters of that other ocean—that consciousness which is no one in particular but which contains everyone and everything" (184). The narrator goes even further, enjoining the reader to suppose that this is when his character experiences the instant, terminal shock of a heart attack. There is, therefore, at least one way for him to connect with entities such as Kenny, Charlotte, and Mrs. Strunk. George, it would appear, no longer needs to "pass" among the minorities of the Living, for he has now joined the majority of the Dead.

NOTES

1. Christopher Isherwood, "Los Angeles" [1947], in *Exhumations: Stories, Articles, Verses* (New York: Simon and Schuster, 1966), 158.

2. Christopher Isherwood, *A Single Man* (New York: Simon and Schuster, 1964), 110.

3. Carola M. Kaplan, "Working through Grief in the Drafts of *A Single Man*," in *The American Isherwood*, ed. James J. Berg and Chris Freeman (Minneapolis: University of Minnesota Press, 2015), 37–47.

4. Christopher Isherwood, "The Englishwoman" [early draft], 1962, Christopher Isherwood Papers, CI 1062, Huntington Library, San Marino, California, 131.

5. Christopher Isherwood, "The Englishman" [early draft], 1962–63, Christopher Isherwood Papers, CI 1061, 6.

6. Arjun Appadurai, *Modernity at Large: Cultural Dimensions of Globalization* (Minneapolis: University of Minnesota Press, 1996), 173.

7. Christopher Isherwood, "A Single Man" [second draft], 1963, Christopher Isherwood Papers, CI 1133.

8. Christopher Isherwood, Writing Notes for *A Single Man*, 1962–63, Christopher Isherwood Papers, CI 1158.

9. The title *A Single Man* was, according to Isherwood's *Sixties* diaries, suggested by Don Bachardy after he read the final version of the manuscript. On August 2, 1963, Isherwood recorded: "In bed, on Monday night, Don was silent for a long while. I thought he had fallen asleep. Then he suddenly asked, 'How about "A Single Man" for a title?' I knew instantly and have had no doubts since that this is the absolutely ideal title" (283). Legally, it's worth noting, "a single man" would be

how George is described on the mortgage of his house in those dark days before "gay marriage." Christopher Isherwood, *The Sixties: Diaries,* vol. 2, *1960–69,* ed. Katherine Bucknell (London: Chatto & Windus, 2010).—Eds.

10. Christopher Isherwood, "A Single Man" [draft], 1962, Christopher Isherwood Papers, CI 1063, 12.

11. Isherwood, *The Sixties,* 186.

12. Becoming Gay in the 1960s

Reading *A Single Man*

Christopher Isherwood's 1964 novel *A Single Man* is surprisingly contemporary when read in the twenty-first century, but it also contains plenty of traces of the past. It is set in that most modern of all states, California, and in Los Angeles, which (unlike the pedestrian city, San Francisco) was built after the invention of the car and from the air looks like a vast collection of villages. As Allan Bérubé pointed out in his 1990 book, *Coming Out under Fire*, World War II was one of the first occasions when young gay American men were far from home, were thrown together in an all-male world, had some money, and feared they might die tomorrow—all the ingredients necessary for coming out. Many of them settled after the war in the welcoming gay beach communities along the Pacific. This is the period, if we include the 1960s, when David Hockney moved to Los Angeles and did all those paintings of young men showering or swimming in a sun-dazzled pool, the nude images of men often derived from erotic physique magazines of the period.

In *A Single Man,* Isherwood refers to the period in uncharacteristically ecstatic tones: "That summer of 1945!" He speaks of his favorite bar, the Starboard Side:

> You pushed aside the blackout curtain and elbowed your way through a jam-packed bar crowd, scarcely able to breathe or see for smoke. Here, in the complete privacy of the din and the crowd, you and your pickup yelled the preliminary sex advances at each other. . . . Hitch-hiking ser-

vicemen delayed at this corner for hours, nights, days; proceeding at last on their journey with black eyes, crab-lice, clap, and only the dimmest memory of their hostess or host. . . . And then the beach-months of 1946. The magic squalor of those hot nights, when the whole shore was alive with tongues of flame, the watchfires of a vast naked barbarian tribe—each group or pair to itself and bothering no one, yet all a part of the life of the tribal encampment—swimming in the darkness, cooking fish, dancing to the radio, coupling without shame on the sand. George and Jim (who had just met) were out there among them evening after evening, yet not often enough to satisfy the sad fierce appetite of memory, as it looks back hungrily on that glorious Indian summer of lust.[1]

This is the very bar where, not long after Jim's sudden death, George returns, drunkenly, and meets up with one of his students, an inquisitive, friendly, handsome, hung guy named Kenny. Kenny's Japanese-American girl-friend, Lois, has driven Kenny all the way out to this louche bar; he's tried to convince her to go to a nearby motel with him (for the second time); she refuses because the first experience was so sordid. They've fought, and Kenny has gone to George's neighborhood bar. Privately, George thinks Kenny, without quite admitting it to himself, has come to this remote bar precisely in hopes of meeting George.

The two men get very drunk and soon the sort of "democracy" has been established between them that George likes so much at the gym, where young and old are equal, interested only in their "routines." No mention is made of the intergenerational love that sprang up in the ancient Greek gymnasium, but Isherwood clearly has that in mind, just as the classical unities of time and place suggest Greek drama.

George supposes Kenny has sought him out because he wants his professor to tell him something, to impart some wisdom. But George insists he can't convey any wisdom since "what I know is what I am" (176). George thinks of himself as "a book you have to read." And indeed the fact that knowledge is incommunicable except through experience, lived or fictional, is one of the best reasons for writing or reading fiction of the very sort of *A Single Man*. If a guru told us the secret of life, the meaning of the universe, the words would be banal or meaningless: it's the trip to Ithaca that counts, not Ithaca itself. To the degree a novel or memoir can approximate the triumphs and defeats, or quiet pleasures and disappointments, of a life, to that degree it can communicate ethical and aesthetic knowledge—in a way that nothing else written can do. This enthusiastic passage might count as Isherwood's *ars poetica*.

In the words of Krishnamurti, whom Isherwood was familiar with, "That depends on you, and not on someone else, because in this there is no teacher, no pupil; there is no leader; there is no guru; there is no Master, no Savior. You yourself are the teacher and the pupil; you are the Master; you are the guru; you are the leader; you are everything."[2]

There are old-fashioned aspects of the novel; I suppose its mild scorn toward women seems a gay attitude out of the past. True to the background reference to the *erastes* and *eromenos*, George fantasizes about engaging in a Platonic dialogue with Kenny. "George can't imagine having a dialogue of this kind with a woman, because women can only talk in terms of the personal" (as we've just seen in the scene with George's woman friend and fellow Brit, Charley, who is too needy for a rational friendship and who hopes to seduce George after all these years). "A man of his own age would do, if there was some sort of polarity; for instance, if he was a Negro. You and your dialogue-partner have to be somehow opposites. Why? Because you have to be symbolic figures—like, in this case, Youth and Age. Why do you have to be symbolic? Because the dialogue is by its nature impersonal. It's a symbolic encounter" (154).

While writing this book, Isherwood seemed to be anticipating an idea presented in 1985 in *The Homosexual Matrix*, by C. A. Tripp, who argued that the best gay relationships reproduced the dichotomy of male–female couples by pairing men who were of different races or ages. I wonder if Isherwood ever met Tripp, whose book sold half a million copies and who was a student of Alfred Kinsey. Isherwood had met Kinsey as early as 1951; they were introduced by the New York writer Glenway Wescott. Isherwood in turn introduced Kinsey to several other gay writers, including Tennessee Williams, and to members of the Mattachine Society, the homophile organization founded in 1950 and that counted two thousand members by 1953.[3]

At one point early in *A Single Man*, George toys with the idea of symbolic experience, but it's never quite clear what he means. He might be talking about Plato's idea that everything in the world around us is just a shadow in the cave, a mere material and inferior representation of the notion that that shadow reflects or imperfectly exemplifies. But the novel also contains a much more original and amusing formulation, which George articulates in a heated exchange with colleagues. He describes an expression of impatience with the European scorn for American materialism:

> "We've reduced the things of the material plane to mere symbolic conveniences. . . . But the Europeans call us inhuman . . . because we've renounced their world of individual differences and romantic inefficiency and objects-for-the-sake-of-objects. All that dead old cult of cathedrals and first editions and Paris models and vintage wines. . . . The Europeans hate us because we've retired to live inside our advertisements, like hermits going into caves to contemplate. We sleep in symbolic bedrooms, eat symbolic meals, are symbolically entertained—and that terrifies them. . . . Essentially we're creatures of spirit. Our life is all in the mind. That's why we're completely at home with symbols like the American motel room. Whereas the European has a horror of symbols because he's such a groveling little materialist." (91–92)

You have to admit that this is a very funny reversal, in which Americans build skyscrapers but Europeans worship them. Perhaps it is true that with our primitive Christian distrust of this world and its pleasures, we are relatively free of commodity fetishism, which has become so deeply instilled in Europe as a class marker. But then the opposite may also be true: one could argue that Americans build their identities by buying things.

At other times Isherwood himself seems to be that very European with a scorn for the American culture of "conspicuous consumption" worthy of the sociologist Thorsten Veblen, who is of course best known as the author of *The Theory of the Leisure Class* (1899). Certainly, many of Isherwood's negative opinions of permissive parents, smug mothers, hateful, bratty children, and of the family itself seem very much of the period, with a dash of gay resentment added. The dislike of children is reminiscent of the "no-neck monsters" in Tennessee Williams's 1955 play *Cat on a Hot Tin Roof.* This dislike of children seemed smart and intellectual and sophisticated back then.

Against these retrograde elements, what's new in the novel is Isherwood's sharp, satirical denunciation of enlightened homophobia:

> (Shame on those possessive mothers, those sex-segregated British schools!) . . . Here we have a misfit, debarred forever from the best things of life, to be pitied, not blamed. Some cases, caught young enough, *may* respond to therapy. As for the rest—ah, it's so sad;

especially when it happens, as let's face it it does, to truly worthwhile people, people who might have had so much to offer. (Even when they are geniuses in spite of it, their masterpieces are invariably *warped*.) So let us be understanding, shall we, and remember that, after all, there *were* the Greeks (though that was a bit different, because they were pagans rather than neurotics). Let us even go so far as to say that this kind of relationship can sometimes be almost beautiful—particularly if one of the parties is already dead, or, better yet, both. (28)

In my gay adolescence in the 1950s I frequently heard this kind of condescending pity for gays, especially from enlightened straights like George's neighbor, Mrs. Strunk. Our only hope was therapy, and I wasted nearly twenty years on the couch. I was particularly worried about the warped books I might write, excluded as I was from the great rites of heterosexual marriage, parenting, adultery, and divorce. Isherwood is light-years ahead of his gay contemporaries in this passage in which he is able to parody this damaging "acceptance," even if he is not quite ready to foresee the moment when gays would redefine themselves as a minority rather than a diagnosis.

Although Jean Genet had embraced the idea that gays were criminals and sinners—a stronger position than the liberal notion that they were "sick"—and Edgar Rice Burroughs had portrayed gays as creepy Saurians, scary but not quite human—Isherwood was unusually advanced in picturing George as a man in mourning, perhaps, but not neurotic, not in search of medical help, not begging society to "forgive" him for his defect or transgression. In *A Single Man* there is no etiology, no talk about how George became gay (always a retrogressive pursuit, since it implies the process could be reversed and the result needs explaining). George isn't exactly "out," except to a few intimates, but he's not closeted either. He does die, but he doesn't commit suicide.

Nor is homosexuality the exclusive or even the main theme of *A Single Man*. Particularly compelling is the gradual assembly of George's self upon awakening and the subsequent dissolution of those elements in death. Although it never directly names Hinduism or Vedanta, the novel conforms to ideas of Eastern religion—though curiously more to Buddhism than Hinduism. The Buddha taught that the self, which is only an illusion, is made up of five "aggregates" or skandhas, and that the true state of no-soul, anatta, is perceived when the various aggregates dissolve, such as feelings, perception, and consciousness, to name just three. Whereas Hinduism believes in a soul, an Atman, which can be reincarnated, Buddhism is built on the idea of no-soul. All that is passed on is one's moral record, one's karma, which influences rebirth. In Buddhism, there is rebirth without souls, just the cause-and-effect of karmic virtues and defects (such as greed and anger). The consequences of these faults must be worked out so that the long, painful cycle of rebirth can come to an end in enlightenment, Nirvana.

We know Isherwood's powerful sexual drives were always in conflict with the practice of Vedanta, as explored in his final completed book *My Guru and His Disciple*. Perhaps George, who feels such a deep hankering after Kenny and who hasn't resolved his mourning of Jim, will be reborn, in part through his intense desire for Kenny.

Of course none of this is mentioned explicitly in *A Single Man*, but in the last words of the novel we read: "And if some part of the nonentity we called George has indeed been absent at this moment of terminal shock, away out there on the deep waters, then it will return to find itself homeless. For it can associate no longer with what lies here, unsnoring, on the bed. This is now cousin to the garbage in the container on the back porch. Both will have to be carted away and disposed of, before too long" (186). There has never been a less sentimental or "spiritual" account of dying. Instead of seeing the nonsoul as Buddhists might, Isherwood talks of an oversoul, "that consciousness which is no one in particular but which contains everyone and everything, past, present and future, and extends unbroken beyond the uttermost stars" (184). He compares individuals to rock pools, which contain the waters of the ocean, the totality of all this is or was or will be. Krishnamurti may have taught this brand of Vedanta, but on the issue of rebirth he sounds like a Buddhist: "Immortality is not the continuance of identified thought. The mortal cannot seek the immortal. Immortality comes into being when the thought process as the 'me' and the 'mine' ceases."[4]

As a self-doubting homosexual adolescent and young man, I suffered terribly. I not only sought to go straight, but I also tried to extinguish all desire through Buddhism. I would meditate for hours and attempt to control my breathing. I was convinced I even levitated once about a foot off the bed. Gay desire wasn't the problem; all desire was to be extirpated. Like Isherwood, I found comfort in the calm acceptance of homosexuality in both Vedanta and Buddhism. Like Isherwood, I had a great need for sexual expression, which I regarded as a block to enlightenment.

A Single Man, as the work of a sophisticated but pious writer, endlessly alert to self-irony and comic possibility, driven by sexual desire, spoke to me fervently, intimately.

NOTES

This essay is based on the inaugural Isherwood–Bachardy Lecture, which Edmund White gave at the Huntington Library on September 29, 2016.—Eds.

1. Christopher Isherwood, *A Single Man* (Minneapolis: University of Minnesota Press, 2001), 147–48.

2. J. Krishnamurti, *The Collected Works of J. Krishnamurti, 1966–1967,* vol. 17, *Perennial Questions* (Ojai, Calif.: Krishnamurti Foundation of America, 2018), n.p.

3. For more on these connections, see Henry L. Minton, *Departing from Deviance: A History of Homosexual Rights and Emancipatory Science in America* (Chicago: University of Chicago Press, 2001), 172ff.—Eds.

4. J. Krishnamurti, *The Collected Works of J. Krishnamurti, 1945–1948,* vol. 4, *The Observer Is Observed* (Ojai, Calif.: Krishnamurti Foundation of America, 2012), 190.

BARRIE JEAN BORICH

13. "Three Quite Different People"

Christopher and His Nonfictions

YOU ARE A DIFFERENT PERSON

At the end of *Christopher and His Kind,* in that moment on the ship when Isherwood and Auden lean against the rail as Miss Liberty—the "giant-ess," Christopher calls her—swells into view, the memoir returns themati-cally to where it began, to a point of rebecoming. We've seen such images before, as Christopher and Wystan must have as well, transit as remaking, that iconic arrival as marker of the American freedom narrative.[1]

In early twentieth-century stock photographs, it's the workers from Southern and Eastern Europe we see on that boat deck, including the rough young men who could have been the object of Christopher's admirations—the bearers of hoped-for bodily affections but also the not-upper-class-English, not-bound-to-propriety life Isherwood hoped to immigrate to. The promise of actual freedom for the working immi-grant, then and now, may well be illusory, but for Isherwood the horizon was coming clear, the homo-foreigner's yellow brick road to liberation in America. The most American of migration tales is also the classic queer narrative. As beleaguered as LGBT people have been in this country, we are so often also the first ones to relocate our bodies, from within and without, in order both to embody new versions of self and inhabit new definitions of homeland.

In a 1977 interview with Chicago oral historian and man-of-the-people radio host Studs Terkel, Isherwood said, "You are a different person

175

in different places."[2] Indeed, and these "different persons" write quite different sorts of books.

PERMANENT FOREIGNER

How many authors, particularly memoirists, have, from book to book, shape-shifted both voice and point of view on the page as dramatically as did Isherwood? For literary writers, style and form are a kind of homeland, as in a residential space of open thought and access to both chosen and foundational expression. Form might be the writer's most significant and hard-won homeland—in which case we can see in Isherwood's story a slowly evolving arrival. From the Herr Issyvoo of his autobiographical documentary fiction in which homosexuality is merely implicit, to the openly queer and multiply voiced narrator of *Christopher and His Kind,* the narrator's body and identity continually shift position, like that of a voyager or pilgrim, perpetually, if only temporarily, making themselves at home.

In the same radio interview with Studs Terkel, Isherwood described himself as a permanent foreigner:

CI: While I'm in England, my American half—after all I have lived here more than half my life—comes out; but while I'm here, my English half comes out. . . . So, I suppose the answer is that I think of myself as a foreigner.

ST: So, wherever you may be, you're a foreigner, a foreigner and yet at home.

CI: Yes, I don't mind. I like being a foreigner. I don't understand this thing very well about roots. . . . I mean, I have roots, very strong roots—I'm very, very British in many ways—but I can replant them anywhere in a moment. It's no problem. (167)

Foreigners replant themselves outside the community within which they originally resided. Memoir is the merging of memory and reflection, and literary hybrid is an uncommon form made of the union of familiar genre characteristics. The writer of witness is one who collects and observes that which others overlook. With all this in the mix, it's perhaps unsurprising that the narrator in *Christopher and His Kind* came to be so strategically and eloquently fractured.

Interlude of Her Kind

She believes she will understand his fragmented narrator better if she can see what he saw, first from the boat in New York Harbor yes, but that one is easy. The actual and figurative urban blizzard, the lurch of the ferry, the gray skyline, what he called "rude steel nudity" bursting through. She's seen that newsreel. He hated New York City, but Southern California would be the opposite, all windows and green cliffs. All cars and lemon trees and sunlit sea. All that fragrance and cinematic sweep. How do bodies change to meet such shifts in the weather?

BREAKING THROUGH GATES

I don't mean to suggest that literary form is always the direct product of design. It's not, for instance, accurate to claim that any of the creative nonfiction breakthroughs of the mid- to late twentieth century, spanning a good fifty years, were the product of an organized artistic movement.

The mid- to late twentieth-century literary nonfiction innovators were many, though they were very much *not* gathered in the same rooms. Mary McCarthy's *Memories of a Catholic Girlhood* (1957), for instance, used self-interrogating inner chapters to critique the "truthiness" of the coming-of-age stories she originally published in the *New Yorker*. Both John Hersey and Truman Capote invented the "nonfiction novel" by transforming reportage to third-person fiction-like narration. Hersey, in *Hiroshima* (1946), kept his presence off page, truly the open shutter of a deeply observant camera, while the shaping sensibility of Capote's *In Cold Blood* (1966) inhabited the narration of a small-town Kansas murder. It became at once a masterpiece of literary witness and a barely veiled crush letter to a hunky murderer. Maxine Hong Kingston's *The Woman Warrior* (1975) and *China Men* (1977)—books she has described as a matched set, rendering a split but unified biography of her people—used accretion rather than plot to achieve an American arrival arc. In *Pilgrim at Tinker Creek* (1974), Annie Dillard used segment and symphonic structure to essay nature and God from the inside of the natural and observed world. Audre Lorde's partly documentary, partly narrative, and partly mythologized *Zami: A New Spelling of My Name* (1982)—a form she dubbed "biomythography"—honored lives and intersections of the marginalized and re-created the home of self. John Edgar Wideman moved as if through walls in his *Brothers and Keepers*

(1984), sometimes bringing family and community to the page in sweepingly lyric summary, sometimes immersing himself into the scene-based first-person narrative of his incarcerated brother, sometimes caustically ranting against the racist American penal culture.

These breakthrough books, and many more, emerged on the literary scene between 1950 and 1990 as if just let out of genre jail, but if they are related, it's less a matter of shared literary conversation than as markers of a shifting sense of the American self—the personal becoming public, the margins breaking through the gates to the center, and perhaps even the democratization of personal liberation. Although it's also not accurate to say Isherwood (who published *Christopher and His Kind* in 1976) was in direct conversation with any of these writers about autobiographical practice, they do all write out of the same zeitgeist. What these works share is a sense of coming into liberatory space through breaking out of the constrictions of both social constraint and genre convention.

TOWARD A HOMELAND

Literary memoir is much older than any of these examples, though contemporary writers often talk about the form as if it were invented in the late twentieth century. If we track the act of writing about the events of one's life in order to better understand one's place in the world, then we might even date the form back four thousand years or so to Egyptian autobiographical tomb inscriptions, where the scholars' descriptions sound remarkably like how we describe memoir today. In *Ancient Egyptian Autobiographies Chiefly of the Middle Kingdom*, Miriam Lichtheim writes, "If autobiography is the relation of bits of one's life from a position of self-awareness and reflection, then ancient Egyptian autobiographic inscriptions were real autobiographies."[3]

But autobiography is not quite the same thing as memoir; an autobiography is a first-person biography seeking to record the full story of a life, whereas a memoir examines aspects of a life as understood through the particular lens of some question or topical discernment.

The ancient text most commonly cited by scholars of autobiography and contemporary memoirists interested in the history of the form is Saint Augustine's *Confessions*, often mentioned as the West's first redemption memoir. Augustine, by then the bishop of Hippo, describes his lusty youth, which he forgoes in the process of converting to what was still, in the fourth and fifth centuries, the radical sect of Christianity.

The narrative of converting the self from one kind of human to a purportedly better self is recognizable to our contemporary sensibilities and one we've seen over and over again in present-day memoirs of recovery from addiction, compulsive sexuality or sexual violation, as well as in queer stories of coming-of-age, coming out, and affirming gender identity. All of these "confessions" are reclamation tales, the story of being saved from one kind of life and embraced by another. But if we are to read *Christopher and His Kind* as a conversion narrative in the tradition of Augustine's *Confessions,* then we must acknowledge that what one converts to is in the eye of the converted. A "confession," in both the spiritual and literary sense, suggests subsequent redemption, the notion of being saved from sin or error or captivity—an autobiographical tradition that both defines and plagues the memoir. Isherwood's memoirs trouble that tradition, in ways that most queer memoirs have come to defy heteronormativity in their insistence on creating families and communities within which unconventional genders and sexualities flourish.

Augustine wished to escape into a transformed self when writing those famous words "Grant me chastity and self-control, but please not yet."[4] In *Christopher and His Kind,* the narrator/primary character does not wish in the least for this sort of redemption. Even later, in the memoir *My Guru and His Disciple,* while he might wonder if Swami will accept a homosexual acolyte into the fold, Isherwood never considers his lust for men a burden to be relieved of. Quite the opposite.

What this means, in terms of Isherwood's work, has to do with the difficulties of memoir craft, in particular that of writing more than one memoir, over time, during which the body and mind progress. Not only did Isherwood make himself into a character on the page in many of his works, but he also continually repositioned that narrator in regards to the story and to the reader, as his own position in love and place continued to progress toward a homeland of liberation. He was not looking for a better self. We might even say his "different selves" were the same self, but seen better in a new context. He was in pursuit of a place where this unabashedly queer self might comfortably reside, writing his way into a re-creation, not of self but of home.

WHAT YOU CAN SEE FROM HERE

There is a tenet about contemporary memoir writing that I constantly repeat to my students. These two sentences are from British writer V. S. Pritchett: "It's all in the art. You get no credit for living."[5] This is the difference between merely testifying and doing what Annie Dillard called "fashioning a text," meaning that, for the writer, the making of the object is as important as, perhaps even more important than, the story the writer means to tell, and that the autobiographical figure on the page is a version of the self, but not the self complete.[6] While *Christopher and His Kind* matters in that it was one of the earliest explicitly gay memoirs, it's also a work that forthrightly states it has been written to speak to what had previously been unspoken. The facts of a young person may not be the same facts as those of an old person. Speaking the unspoken is the act of refashioning what has already been said, and then speaking again.

The directness of *Christopher and His Kind* was widely praised. Terkel, for instance, in his interview with the author, exclaimed over the book's candor, referring to Isherwood's unapologetic coming out as far on the page as he was in actual life. Still, the revelations of sexuality may not be the truest thing about this book, particularly as those likely to have an ear for such things already knew that the thinly veiled narrator of *The Berlin Stories* was a homosexual man, or a *queer*, as Isherwood liked to self-describe. I suggest the most radically true aspect of this rendering of Isherwood's salad days in Berlin is the work's grand experiment with point of view. Point of view is, of course, a literary element, but it's also a statement of position: where in time and space is the author standing and what is visible from that vantage point that was not visible from where the author stood before?

Interlude of Her Kind

The first time she attempts to find the author's address on Adelaide Drive, she gets lost. She is driving an unfamiliar rental car, which is part of the problem. She visits from one of the dense cities back east, where it's been too long since she's owned a car; she has lost her driving reflexes. And it's so hilly on that side of Santa Monica. In her first attempt she misses the street entirely, shooting off into the canyons, and has to navigate a series of one ways until getting back to the beach, past the building with the Camera Obscura, as if the whole neighborhood says "I am a camera," and then making sure to turn up the hill before those glass apartments on the waterfront. She would have been content to just drive by his house, but friends had told her to be sure and peek over the fence. Which fence? And where could she park? And really, she's not a stalker. She just wants to see what he saw. Every author is a camera, but in the human body, images do not merely process but impress. Voice is both what we come from and what we come to. All she wants is to see his view.

UNTIL WE ARE AT HOME

Who, then, is this transitory, place-shifting "I" on the memoirist's and personal essayist's page, and what geographies made them that way?

Studs Terkel asked Christopher about that relationship of location to identity:

ST: Being in a different land, a different culture, you as a writer could know more about your home there than in England, which is why so many writers went to Paris in the 1920s and realized so much about America.

She just wants to see what he saw. View of the Pacific Ocean from Adelaide Drive. Photograph by Barrie Jean Borich.

CI: Oh, that's very true. . . . You see, you go to Berlin, and suddenly you are a "German Studs," and it's very interesting to find out what the German Studs is like. (167)

By that measure *Christopher and His Kind* is a peculiar kind of conversion memoir, as the tale it retells is of the time the British Isherwood became the German Christopher, a young man in search of that free place capable of providing, for both his work and his homosexuality, a home that might well have been Berlin if not for the Nazis.

Any one of us can change location to become another variation of self, but at the same time the characteristics acquired in any new place exist only against the tension of who we were before we got there. Our place-based identities accrete rather than replace.

The self that speaks from *Christopher and His Kind* is an inherited British and adopted German self that revised himself yet again, years later, against the wide, blue expanse of the Santa Monica saltwater and the cragged, burnished cliffs of the Pacific Palisades. He immigrated to California having just lost a lover, his Heinz, to a Germany that didn't want his kind. It's hard to stay true to a homeland, particularly a chosen homeland, one that doesn't love you back. But this then is the twentieth-century queer narrative, the slow bringing of the self from overcast to sunshine, from obscurity to transparency, from unspokenness to language, from refugee to citizen. We are not citizens until we are at home, and we can't be at home if our homelands are unwilling to take us in.

UP THAT SUNNY HILL

What, then, is a homeland, and how can we know if we've written ourselves there?

Some homelands are that original location that made us, but other homelands, the ones we seek out as adults, are those places where we imagine we can remake ourselves, a sanctuary where we might not worry about presentation or judgment. Particular location is central to homeland, even if the actual experience is ephemeral. Some leave, some return, some perpetually quest. Homeland is always the half-mythical, wholly unreachable, shining hillside on the horizon, more process than destination. The climb up that sunny hill where the view spills out is less a destination than just the daily trudge.

Interlude of Her Kind

She does finally park the car at the end of the block, on another street entirely, and walks up to the sprawling, ocean-view houses. When she can't find the house number she stops in puzzlement. It's the middle of the day and no one is driving up or down the hill but workmen, gunning the gas, slamming on the brakes so as not to hit the blond woman wearing a cactus-green dress that matches her tattoos, standing on a road lined with desert landscaping, trying to peer over fences unobtrusively, looking for what? The houses don't interest her, but when she gives them her back, what she sees is that wild and marvelous sea. To look at this sea every day, do you pause and consider how you got to this view? Because this is the view that fills windows? Because you met your love on this beach?

A QUEER-NORMATIVE ARC

The liberation those of us studying creative writing in academic settings in the late 1980s were so attracted to was the variation and experiment of literary nonfiction—the breadth and capacity to create a form that matched the anti-arcs of our lives. Here was a form that held all the craft delights of fiction and poetry, and yet wasn't bound to a static canon. The possibilities were ever evolving, even as the lack of agreed-upon structure was daunting. But if we needed tradition, we had all sorts to choose between, from before we called nonfiction an art. The essayists tend to claim the prismatic questions of Michel de Montaigne, and memoirists relate to the change arc of Augustine, while the lyric nonfiction writers align with the spare lists of observation and complaint penned by the Japanese courtier Sei Shōnagon, in what came to be known as *The Pillow Book* (ca. 1000), and the journalists refer to the participatory reportage of Gay Talese. Furthermore, when offering the definition of creative nonfiction to any literate lesbian who came out before the end of the twentieth century (but did not do time in an MFA writing program), she will likely call forth Audre Lorde when she says, "Oh, you mean biomythography?"

When I first read *Christopher and His Kind*, I was already long in love with *The Berlin Stories* for the same reason as so many others—that fast credit line at the start of the film version of *Cabaret*: "Based on stories by Christopher Isherwood." *There's a book?* My first reading of *The Berlin Stories* was long before I'd heard of the myriad subgenres of nonfiction, yet I knew Isherwood had written some sort of nonfiction, as well as some sort of queer coming-to-knowledge tale.

I had already begun to write creative nonfiction when I read *Christopher and His Kind* the first time, and I did not find it a perfectly formed gem of a book, as I had *The Berlin Stories,* and I still don't. But the book's formal imperfections may well be because *Christopher and His Kind* is so true to actuality it resists form. The book is a hybrid of first- and third-person narrations and quotations from earlier books, accurate but at times choppy, a memoir of both living and writing a sexual coming of age that keeps breaking out of any recognizable structure—in the time before nonfiction writers were really talking to each other about form, and on the cusp of the time when we began to consider memoirs fully "literary."

Clearly *Christopher and His Kind* is literary and is a memoir. Still, Isherwood's name (as well as Audre Lorde's name) was not included on the nearly exhaustive list of memoirists in Ben Yagoda's 2009 book *Memoir: A History,* though nearly every other author I've mentioned here is, along with many others, including even celebrity memoirists such as actress Valerie Bertinelli and Hollywood hoofer Fred Astaire. The absence of Isherwood and Lorde on this list, two significant early game changers, annoys but does not surprise me, as creative writing workshop genre discussions generally didn't include LGBTQ authors until the 1990s publication of memoirs by Paul Monette, Bernard Cooper, and Mark Doty (all of whom are on Yagoda's list), and in the 2000s, of course, Alison Bechdel (also *not* on Yagoda's list), whose revolutionary graphic memoir *Fun Home* is still changing everything.

When I make my own lists of the scattered history of the form, I do include Isherwood and Lorde—and especially Bechdel—not just to be inclusive, not just to fill in the overlooked lesbian gaps, but also because of what everyone misses if we leave queer innovation out of the conversation. Queer nonfiction is particularly queer because queers have long been happy to try to make forms that can hold queer-normative lives. Which brings us back to that layered and self-interrogative autobiographical third person.

THE TRANSPARENT MASK

Why then all those pronoun gymnastics in *Christopher and His Kind*? Because to know home you have to know the self. For authors to know and

write the self, they must remove fictive masks while retaining an authorial voice, and at the same time be able to operate as characters on the
page—still a mask, but a transparent disguise. In his book *The Made-Up
Self: Impersonation in the Personal Essay*, Carl Klaus writes (in which, for the
purposes of this discussion, I've replaced "personal essay" with "memoir"):

> Voice . . . is both an authentic and a fictionalized projection of personal-
> ity, a resonance that is indisputably related to its author's sense of self but
> that is also a complex illusion of self. . . . The ultimate source of imper-
> sonation probably should be traced to the paradox that exists at the heart
> of any [memoir], which by virtue of being an act of self-dramatization is
> at once a masking and an unveiling, a creation and an evocation of self.[7]

The difference that comes of not saying and saying the once-forbidden
words is like the difference between the dense obscuring snow of an
old-world city and the sunny cliffside view of the Pacific. The difference
between the protagonist of *Christopher and His Kind* and the protagonist of
The Berlin Stories is that transparency. "It was Berlin itself he was hungry to
meet; the Berlin Wystan had promised him. To Christopher, Berlin meant
boys" (*Christopher and His Kind* 2).

But the boys in Berlin gathered in the dark, in the underground places:
"I can still make myself faintly feel the delicious nausea of initiation ter-
ror which Christopher felt as Wystan pushed back the heavy leather door
curtain of a boy bar called The Cosy Corner and led the way inside" (3).
The liberation of the city has always been that which comes in the night,
behind heavy curtains, and isn't that how queers once learned to recognize
each other?

We stay outside this particular curtain in *The Berlin Stories*, but we
know it's there, which means perhaps we read Isherwood's earlier works
not so much as fiction, but as memoir with a secret. Many would argue that
memoir with a secret is not a memoir, but consider the range in the history of the form. Audre Lorde mentions all manner of lesbian love in *Zami*
but doesn't bring up the fact that she strayed from the gay girl life of the
1950s Greenwich Village long enough to acquire a husband and two kids.
And what of Bernard Cooper's omission of three dead brothers in *Truth
Serum*, his memoir of growing up gay in Los Angeles, story points he left
out because the youngest was fifteen years older than he was and lived away
from home for most of the author's childhood, and because he'd already

told their stories in other books, and because *Truth Serum* was about coming of age as a gay man in the AIDS era, and "very early in the writing . . . I knew that a book concerned with homosexual awakening would sooner or later deal with AIDS and the population of friends I'd lost to the disease. . . . To be blunt, I decided to limit the body count in this book in order to prevent it from collapsing under the threat of death."[8] Omission is common enough in memoir to be a characteristic.

That gap between *The Berlin Stories* and *Christopher and His Kind* is significant enough in his own evolution for Isherwood to bring it up on the opening page of the later book. "The book I am now going to write will be as frank and factual as I can make it, especially as far as I myself am concerned." Which brings us back to his pronoun gymnastics. In *Liberation,* the final volume of his published diaries, in an entry dated October 29, 1973, we find these notes on how he wrestled with the problems of pronouns and transparency:

> I have now realized that I can only put our departure in perspective if I begin with Germany—why I went there—"to find my sexual homeland." . . . I'm also much bothered by the first-person-third-person problem. . . . "Christopher" is such a cumbersome name to keep repeating and the use of it has a dangerous cuteness. I think I'll probably end up by writing "I."[9]

But Christopher's "I" was not yet wide enough to bring all his fragmentations to the page at once. In *Christopher and His Kind,* he achieved memoiristic transparency by using a shifting point of view to embrace a multiple self. Terkel asked him about this multiplicity:

ST: What's moving to me about *Christopher and His Kind,* which you call a revisionist autobiography because—in a way you are a camera—you are looking at yourself now and saying here is the real Christopher Isherwood, not the one you've read about earlier. In a sense you are still outside looking at yourself.

CI: There are actually three, aren't there? There's the author, now, seventy-two; there's the character who appears in *The Berlin Stories,* in his thirties; and there's also the real Christopher—not as he's presented in *The Berlin Stories*—in his thirties. Those are three quite different people.

ST: And in a way you use the second person and the third person—and the first. You use all three, which makes it very exciting. But what's very moving to me is the candor and the good humor. There's a joy to it. You're free; you've always been a free man, but within limitations, haven't you? Certain things you always had to hide. (168)

"WE CAN SEE THE HILLS FROM OUR BED"

Christopher's autobiographical transparency and collage of self can only be fully understood through the clarifying lens of place. If California is his liberation, then Berlin was his transgression. We disobey the rules of home to obey the demands of the body, but then how does one inhabit that disobedience? Some would forgo home, or would forgo bringing the body home. But for Isherwood, even his reinvented home was a complex enterprise: material, demanding, and constant, and—to this permanent foreigner—not monogamous and never unchanging. Homes change. Bodies change. The ways bodies inhabit homes change. His Santa Monica move is a carrying away from the urban fog of his first sexual homeland, into another place in which the landscape itself is clear and sunny—transparent. The view conveys both ground and horizon, including how any looker's perception of that geography may have shifted over the course of Isherwood's time there, and later, after his death, the course of his lover's time alone there.

He writes himself and his love Don Bachardy into the beginning of this new homeland in the completely unmasked voice of his diaries, October 2, 1959:

> The day before yesterday we moved here.... We are both still in the first delight of being here. Principally, it's the view—being able to see the sky and the hills and the ocean. We can see the hills from our bed. Don is so delighted, it warms my heart. But this is a real house, a long in-and-out place of many rooms and half-rooms, passageways and alcoves. And in spite of the power pole and power lines and TV aerials, there really is a hillside privacy and snugness—something that suggests a run-down villa above Positano.[10]

Interlude of Her Kind

She climbs partway down and up that hill still trying see what they saw. She has to turn around and around before she understands: she can't see the house

All cars and lemon trees and sunlit sea. View of the house. Photograph by Barrie Jean Borich.

because it's embedded into the hillside that falls away toward the sea, shielded from the eyes of the lookers. Yet she does look over the fence, as her friend advised, and sees the cactus gardens, a tender green moat between the house and the world. This is a California August sun, clear and sharpening, and afternoon so the light has just started to bend. She leans into the rail at the curve of the road, toward the water. She isn't the first one to see this. Oh how the right light can liberate.

NOTES

1. Christopher Isherwood, *Christopher and His Kind* (Minneapolis: University of Minnesota Press, 2001), 338.

2. Studs Terkel, "Christopher Isherwood," in *Conversations with Christopher Isherwood*, ed. James J. Berg and Chris Freeman (Jackson: University Press of Mississippi, 2001), 167.

3. Miriam Lichtheim, *Ancient Egyptian Autobiographies Chiefly of the Middle Kingdom: A Study and an Anthology*, vol. 84 of *Orbis biblicus et orientalis* (Heidelberg: Universitätsverlag, 1988), 2.

4. Augustine, *The Confessions*, trans. Maria Boulding, ed. John E. Rotelle and William Harmless (Hyde Park, N.Y.: New City Press, 2012), 198.

5. Quoted in Judith Barrington, *Writing the Memoir* (Portland, Ore.: Eighth Mountain Press, 2002), 72.

6. Annie Dillard, "To Fashion a Text," in *Inventing the Truth: The Art and Craft of Memoir*, ed. William Zinsser (New York: Houghton Mifflin Harcourt, 1998), 141.

7. Carl H. Klaus, *The Made-Up Self: Impersonation in the Personal Essay* (Iowa City: University of Iowa Press, 2010), 47.

8. Bernard Cooper, "Marketing Memory," in *The Business of Memory: The Art of Remembering in an Age of Forgetting*, ed. Charles Baxter (St. Paul, Minn.: Graywolf Press, 1999), 111.

9. Christopher Isherwood, *Liberation: Diaries*, vol. 3, *1970–1983*, ed. Katherine Bucknell (London: Chatto & Windus, 2012), 398.

10. Christopher Isherwood, *Diaries*, vol. 1, *1939–1960*, ed. Katherine Bucknell (London: Chatto & Windus, 2011), 829.

14. In Search of a Spiritual Home

Christopher Isherwood, *The Perennial Philosophy*, and Vedanta

After he left Europe, a few months prior to the onset of World War II, and moved to Los Angeles, Christopher Isherwood's search for a new home proved to be not only material but also spiritual, following his introduction to Vedanta by Aldous Huxley and Gerald Heard. In his attempt to realize this spiritual sense of "home," Isherwood embarked on what was to become a lifelong study of Vedanta and practice of meditation with his guru, Swami Prabhavananda. He spent a considerable part of his time in Los Angeles translating Vedic texts into English. His formal study of Vedanta yielded a large body of nonfiction writing on Vedanta, but perhaps more interesting than his considerable nonfiction output on Vedanta are other formulations of a spiritual vision that emerge in his journals and literary production during the period. Not surprisingly, in these writings the conception of a spiritual vision is far more ambivalent and conflicted, as Isherwood grapples with how to represent such a consciousness more richly in literature and to actualize it in his own complex life. This essay explores how we might read this indirect engagement with Vedanta through contemporary reformulations of Huxley's and Isherwood's perennial philosophical outlook. From this perspective, Isherwood's fiction becomes an important representation of what the theological philosopher David Bentley Hart calls "the experience of God" that recognizes the "mystery of our being" and its "absolute contingency."[1]

Isherwood developed his conception of Vedanta in the context of the perennial philosophical outlook of the period. Particularly influential in establishing this view was Isherwood's friend Aldous Huxley, who popularized it in his seminal book *The Perennial Philosophy* (1945). Huxley's version of the Renaissance idea of *philosophia perennis* involved taking a syncretic approach to different religions, regarding them all as ultimately expressing a number of universal truths behind their apparent differences. This consisted of three common truths: (1) the self is by nature divine; (2) this nature is identical with the divine Ground of Being; (3) the ultimate goal of life is to come to the realization of such nonduality through mystical union. *The Perennial Philosophy* illustrated this through quotations from diverse religious traditions, including Taoism, Hinduism, Buddhism, Islam, and Christianity. Huxley's perennial philosophy, like Theosophy, was a hybrid belief system. Huxley argues for an apparently theist "divine Reality," and a "soul" that is congruent with that reality, as being among his universal truths.[2] According to Huxley, in the Vedic traditions the "Divine Ground is Brahman, whose creative, sustaining and transforming aspects are manifested in the Hindu trinity," whereas in "Mahayana Buddhism the Divine Ground is called Mind or the Pure Light of the Void" (13–14). From this perspective, while the mystical experience is beyond the "phenomenal ego," it is deliberately ambiguous whether such a state represents the dissolution of the self (as in the Buddhist concept of no-self), or whether it represents the union of the individual, eternal self (atman) with the "Divine Ground," as is common in many Vedic traditions (13). This broad perennial philosophical outlook, which places mystical experience at the heart of all religions, was so prevalent during Isherwood's lifetime that it was not only shared by Isherwood but also by the major figures promoting Vedanta and Buddhism in America at the time, most prominently Swami Prabhavananda, Alan Watts, and D. T. Suzuki.

In our contemporary moment, there has been a range of responses to this version of the perennial philosophy. Various theorists within cultural studies have challenged a perennial philosophical approach, owing to its universalist claims and historical connections to European colonialism. In the field of postcolonialism, for example, the perennial philosophy is seen as a function of Edward Said's concept of Orientalism—a critical approach which argues that Western academic and cultural representations of the "Orient" establish a boundary between the West and the "Orient." From this perspective, the "mysticism" of the "Orient" is contrasted to the rationality of the West, the laziness of "Orientals" is contrasted to the industriousness of Westerners, and so on. Drawing upon the work of Michel Foucault, Said's *Orientalism* (1978) argues that such (mis)representations of the "Orient" go beyond mere stereotypes because they produce a systematic knowledge about the "Orient" and, consequently, masquerade as fact within Western discourse. Indeed, so powerful is Orientalism in shaping representations of the East that, when applied to Vedanta, the mystical or "spiritual has not only become a prevalent theme in contemporary Western images of India," but also "exerted a great deal of influence upon the self-awareness of the very Indians it purports to describe."[3] But the Orientalist position raises two issues with respect to Vedanta: first, how is it possible to produce anything that is not Orientalist if the system is so all-encompassing? And second, Orientalism denies Vedanta meaningful religious ontological space by conceiving of religion as an entirely cultural phenomenon. In other words, while representations of religious experience may fall back on Orientalist tropes, this does not mean there is no such thing as religious experience. Both Huxley and Isherwood were, for example, adamant that language and culture could only point to—but never fully grasp—religious experience, a point I will explore later in this essay.

More useful responses for my purpose here are recent attempts to rework a perennial philosophical approach in light of its evident shortcomings. A number of thinkers have addressed the problems with Huxley's version of the perennial philosophy, such as the lack of texts in translation at the time, its weak universalist position, as well as its tendency to conflate significant differences between religious traditions. One of the most successful attempts to reconceive a version of perennial philosophy comes from the theological philosopher I mentioned earlier, David Bentley Hart. In *The Experience of God*, Hart makes the case that all serious religious and philosophical thought lies in the child's experience of the wonder of being—a foundational idea that gets forgotten as we move toward adulthood and inevitably "displace awe" and "banish delight" (88). Hart's argument makes a more convincing case for a perennial philosophy than that conceived during Huxley and Isherwood's time, not only because there is now a much broader range of well-translated religious texts available but also because of the sophistication of Hart's approach.

Drawing upon his training in analytical philosophy, Hart argues that if we trace back the material world to even the smallest subatomic quanta, we still find it is made of some kind of matter, however infinitesimally small it may be. It is therefore impossible for us to use this method to reach some point of absolute origin, as it is logically impossible for something to come from nothing. Hence nothing in our world possesses the cause of its own existence—all things are produced from something else. This is what Hart regards as the absolute contingency of the material world. It follows from this that there must be a different ontological category from which all being proceeds but that also can cause its own existence—that is not contingent upon something prior to produce it. This ontological category is what Hart calls "God": a category beyond our full intellectual grasp foundational to all religions. Hart argues that the phenomenological encounter with this category—the experience of God—is beyond language, as it was for both Huxley and Isherwood, and therefore mystical experience lies at the heart of all religions. It is this ineffable nature of God that explains the deconstruction of religious certainty in all religious traditions: from the *via negativa* in Christianity (fruitful negations), *lahoot salbi* in Islam (negative theology), to *neti neti* in the Vedic tradition (not this, not this). The idea here is that, because God cannot be fully grasped through language, we must always sweep the rug out from under us when we start to become too certain in our conceptions. If God is an ontological category beyond human conception—we can point to it and experience but never fully grasp or represent it—then we must always deconstruct our representations and conceptions of God.[4] Or as Saint Augustine puts it, "If you comprehend it, it is not God" (142). Conversely, we can also have the experience of God simply by contemplating the nature of our being. If we do so, the world becomes one of wonder and awe—we encounter essential strangeness of our being. This is why silence and meditation are central to spiritual practice: God is a phenomenological encounter and, therefore, intellect and abstraction can only take us so far. So, from complex logical reasoning we return to a simple childlike idea: the experience of wonder at the world that Hart argues is at the heart of all philosophical inquiry.

Hart's reformulation of the perennial philosophy is a productive framework from which to read Isherwood's engagement with Vedanta because, in his most effective fiction, it is precisely this strangeness of being and sense of awe and wonder at the world that Isherwood evokes.[5] Yet he was fully aware of the challenges he faced in writing a novel about Vedanta. He reflects upon these challenges in his essay "The Problem of the Religious Novel" (1951), in which he argues that the problem of representing the mystical experience is sidestepped in nonfiction by using the "accepted terminology" of religious traditions, but that in fiction this "kind of shorthand is never permissible for the novelist."[6] Accordingly, the religious novel must show that "the average man and woman of this world" are searching for the kind of mystical experience described by the perennial philosophy, but they are "looking for it in the wrong places." The successful religious novel, then, is not so much one that directly engages with religious ideas but one that strips away the illusions of "surface consciousness" in order to expose the suffering inherent in the world of sensory experience, and point to, if not define, an alternative experience (166).

Significantly, Isherwood was working on his nonfiction representations of Vedanta at the same time that he was writing some of his best fiction. In 1963, for example, he was occupied with both *A Single Man* (1964) and *Ramakrishna and His Disciples* (1965), and his diaries detail his switching back and forth between the two projects. The cross-fertilization produced an imprint of Vedanta on his fiction during this period—an indirect expression of Vedanta that comes closer to Hart's version of the perennial philosophy than Huxley's. In his fiction, Isherwood achieves what Hart understands as the displacement of habit with awe and wonder, and produces very different representations of Vedic concepts than his nonfiction writing on Vedanta, because his own voice emerges in these fictional works. More specifically, Isherwood utilizes three main tropes to express his perennial philosophical version of Vedanta in his fiction. The first is representation of film to indicate that our habitual perception of the world is an illusion. In *Prater Violet* (1945), for example, the narrator (a fictional version of Isherwood) is a writer on a movie with a well-known director who flees to London from the Nazis during World War II. The novel centers on the filming of a movie but also uses the trope of movie production to reflect upon the nature of existence. The narrator comes to realize that he and the director both have defined roles in a drama they have created for themselves in their relationship: "I might have turned to Bergmann and asked; who are you? Who am I? What are we doing here? But actors cannot ask questions during the performance. We had written each other's parts, Christopher's Frederick, Frederick's Christopher, and we had to go on playing them as long as we were together."[7]

The second is a sense of "unhoming" that often involves destabilization and/or refutation of traditional family relationships, enabling recognition of a more profound spiritual home. In Isherwood's final novel, *A Meeting by the River* (1967), for example, the family is contrasted with the freedom experienced by the two protagonists (brothers) in the outside world. There are obvious social reasons for this unhoming in the novel, foremost among these, the repressive sexuality and gender roles of the period. The novel, however, centers on Patrick, a young man who moves to India to become a monk, placing this process of unhoming within a religious context and suggesting the process as a metaphor for the search for a spiritual home.[8]

Finally, perhaps the most compelling contribution to the translation of Vedic texts for a Western audience is not so much his translation of the Gita or the book on Ramakrishna, but rather Isherwood's ability to produce a sense of wonder and awe of being in his fiction by questioning the ontological certainty of who we are as human beings. In *Prater Violet*, for example, he writes, "It was that hour of night at which man's ego almost sleeps. The sense of identity, of possession, of name and address and telephone number grows faint. It was the hour at which man shivers, pulls up his shirt collar and thinks, I am a traveler. I have no home" (122). This strangeness of being is most actualized in *A Single Man*. The novel is bookended by two remarkable passages that contrast sharply with the conventional realist narrative mode employed for much of the novel. The first of these passages, the novel's opening, establishes unfixed, unsettling points of view:

> Waking up begins with saying *am* and *now*. That which has awoken then lies for a while staring up at the ceiling and down into itself until it has recognized *I*, and therefrom, deduced *I am, I am now. Here* comes next, and is at least negatively reassuring; because *here,* this morning, is where it has expected to find itself: what's called *at home.*[9]

The unusual phrasing of the novel's first sentence raises questions of who or what is waking and "saying *am* and *now.*" What is the consciousness that precedes the recognition of self and thinks, "*I am, I am now*"?

As the text proceeds, Isherwood goes on to complicate the "I" of the narrative further by representing the body as a semiautonomous object that is controlled by "the cortex, that grim disciplinarian" (9). When this "creature we are watching" then examines itself by staring into the mirror, "it sees many faces within its face—the face of the child, the boy, the young man, the not-so-young man—all present still, preserved like fossils on superimposed layers, and, like fossils, dead. Their message to this live dying creature is: Look at us—we have died—what is there to be afraid of?" (11). Here, memory is represented as a palimpsest in which the self of the present is layered upon previous selves that are "dead" but remain "present still, preserved." The text's shifting narrative mode further destabilizes the sense of self by changing from the objective point of view used to describe "the creature we are watching" to an omniscient mode that gives voice to the memory of George's past selves, as well as the "it" that "answers them" by confessing *I'm afraid of being rushed* (11). While the objective exterior perspective offers a view of "the creature" as a single being, the omniscient interior narration opens up a series of questions: Who is the "I" that responds to the body's reflection in the mirror? How is the self transformed from an "it" to "I"? What is the consciousness(es) that make such voices possible? The "George" that inhabits the novel is at once the depersonalized being of the opening sentence, the Cartesian individual who deduces *I am, I am now,* the "it" commanded by the cortex, the past selves of memory, and the socially constructed "George," who is "all actor" (44). As the novel progresses and the publicly recognized "George" emerges to move through his daily life in Los Angeles, this socially constructed identity is never able to eclipse fully these other forms of consciousness in order to complete the illusion of individuality it demands. The "George" that inhabits the majority of the novel is shown to be a construct created by social performance, and not the ontologically substantive character of a traditional novel.

Consider, for example, the following passage:

> For it obviously *has* been talking. George realizes this with the same discomfiture he felt on the freeway, when the chauffeur-figure got them clear downtown. Oh yes, he knows from experience what the talking-head can do, late in the evening, when he is bored and tired and drunk, to help him through a dull party. It can play back all of George's favorite theories—just as long as it isn't argued with; then it may become confused. . . . But *here,* in broad daylight, during campus-hours, when George should be on-stage every second, in full control of his performance! Can it be that [the] talking-head and the chauffeur are in league? *Are they maybe planning a merger?* (54; emphasis in original)

Here the "chauffeur-figure" aspect of George's self and the "talking head"

that lectures students are suspected of being different aspects of a constructed version of reality—George's "performance" (36). But while
aspects of George's consciousness resurface and create a dissonance in
his perceived individuality, as the passage progresses it becomes less clear
whether it is the narrator or some aspect of George who is observing
George's performance. On a formal level, Isherwood's use of free indirect
discourse to end the passage blurs the distinction between George's speech
and the narrative voice—a technique that is used repeatedly throughout
the novel. This technical device allows Isherwood to present the last sentences of the passage in such a way that they appear to come from inside
and outside the character simultaneously. This technique adds to the effect
of George losing "full control of his performance" because the last three
sentences come from an ambivalent source (36). They seem to dissolve
the boundaries of George's individual consciousness and float in undefined
space, undermining any stable authority of narrative voice by confusing the
reader as to whether they belong to the narrator, to George (and, if so, what
aspect of his self), or to Isherwood himself.

This process of questioning surface consciousness is brought into
sharp focus at the novel's conclusion, which asks as "this body known as
George's body sleeps . . . *is* all of George altogether present here?" (183).
The novel responds to this rhetorical question with the image of a rock
pool when "the tide is out," developed in the following way:

> Each pool is separate and different, and you can, if you are fanciful,
> give them names, such as George, Charlotte, Kenny, Mrs. Strunk. Just
> as George and the others are thought of, for convenience, as individual
> entities, so you may think of a rock pool as an entity; though, of course,
> it is not. The waters of its consciousness—so to speak—are swarming
> with hunted anxieties, grim-jawed greeds, dartingly vivid intuitions, old
> crusty-shelled rock-gripping obstinacies, deep-down sparkling undis-
> covered secrets, ominous protean organisms motioning mysteriously,
> perhaps warningly, toward the surface light. How can such a variety of
> creatures coexist at all? Because they have to. The rocks of the pool hold
> their world together. And, throughout the day of the ebb tide, they know
> no other. (183–84)

Here is the final vanquishing of the idea of *A Single Man* in which the simile
of a rock pool exposes the illusion of the individual self at the heart of the
perennial philosophical outlook.

By contrast, the metaphor of the ocean provides an expansive view of consciousness in which there is no individual self. Isherwood writes:

> But that long day ends at last; yields to the nighttime of the flood. And, just as the waters of the ocean come flooding, darkening over the pools, so over George and the others in sleep come the waters of that other ocean—that consciousness which is no one in particular but which contains everyone and everything, past, present and future, and extends unbroken beyond the uttermost stars. (184)

As the aspect of George's consciousness associated with his public identity sleeps, a different part awakes, one the novel foreshadows through its destabilization of the self. Isherwood depicts a spiritual vision, one that is spatially all-encompassing ("extends unbroken beyond the uttermost stars"), encompassing all beings and matter ("contains everyone and everything"), but that also operates simultaneously on a temporal axis ("past, present and future"). This temporal axis is significant because it indicates that the novel is not the linear narrative it first appears to be, moving chronologically through a day in George's life. Rather, because "that other ocean" contains "everyone and everything, past, present and future," it is part of the *event-ness* of the novel throughout. Hence, the image of "that other ocean" is not so much an ending to the novel—a finality—but instead a presence throughout: it is simply an expanded awareness of something that has been there all along. This recursive quality, this looping back, invites us to *re-see* the mundane aspects of George's life as what cultural theorist Ira Livingstone calls "the pedestrian sublime."[10] From this perspective, the novel is not so much a series of present moments linked through narrative; I see it more as a complexly interwoven fabric of experience with multiple overlaps. The strange me and not-me moments that George experiences throughout the novel—"For it obviously *has* been talking. George realizes this with the same discomfiture he felt on the freeway, when the chauffeur-figure got them clear downtown"—might be understood as the consciousness of "that other ocean" looping back upon itself (54). Recognition of this recursive quality of Isherwood's spiritual vision requires us to return to the previous pages and realize that *All* is part of this encompassing spiritual vision—including George's sexuality and love for Jim that forms the heart of the novel. Nothing is more or less part of "that other ocean" than anything else. The novel is, in other words, a literary expression of Isherwood's understanding of Vedic reality outlined in "What Is Vedanta?," in which the illusion of the universe may lead us to perceive ourselves as separate from this reality but that we are, in fact, "never separated from it for an instant" (24).

In this respect, Isherwood's grand spiritual vision in *A Single Man* represents a somewhat ambivalent relationship to Victor Marsh's idea of reclaiming "the possibility of a queer spirituality," as outlined in his essay in this volume. On the one hand, as Marsh articulates, given the vexed historical context of queer spiritual experience, the category of queer spirituality can be seen as a corrective to religious discourse, and *A Single Man* might be read as a profound spiritual vision articulated from a position of queer experience. To use the taxonomy of a "queer spirituality" for *A Single Man* is useful to the extent that it reminds us that meaningful queer spiritual experience has been occluded from traditional religious discourse and experience. On the other hand, to categorize the spiritual vision of the novel as evidence of queer spirituality appears reductive, or even contradictory, to the vision itself, as well as to how it functions in the novel. Because "that other ocean" appears at the end of the novel, it forces us to realize that "George and the others" as well as "everything and everyone" are part of this same consciousness in the preceding pages—they are simply not awake to this reality (184). The significance of this formal recursive device is that it renders queer experience both as ordinary and as spiritual as anything else. All categories of identity and experience are leveled from the perspective of this expanded consciousness. The novel does not require George to transcend or repudiate his queerness to realize this spiritual vision: this consciousness always has and always will permeate the phenomenal world, and hence George's queerness in the novel is inescapably part of this grand spiritual vision. Thus, the novel challenges not only the attitudes of characters like Mr. and Mrs. Strunk toward George's sexuality but also the prevailing religious views that privilege, as Marsh says, "forms of (hetero)sexuality authorized by religious doctrine": In *A Single Man*, homosexuality is not a sin to be renounced and, therefore, framed as a barrier to the consciousness of "that other ocean." It is not a separate category of being to the spiritual; it is inexorably part of the novel's spiritual vision.

To read *A Single Man* in light of Isherwood's perennial philosophical approach to Vedanta, then, is to recognize how it gives form to the concept of nonduality. It is a queer spiritual vision insofar as it enables Isherwood to make his sexuality part of this vision in a way that is not evident in most representations of Vedanta, including his own nonfiction writings on the subject. But it is also a spiritual vision that is, in its own terms, irreducible to categories of identity: its radicalness lies in its inclusive vision of non-duality, not in its particularization of it. On a formal level, *A Single Man* confronts one of the biggest challenges that faced Isherwood in bringing Vedanta to a Western audience—that of translating the Vedic concept of nondualism in a culture grounded in conceptions of the individual—by using the image of "that other ocean" at the end of the novel as a recursive device that destabilizes conceptions of individual character (184). Consequently, as a novelist Isherwood addresses much of the criticism leveled against his approach to Vedanta in his nonfiction writing, as well as the broader perennial philosophy of the period, in which Vedic concepts, such as Atman, are translated into categories of the soul, or true self, in order to appeal to European and American audiences. In *A Single Man,* this sense of a bounded self is radically disturbed. Instead, we are left with an oceanic image of nonduality that resists containment and offers a sense of awe and wonder of the irreducible strangeness and absolute contingency of being. In this way, the novel points beyond itself and the limits of thought and language to a phenomenological encounter with a consciousness that Hart calls the "experience of God" and that Isherwood imagines poetically as "the waters of that other ocean" (184).

NOTES

1. David Bentley Hart, *The Experience of God: Being, Consciousness, Bliss* (New Haven, Conn.: Yale University Press, 2013), 9, 90.

2. Aldous Huxley, *The Perennial Philosophy* (New York: Harper and Row, 1945), vii.

3. Richard King, *Orientalism and Religion: Postcolonial Theory, India and "The Mystic East"* (London and New York: Routledge, 1999), 92.

4. For Hart, the sorts of attacks on religion advanced by scientists such as Richard Dawkins overlook these qualitative experiences of being and, as such, "fail to engage the truly essential and abiding mystery of qualitative experience" (178). What for Dawkins underpins the illusion of god that will eventually be explained away by science remains for Hart "an encounter with an enigma that no mere physical explanation can resolve" (89). To try to explain away this experience

of strangeness and wonder misses "a genuine if tantalizingly brief glimpse into a inexhaustibly profound truth about reality" (90).

5. Isherwood's nonfictional attempts to depict Vedanta appear less successful in representing it from the perennial philosophical approach Hart outlines because of the stylistic choices that Isherwood makes in attempting to introduce Vedic concepts to new audiences outside India. For example, in "What Is Vedanta?" he writes, "The ego sense which is the base of individuality will continue to work its way upward, through inanimate matter, through plant life, through the lower animals, into human form and consciousness. . . . But how can we discuss these things? We stumble over our own words. The universe is an illusion. Our essential nature is reality. We are never separated from it for an instant." The problem with this kind of writing is that one can almost feel Swami Prabhavananda standing over Isherwood's shoulder, resulting in a voice too direct and foreclosing—too tight in its conclusions. The challenge for Isherwood here is that he is trying to introduce Vedanta to a new, skeptical audiences who are unfamiliar with its outlook and, therefore, not ready to have it deconstructed or negated. However, in so doing all senses of wonder and mystery are lost—in both content and style. "What Is Vedanta?," in *Living Wisdom: Vedanta in the West,* ed. P. Vrajaprana (Hollywood, Calif.: Vedanta Press, 1994), 13–36.

6. Christopher Isherwood, "The Problem of the Religious Novel," in *Vedanta for Modern Man* (New York: Harper & Brothers, 1951), 166.

7. Christopher Isherwood, *Prater Violet* (Minneapolis: University of Minnesota Press, 2001), 127.

8. In the Upanishads, for example, we read, "Within the city of Brahman, which is the body, there is the heart, and within the heart there is a little house. This house has the shape of a lotus, and within it dwells that which is to be sought after, inquired about, and realized. What then is that which, dwelling within this little house, this lotus of the heart, is to be sought after, inquired about, and realized?" (Chandogya Upanishad 8:1:1, 2).

9. Christopher Isherwood, *A Single Man* (Minneapolis: University of Minnesota Press, 2001), 9; italics in original.

10. Ira Livingstone, *Where God Comes From: Reflections on Science Systems and the Sublime* (Alresford, UK: Zero Books, 2012), 57.

15. "Enlarging Their Clearing in the Jungle"

The Political Significance of Christopher Isherwood's
My Guru and His Disciple

> Religion isn't a course of passive indoctrination. It is an active
> search for awareness.
> —CHRISTOPHER ISHERWOOD, *THE WISHING TREE*

If Isherwood had "come out" as a queer man to his readership with
the publication in 1976 of his landmark autobiography *Christopher and His
Kind*, then his final completed book, *My Guru and His Disciple* (published in
1980, when he was seventy-six), effected a bold "coming out spiritually," to
use Christian de la Huerta's term.[1] Isherwood was acutely aware that this late
text would provoke scornful criticism, even from close associates, so its publication was an assertive move, consciously pushing back the "jungle" of religious prejudice to permit the fullest possible exploration of queer potential.

In *My Guru and His Disciple* Isherwood pointed toward the reclamation of a queer *spiritual* intelligence, and he drew on resources beyond
the characteristic and deep-rooted homophobia of the Abrahamic traditions. As well as the literary and historical resonances of such a text, his
assertion of the value of spiritual inquiry had political repercussions that
continue to provide testimony of queer consciousness moving beyond the
usual markers of selfhood and constituting "sites of political contestation"[2]
against toxic representations of the meaning of queer lives, queer identity,
and queer intelligence. *My Guru and His Disciple* is a significant *testimonio*
that reconfigures conventional constructions of a queerness, with critical
implications in literary, political, and religious spheres.

THE VISION

The image of "enlarging their clearing in the jungle" is taken from *Christopher and His Kind*, where Isherwood discusses E. M. Forster's novel *Maurice*, which he was eventually to assist in getting published.[3] Isherwood praised the same-sex partners Edward Carpenter and George Merrill as "boldly enlarging their clearing in the jungle" (130). Carpenter (1844–1929) was an influential figure across the turn of the twentieth century, not simply because of his nonconformist sexuality. He also developed a positive vision of the place of an intermediate or "third" sex in human societies, according it a special role in the vanguard of social change.[4] He and Merrill lived openly in a loving partnership in the aftermath of the 1895 Oscar Wilde trials and the criminalization of all forms of male homosexual contact in Britain. Carpenter also developed an abiding interest in mysticism and Vedanta philosophy.[5]

I place Isherwood as a significant figure in the tradition of Carpenter, with a positive vision for "homogenic love" that pushes beyond the exclusivist, two-dimensional modelings of conventional gender roles and the propaganda of "family values." Isherwood was comfortable with his own sexuality from the earliest years. He took courage from Carpenter's example, especially after the publication of *Christopher and His Kind*, when he became an avuncular literary icon during the heady days of "gay liberation." I believe, however, that he was "enlarging the clearing in the jungle" beyond simple tolerance for sexual dissidents as part of the ongoing struggle for gay liberation.

I contend that "gay liberation" might now be construed as a subset of a much broader quest that includes liberation even from incomplete identifications as "gay" or "homosexual" as markers of identity, in fact, *without in any way requiring the repudiation of their sexuality*. This quest pushes beyond sexuality itself as an identifier of a human "type" toward an enhanced, integrative sense of personhood. In this reading, "liberation" can be seen as a breakthrough from all toxic concepts and values that crush human potential and as a process of freeing the questing intelligence from erroneous thinking, no matter how ancient its roots. And, given this influential writer's controversial adoption of practices from the Vedanta tradition that he studied in its Advaita, or nondual form,[6] liberation may be defined as freedom from any construction built up in ignorance of the all-embracing reality, Brahman. According to this philosophy, separation from the consciousness of that unified reality is delusional. Compare this with the moral teachings framed in religious traditions based on narrowly conceived, two-dimensional binary views of human potential: the good/bad, gay/straight, sinners/saved constructions. The fundamental roots of homophobia derive from this divisive labeling system.

Following Advaitist principles, on the contrary, allowed Isherwood, the erstwhile atheist, to engage with spiritual praxis even as he was trying to explore and discover both the nature of his sexuality and his *dharma* as a writer. He persevered with Vedanta practices over several decades, and, after a long journey of transition and transformation, he was able to exceed the discursive parameters that supposedly constituted him, even to himself, in the process becoming a "disobedient subject"[7] of those discourses that would cast him outside the fold of conventional religious morality. In learning how his finite personal ego-self related to the deepest stratum of the universal "Self" (in Vedanta, *Param Brahman*; for Aldous Huxley, the "Divine Ground"; what Paul Tillich termed the "Absolute Ground of Being"), Isherwood came to recognize a continuity of being within an integrative experience that ultimately subsumes even the identification as "homosexual."[8]

Thus, the outcomes of spiritual inquiry may also reverberate politically, not only by their insistence on the complex diversity among human "types" but also by reclaiming, through empirical spiritual praxis, the sense of ultimate belonging that resolves the toxic alienation that often results from such deeply flawed dualistic teachings. The political ramifications extend so far as shifting the basis of the construction of Meaning itself, foreshadowing some current challenges to narrowly conceived notions of gender and sexuality taken as Truth in standard framings, especially among orthodox religious belief systems.

For Isherwood, this transformation of consciousness did not happen overnight, and it was tested against his lived experience over decades. By the 1930s Isherwood viewed himself, like Carpenter, as a socialist; he was opposed to the rise of the Fascists, and he was a conscientious pacifist at the time of the Second World War. He was an unlikely candidate for conversion to "religion" in any form:

> My interpretation of the word "God" had been taken quite simplemind-
> edly from left-wing anti-religious propaganda. God has no existence

except as a symbol of the capitalist superboss. He has been deified by the capitalists so that he can rule from on high in the sky over the working-class masses, doping them with the opium of the people, which is religion, and thus making them content with their long working hours and starvation wages.[9]

His odyssey as a "queer" man (this is the term he used to describe himself) was later recounted in *Christopher and His Kind,* but it was his journey as a queer *spiritual* man, meditating under the guidance of a swami in the Ramakrishna Order of monks, that produced this fourth and final autobiography *My Guru and His Disciple,* which gave the record of the life a deeper resonance that many commentators have been loath to recognize.

The book was unpopular at the time. While there would be later calls for Isherwood to be reevaluated as a serious religious writer,[10] that proposal met with a certain amount of skepticism, both from his literary readership and his gay following. For this possibility did not square with the standard view of Isherwood, dominated by a set of stereotyped views that paid little attention and even less respect to his religious life. Nor did it sit easily with the dominant construction of queer men as religious pariahs, an ancient prejudice that lingers in some circles today. To inscribe a life narrative that presents a differently ordered view of reality, such as in *My Guru and His Disciple,* gently wrests control away from dominant discursive constructions of what is "normal" and what is "sinful"; it assertively reconfigures the potential of queer intelligent inquiry into the nature of being in the world.

Some among his queer readership, having identified religious discourse as the major and abiding source of homophobia, refused to recognize any positive resources for queer intelligence there, even from traditions and practices beyond the Abrahamic models. Isherwood had rejected the Anglicanism of his childhood and had been through a bruising disillusionment with politics, too, when he witnessed the collapse of Marxist idealism and its promise of equality (for women and homosexuals) as the aftermath of the Russian Revolution soon abrogated those ideals. As he explained in a 1971 interview with Len Webster:

> The tremendous stumbling block to me personally was the homosexual question: the treatment of homosexuals in Russia—which was absolutely in contravention to their original declarations, that the private life was no concern. . . . The Russians started to equate homosexuality with fascism. And this in itself was such a loathsome piece of hypocrisy that,

while I hardly admitted it to myself at the time, I see now that a government that can lie like that about one thing is really profoundly rotten all the way through, and just like any other government, in fact—and not at all the Kingdom of Heaven![11]

THE GENRE ISSUE

Isherwood was accused of narcissism by some of his critics, due to his characteristic mining of his own life experience to construct original textual narratives, but Isherwood was not as shortsighted as some of his critics. If autobiography—writing the life oneself—is a form of testimony, I would shift the descriptor further to align Isherwood's work, in this context, with the genre of *testimonio*, consciously using the Spanish-language term to invoke the political contexts usually associated with the genre (in spite of the controversies, literary and otherwise, that have aggregated around the term). *Testimonio* has been defined as "a first-person narration of socially significant experiences in which the narrative voice is that of a typical or extraordinary witness or protagonist who metonymically represents others who have lived through similar situations and who have rarely given written expression to them."[12]

Autobiographical texts are labeled thus when they present first-person accounts of human rights abuses and would usually be applied to certain forms of political protests, as if that makes them less than "literary." But any work at "clearing the jungle" of oppression—including bullying by religious professionals, who sometimes seem preoccupied with nothing so much as the policing of gender boundaries—and challenging the control of the moral imaginary deriving from conventional religious teachings, has acutely political ramifications.

Isherwood's "out" texts are more than just chronicles of a particular life; they are acts of political resistance. For, among its various levers of power and control, the hegemon, or dominant order, will always attempt to control the production of meaning. Through life narratives such as these, Isherwood presented a way of living, loving, *and worshipping* beyond the accepted models in societies constructed around heteronormative values and, contrary to the ruthless push toward secularism, also affirmed the value of empirical practices of introspective meditation, under the guidance of his very tolerant guru.

Isherwood made extensive use of his lived experience in his fiction, as well as in his directly autobiographical work, and he was an early exponent of using lived experience as a scalpel to dissect conventional constructions and reconfigure the meaning and value of this material in order to produce what we might call dissident history. People not living through the hostile conditions of twentieth-century homophobia may not recognize the relevance here, but resistance work done to alleviate social oppression has conspicuous and urgent political dimensions, never more so than in the challenge to these intersecting discourses dealing with gender norms and the pejorative religious framing of dissident lifeways.

Recent theoretical work by scholar Jaume Aurell positions such writing as "interventionist autobiography":

> I propose to call these writings *interventional* in the sense that these historians use their autobiographies, with a more or less deliberate authorial intention, to participate, mediate, and intervene in theoretical debates by using the story of their own intellectual and academic trajectory as the source of historiography.[13]

In such framings, the focus of life narratives refers to wider contexts than the solipsism of narcissism, a charge often brought against Isherwood's writing practice, even into the twenty-first century. To illustrate my point: in reviewing Peter Parker's biography of Isherwood for the *Irish Times,* Robert O'Byrne opined that Isherwood "was vainglorious to a ludicrous degree," claiming that "like all self-centred people," Isherwood understood himself very poorly.[14] O'Byrne continues, "Nobody fascinated Christopher Isherwood as much as Christopher Isherwood," arguing that Isherwood's "crystalline prose style managed to conceal that character flaw from readers." He depicts Isherwood as a "fraudulent rebel . . . without much honour or respect."

While acknowledging that some critics today still hold to that construction, it is my position that the confusion about identity, and the "interest in exploring himself" that O'Byrne finds so lamentable was the spur for an interrogation of selfhood that drove Isherwood's writing, and his personal journey into Vedanta philosophy and practice too. It is this very research that has revived interest in Isherwood today, not only from a queer readership but also from an audience for whom the problematized self is a critical postmodern issue.

If queer Isherwood—Isherwood the literary figurehead for gay liberation—has become sufficiently respectable to be mined for literary analysis by scholars and presented at learned conferences and in major international literary journals, have we, even in the process of accommodating what was considered pathologically deviant only a few decades past, fully appreciated the thrust of this very original writer's radicalism?

SPIRITUAL PRAXIS

I believe the queer interrogation of heteronormativity is a project still in process, with important implications into the future for further "clearings of the jungle." A new understanding of the possibility of a queer spirituality is emerging to carry that interrogation beyond the struggle for freedom of sexual expression, civil rights, marriage equality, and so on—as important as these have been as litmus tests for "liberation"—at the social, philosophical, and legal level. To reclaim the possibility of a "queer" spirituality has, in itself, wide-reaching political ramifications in its challenge to the normative order and the acceptable models of meaning and knowledge enshrined therein. Thus, this interrogation leads directly to the further liberation of courageous queer intelligence.

Much emphasis has been placed on the institutional expression of religion as the authorized path to "God" in standard religious constructions. But the representation of "God" figures has been usefully problematized, and oppressive representations of queer folk and their relationship to the "divine" that have themselves had their roots in narrow religious framings, are being interrogated by queer-minded scholars determined to resist their marginalization as religious pariahs, as framed within the old paradigms. Within this context, I use the term "spiritual praxis" to denote a penetrating, empirical inquiry into the nature of being. Furthermore, this inquiry is often precipitated for queer men and women *as a direct result of* their marginalization by "authorized" religion, with (perhaps) unexpectedly fruitful outcomes.

Isherwood's adoption of a long-term study, in theory and practice, of the particular form of *Advaita* Vedanta promulgated within the Ramakrishna tradition, had far-reaching effects on his identity and understanding. Yet, during the decades Isherwood wrote about Vedanta for the West, those effects were not accorded much respect by the literary commentariat, even as such writings introduced a new generation of Western "seekers" to alternative ways of framing the relationship of the individual to a deeper, all-embracing "Self."[15] In the view of the great reformer Shankara, "Brahman—the absolute existence, knowledge and bliss—is real. The universe is not real. Brahman and Atman (man's inner Self) are one."[16] In their translation of this root text, Prabhavananda and Isherwood explain that "Shankara only accepts as 'real' that which neither changes nor ceases to exist . . . No object, no kind of knowledge, can be absolutely real if its existence is only temporary" (13).

The profoundly integrative vision that underpinned his swami's extraordinary acceptance of Isherwood's sexuality is embodied in the famous initial encounter described in *My Guru and His Disciple*, when Isherwood asks, "Can I lead a spiritual life as long as I am having a sexual relationship with a young man?" He recalls that the swami "hadn't shown the least shadow of distaste on hearing me admit to my homosexuality" (25–26).

Conversely, lingering ethnocentric disrespect of the religious traditions of colonized peoples underpinned much of the hostile reception and patronizing dismissal of Isherwood's sincere adherence to the Advaita Vedanta teachings he studied and practiced with Prabhavananda. Perhaps it is not surprising to us today that such wrongheaded treatment would be based on loyalty to the colonial project among the colonizers—especially in Great Britain, the homeland of empire—and that such loyalty should include the empire's concomitant religious presumptions, for the British colonialist project was also the standard-bearer for an imperialistic Christianity, wherein commerce, politics, and religion were characteristically inseparable.

I view spiritual inquiry as an interrogation rather than as a new set of prescriptive beliefs about human nature, and I draw a distinction between accepting an "approved" identity—one that fits smoothly into the structures of belief, doctrine, ritual, and all the paraphernalia of formal religion that position subjectivity within authorized social and political matrices, stamped with the imprimatur of a "God" figure himself—and this kind of inquiry, which seeks a more authentic accommodation with the existential facts of being.

In providing insight into Isherwood's forty-year study of Vedanta, *My Guru and His Disciple* is, then, a significant *testimonio* of a spirituality of lived experience drawn assertively against a backdrop of puzzlement and ridicule, some of that coming even from his closest friends. This was a skepticism he foresaw, as is made very clear in his diary records while writing this book.[17] "Everything I write is written with a consciousness of the opposition and in answer to its prejudices," he reminded himself (*Liberation* 554). As it was published only a few years before his death, *My Guru* has to be read as a major position statement presenting a clear counternarrative to the dualistic assumption that religion and sexuality are always mutually exclusive possibilities for being and knowing.

In *Mr Isherwood Changes Trains*, my 2010 study of Isherwood's odyssey, I proposed that the urgency of a spiritual inquiry is often precipitated in the lives of queer men and women by the marginalization brought about in normative constructions of identity that characterize them as pariahs, or misfits, outlaws, and malcontents, or all of these. Homophobic constructions of queer subjectivity destabilize not only the psychology of the subject but the ontology, as well, and these people often have to undergo a radical reassessment of their identities, and their sense of self-worth, to survive and thrive. Isherwood's odyssey homeward exemplifies this kind of original sense of dislocation and the recovery of an ultimate relocation.

THE POLITICS OF RELIGION

Meaning and power are inextricably related in contemporary constructions of identity, so resistance to culturally prescribed identification has important political dimensions. To reopen the possibilities for newly ordered subject positions entails a struggle with entrenched political *and* epistemic constructions. The privileged forms of (hetero)sexuality authorized by religious doctrine, and rendered as "scientific facts" by medicine, become legitimating norms that "justify themselves," as scholar Kathleen Sands puts it, "by claiming ontological priority over that which they regulate."[18] In this system, "heterosexuality" is presented "as natural, eternal, or God-given, and this supposed ontological priority provides the warrant for compelling people to enact it." Moreover, Sands continues,

> The type of power that courses through sexuality is normative power. The regime of sexuality delimits how people may conceive and represent themselves, how they construe their desires, the regulations to which they are subject, the economic rewards they may receive, the neighbor-

hoods or nations in which they may live, the laws that will or won't apply to them, the medical treatment they'll be given or denied.

Isherwood's experience of the class-based Anglicanism that he rejected early in his life was an example of the kind of conventional religion that entails codes of inclusion in or exclusion from socially and politically privileged faith communities. These codes produce and support what sociologist Peter Berger terms the "plausibility structures" that anchor the sense of belonging in community for its adherents. "One of the fundamental propositions of the sociology of knowledge," writes Berger in *A Rumor of Angels*, is that the "plausibility" of views of reality "depends upon the social support these receive."[19]

In Berger's model, "plausibility structures" are produced by networks of people "in conversation" who hold to a common worldview and set of moral commitments that help to maintain belief. Berger acknowledges that "it is possible to go against the social consensus that surrounds us," but reminds us that there are "powerful pressures (which manifest themselves as psychological pressures within our own consciousness) to conform to the views and beliefs of our fellow men" (50).

For people excluded from religious structures—indeed, cast as religious pariahs—conventional religion is a closed door, unless they repent from their "sins" of deviance from the dominant order, a transgression that is not only about unauthorized forms of sexual behavior, but also against the entire belief system that holds the world in a safe and familiar framing for conformists.

These structures have been undermined in recent decades by the interrogations of feminist and queer analyses, which have not stopped at the borders of religious teaching. Commenting on Judith Butler's critical work on gender, Sara Salih notes how "the violence of exclusion narrows the categories by which subjects 'qualify' for full human status."[20] In other words, this maneuvering for the high moral ground has serious consequences in the lives of people trying to come to terms with their sexuality, so there are quite pragmatic reasons why institutionalized normative discourses have needed to be interrogated and must continue to be challenged.

Italian Marxist Antonio Gramsci focused his analysis on the ideological machinery through which the dominator class is able to project and institutionalize its own meanings—the hegemon (the ruling group) controls the production of meaning.[21] Further, in order to succeed, the set of meanings promulgated and enforced by the hegemon involves the willing and active consent of those subordinated to its control, who may come to accept that configuration of meaning as "common sense" and "natural." This deployment of the trope of the "natural" order has been carried forward into the twenty-first century by church leaders such as Pope Benedict XVI, who tied his 2008 campaign against homosexuality to environmentalist causes, calling for a "human ecology" to protect the species from self-destruction. Benedict averred that "saving humanity from homosexual or transsexual behavior is just as important as saving the rainforest from destruction." Reuters reported that Pope Benedict recommended that humanity needed to "listen to the language of creation" to understand the divinely ordained roles of man and woman.[22] Of course, if the pope were really drawing his teaching from observing the natural world, he would have noticed, along with zoologists, that so-called homosexual acts have been observed among hundreds of species, from insects to mammals, even birds. In fact, such acts are increasingly recognized as "normal" variations of sexual behavior.[23]

Isherwood's memoir *My Guru and His Disciple* thus stands as a landmark *testimonio*, resisting the hegemonic and homophobic authorized religious framings to affirm a more integrative and inclusive vision of human potential that allows full membership for those previously cast outside the fold. It resists the familiar normative constructions that narrow the categories whereby subjects qualify for full human status, as Salih and Butler note. His book pioneers the way to a more inclusive spiritual vision than that sanctioned by supposedly "divinely" authorized discourses. For Isherwood to publish this text—given his articulated awareness of the kind of resistance, skepticism, and hostility he reckoned the book would engender—was a significant move.

"I BECOME DEFIANT"

Even as late as Peter Parker's extensive biography,[24] Isherwood's religious bona fides were much misunderstood, misrepresented, or dismissed lightly. W. H. Auden, one of Isherwood's closest friends, had spoken dismissively of Isherwood's engagement with this "heathen mumbo jumbo" back in 1951 (*My Guru* 204). An avowedly queer man—and one conspicuously active, sexually—being recognized for his religious writings? Isherwood may benefit today from a cultural shift that he himself is at least partially responsible for bringing about. Thus, in addition to his earlier work as a pamphleteer for the Vedanta Society, the translations he published with Swami Prabhavananda, and the biography of Sri Ramakrishna he labored over for several years, there is solid evidence that we should take his claim seriously, that *My Guru and His Disciple* was "the most worthwhile book I have written *and* probably one of the best modern books of its kind" (*Liberation* 627).

Isherwood was quite aware of the resistance he would face in making a public declaration of his religious life. As he mentions in *My Guru and His Disciple,* most of the reviews of his 1965 biography of Sri Ramakrishna were unfavorable. He noted the recurring objection that he, who wrote "worldly novels," was its author, commentators finding it "a bit difficult to regard Herr Issyvoo as a guru-fancier" (*My Guru* 287–88).

In spite of his realistic expectation that *My Guru and His Disciple* would *not* be well received, he pressed boldly ahead. So what was his intention? From a draft of the afterword Isherwood penned for the book, Jaime Harker extracts the following from the Huntington archive:

> Having written it, my first reaction is a sort of defiant embarrassment. I realize how embarrassing, not to say gooey, this material will seem to many, perhaps most, of the people who read it. But then I become defiant and think, well, if it *isn't* embarrassing, that means it has no quality of shock.[25]

Isherwood had shown his awareness of this skeptical readership as early as the 1940s, when he wrote:

> If a member of the so-called intellectual class joins any religious group or openly ascribes to its teaching, he will have to prepare himself for a good deal of criticism from his unconverted and more sceptical friends. Some of these may be sympathetic and genuinely interested; others will be covertly satirical, suspicious, or quite frankly hostile and dismayed. It will be suggested to the convert, with a greater or lesser degree of politeness, that he has sold out, betrayed the cause of reason, retreated in cowardice from "the realities of Life," and so forth.[26]

The issue is thrown into high relief by a piece he wrote for a memorial on Aldous Huxley. Of the "far-reaching effects" of Huxley's involvement with Prabhavananda, Isherwood observed:

It was widely represented as the selling-out of a once brilliant intellect. As a matter of fact, it actually enlarged Huxley's already vast intellectual horizons by introducing him to mystical experience as a fact, a phenomenon of existence. (Parker 630)

The issue was raised again when he was working on the manuscript of *My Guru and His Disciple*. In a diary entry from October 23, 1977, he notes that he was asked by a young man who was to drive him to a meeting of the American Civil Liberties Union, about the influence of Swami Prabhavananda and what his guru's teaching had done for him. Finding himself "stumbling and faking defensively," Isherwood pauses to consider what kind of "block" caused him to stumble so:

Am I perhaps inhibited by a sense of the mocking agnostics all around me—ranging from asses like [John] Lehmann to intelligent bigots like Edward [Upward]? Yes, of course I am. In a sense, they are my most important audience. Everything I write is written with a consciousness of the opposition and in answer to its prejudices. (*Liberation* 554)

"Because of this opposition," he goes on, "I am apt to belittle myself, to try to disarm criticism by treating it with a seriousness it doesn't (in my private opinion) deserve." He is determined not to cave in and bolsters his intention: "I must not, cannot do this here. I must state my beliefs and be quite intransigent about them" (554).

While he wants to be "intransigent," it is clear that he was extremely uncomfortable about being seen as some kind of holy man. He was careful not to overreach, or to make inflated claims about his "spiritual achievements." There are striking descriptions of Isherwood's intense discomfort in traveling to India with his swami in December 1963.[27] In a talk he gave to the Vedanta Society of New York, Isherwood addressed both the discomfort he felt about the issue of the "insider/outsider" phenomenon—of "belonging" to a religious congregation—and the question of being seen as a spiritual "role model" himself:

Ideally, I know, that example should be spotless. Ideally it should inspire others to think: well, what he or she believes in has certainly transformed his or her life, and I think that it must be something that I could believe in too.[28]

So, he decides, "I must also state my doubts, but without exaggerating them."

By insisting on recording his weaknesses and faults, Isherwood exposed himself to his more flat-footed critics, who often took his self-portrayal at face value, using his confessions as ammunition against him. Perhaps this is how an anonymous reviewer in the British newspaper *The Economist* found "very little to convince the reader that he, or even his guru, has become a significantly better or happier man for it."[29]

However, in his review of *Lost Years* for the *London Review of Books*, in 2000, the British psychotherapist Adam Phillips recognized Isherwood's "determination to track down even the most elusive and unappealing aspects of his past in order to understand and honestly portray himself, both as a writer and as a human being." In contrast to the lingering charges of narcissism, Phillips interpreted Isherwood's use of recollection not just as a way to construct the personal myth but as "the best cure for egotism."[30] Phillips observed, astutely, that "we may look better if we rearrange the facts, but rearranging the facts is also moral propaganda." Phillips also recognizes that, as a writer, Isherwood was aware of the need for an ongoing "critique of the self-justifying voice." Phillips is a notably reliable reviewer of literary works, chiefly in the *London Review of Books*. Given his background in psychiatry, his assessment of writers is unusually insightful and less inclined to be influenced by the politics of the literary world.

In a similar vein, Auden said in relation to Isherwood's use of autobiographical material, that he was

> that rarest of all creatures, the objective narcissist; he sees himself altogether plain and does not hesitate to record for us the lines that the face in the mirror has accumulated, the odd shadow that flaws the character.[31]

Nonetheless, the reviewer in *The Economist* attributed what he downplayed as Isherwood's "half-hearted persistence in the religion" to "the guru's persuasive and flattering tongue," displaying a shortsightedness into which even biographer Peter Parker fell. Few of the critics who find him so wretchedly lacking in "commitment" to causes admit that they are prone to take their cue from Isherwood's own critical self-revelation, without giving due weight to the conscientiousness revealed by that scrutiny.

If at times Isherwood's self-portrayal might be construed as "performative"—self-abnegation as part of the charming persona he was noted for—the ability to see himself in a less than flattering light and expose himself this way, even in the public texts (as opposed to the diaries), was a quality Isherwood's guru recognized as essential to the writer's spirituality. That is to say, this rigorous self-scrutiny—what Isherwood characterized as "the knife in the wound," which was part and parcel of his approach to writing and which was deepened by his spiritual practice—could be characterized as a strength. "The knife in the wound" is an image Isherwood invoked in regard to writing in the first person, an insistence that reveals a rather more challenging process at work than the familiar, if facile, charges of narcissistic self-absorption would allow: "When I write a novel in the third person, I write a sentence and then I put the pen down. I am so bored by it. The knife is no longer in the wound, just suspended over it" (letter to Jeremy Kingston, 1961; cited in Parker 583).

Reading the diaries, one becomes aware that Isherwood's stated intention to be "intransigent," and his scrupulous modesty about his spiritual achievements, were factors held in an uneasy balance, for, as the Italian scholar Mario Faraone emphasizes, in many ways Isherwood saw his religion as a "private" matter, which is ironic, given how much work he had done for and about the Vedanta Society.[32] While this might seem at odds with the self-scrutinizing life writing, it has a particular bearing on the tactful reporting of Isherwood's spiritual life. Alongside his involvement with the Vedanta Society, he maintained a social and professional network of acquaintances drawn from literary and movie circles, among whom it would have been "bad form" to thrust his religious beliefs forward. Don Bachardy tells an amusing anecdote about Gore Vidal visiting them at the Adelaide Drive residence for a dinner party:

> He had just read *My Guru* and [he] was telling me that he had never been so shocked in his life. It was like he had discovered that Chris was one of the pod people in "Invasion of the Body Snatchers"! That he was not only tainted, that he was lost, that he could talk such rubbish.[33]

So, even while he was quite prepared to write about his personal experience of Vedanta for a particular audience, Isherwood was inclined to refrain from proselytizing among his friends and professional colleagues, and even a close friend like Vidal could be utterly unaware of this part of Isherwood's life.

This tact was more than just the reserve of a British gentleman. Asked by the journalist and author Mark Thompson for his collection *Gay Spirit,*

"Do you mind being asked about your spiritual life?," Isherwood put the issue more powerfully:

> The Hindus have a marvelous thing that they say: If you've had any real spiritual experience, hide it, as you would hide from other people the fact that your mother was a whore! Strong words! In other words, for God's sake, shut up about it! And I'm mindful of that.[34]

There are other factors that contribute to the modest tone of the autobiography, one of which, for example, one might call, echoing Samuel Beckett in *Watt*, the problem of "effing the ineffable," which Isherwood was acutely aware of: "Mystical experience itself can never be described. It can only be written about, hinted at, dimly reflected in word and deed" (*Exhumations* 120).

Isherwood made a modest intervention into the narrowly framed religious worldview of his own "tribe" by asserting the validity of his training in a so-called alien tradition, and in so doing, realigned the place of queer intelligence within an all-embracing vision of human potential that invites these erstwhile pariahs into the center of the life of the tribe. If it took the Roman Catholic Church more than 350 years to admit it was in error in excommunicating Galileo for his observations of the real state of affairs vis-à-vis the earth and its relation to our sun, then perhaps we shouldn't expect that the deeper significance of the alleged "outsider" in a dualistic religious tradition would come into clear focus in the very near future. Meanwhile, individual "seekers" may take heart that some have already made a start at "enlarging their clearing in the jungle" and pay more respect to that forward vision. As Franciscan priest Richard Rohr has written, "It is those creatures and those humans who are on the edge of what we have defined as normal, proper, or good who often have the most to teach us."[35]

NOTES

1. Christian de la Huerta, *Coming Out Spiritually: The Next Step* (New York: Jeremy P. Tarcher/Putnam, 1999).

2. David Halperin, *Saint Foucault: Towards a Gay Hagiography* (Oxford: Oxford University Press, 1987), 28.

3. Although written around 1913–14, due to the potential controversy regarding its positive treatment of a same-sex love (and that relationship crossing

class boundaries), *Maurice* was not published until 1971, the year of Forster's death. Forster had shown the manuscript to Isherwood much earlier. [For a discussion of Forster and Isherwood related to *Maurice*, see Wendy Moffat's essay in this volume, chapter 4.—Eds.]

4. In fact, the possibility of a "third" sex was present in ancient times, including in precolonial India. See Ruth Vanita and Saleem Kidwai's *Same-Sex Love in India: Readings from Literature and History* (New York: St. Martin's Press, 2000), and Amara Das Wilhelm, *Tritiya-Prakriti: People of the Third Sex* (2010), referencing the Kama Shastra and other ancient writings from the subcontinent. Das Wilhelm provides a very useful survey of ancient traditions that honored diverse expressions of gender "types" beyond the two-dimensional binary construction, both in his book and at the website www.galva108.org. This is why I regard the renewed interest in spirituality as a "recuperation" of what was once a widely known and even honored state of affairs.

5. Carpenter was engaged with many other leading-edge causes of his day: women's rights; birth control; the beginnings of the study of sexual psychology; broadening educational opportunities for the working classes; more egalitarian forms of political systems, including grassroots socialism; the Fabian Society and the beginnings of the British Labour Party; a return to a lifestyle closer to the earth and protection of the environment; animal rights; the crafts movement . . . the list goes on.

6. In 1947, Isherwood published a translation of *Crest-Jewel of Discrimination* (the Viveka Chudamani), the seminal work by the great reformer Shankara, with his own guru, Swami Prabhavananda.

7. Professor Gillian Whitlock first used the term in "Introduction: Disobedient Subjects," *Autographs: Contemporary Australian Autobiography* (St. Lucia: University of Queensland Press, 1996), ix–xxx.

8. This statement of principles comes from the Ramakrishna Vedanta Society's website, which cites Swami Vivekananda, the pioneer who first brought the Ramakrishna message to the United States: "This grand preaching, the oneness of things, making us one with everything that exists, is the great lesson to learn. . . . Happiness belongs to him who knows this oneness, who knows he is one with this universe" (https://vedanta.org/what-is-vedanta/the-oneness-of-existence). Against this backdrop, divisive teachings seem particularly mean-spirited, even toxic.

9. Christopher Isherwood, *My Guru and His Disciple* (New York: Farrar, Straus, and Giroux, 1980), 11.

10. See, for example, Stephen Wade, "Christophananda Writes His Religion: Isherwood's Purgatory," *Critical Survey* 13, no. 3 (2001): 3–18.

11. Len Webster, "A Very Individualistic Old Liberal: Interview with Christopher Isherwood," in *Conversations with Christopher Isherwood,* ed. James J. Berg and Chris Freeman (Jackson: University Press of Mississippi, 2001), 65.

12. Marc Zimmerman, "Testimonio," in *The SAGE Encyclopedia of Social Science Research Methods,* vol. 3, ed. Michael S. Lewis-Beck, Alan Bryman, and Tim Futing Liao (Thousand Oaks, Calif.: SAGE Publishing, 2004), 118–19.

13. Jaume Aurell, "Making History by Contextualizing Oneself: Autobiography as Historiographical Intervention," *History and Theory* 54 (May 2015): 244–68. I must thank Dr. Ashma Sharma for alerting me to Professor Aurell's work.

14. Robert O'Byrne, "A Fraudulent Rebel," review of *Isherwood: A Life,* by Peter Parker, *Irish Times,* June 26, 2004, 13.

15. For more on contemporary religious trends, see Wade Clark Roof, *Spiritual Marketplace: Baby Boomers and the Remaking of American Religion* (Princeton, N.J.: Princeton University Press, 1999).

16. *Shankara's Crest Jewel of Discrimination,* trans. Christopher Isherwood and Swami Prabhavananda (Los Angeles: Vedanta Press, 1947), 13.

17. See *Liberation: Diaries,* vol. 3, *1970–1983,* ed. Katherine Bucknell (London: Chatto and Windus, 2012), for example, the entry for February 17, 1980: "I don't know what to think of *My Guru.* I can imagine really savage attacks on it and yet in a way I think it is the most worthwhile book I have written *and* probably one of the best modern books of its kind" (627). I list some of the negative and positive criticisms in my *Mr Isherwood Changes Trains: Christopher Isherwood and the Search for the "Home Self"* (Melbourne: Clouds of Magellan, 2010), 193ff.

18. Kathleen Sands, "Mixing It Up: Religion, Lesbian Feminism, and Queerness" (conference paper, Annual Meeting of the American Academy of Religion, Chicago, November 3, 2008).

19. Peter L. Berger, *A Rumor of Angels: Modern Society and the Rediscovery of the Supernatural* (New York: Anchor Books, 1990), 50.

20. Judith Butler, *The Judith Butler Reader,* ed. Sara Salih (Malden, Mass.: Blackwell, 2004), 12.

21. For more on this, see Antonio Gramsci, *Selections from the Prison Notebooks,* ed. and trans. Quintin Hoare and Geoffrey Nowell Smith (New York: International Publishers, 1971), and Peter D. Thomas, *The Gramscian Moment: Philosophy, Hegemony and Marxism* (Leiden: Brill, 2009).—Eds.

22. "Pope Benedict on Homosexuality," *Sunday Times,* December 23, 2008.

23. For examples, see Bruce Bagemihl, *Biological Exuberance: Animal Homosexuality and Natural Diversity* (New York: St. Martin's Press, 1999).

24. Peter Parker, *Isherwood: A Life Revealed* (New York: Random House, 2004).

25. Jaime Harker, *Middlebrow Queer: Christopher Isherwood in America* (Minneapolis: University of Minnesota Press, 2013), 160. One of eight drafts, Isherwood's afterword was ultimately dropped altogether. But his intention is clear.

26. Christopher Isherwood, "Hypothesis and Belief," in *Exhumations* (New York: Simon and Schuster, 1966), 99.

27. For example, see *My Guru and His Disciple*, 258ff, and *The Sixties: Diaries*, vol. 2, *1960–1969*, ed. Katherine Bucknell (New York: HarperCollins, 2010), 99 on.

28. "Address to the Vedanta Society of New York," March 26, 1952. His notes for the talk are included in the papers archived at the Huntington Library in San Marino, California. Isherwood Papers, CI 1014.

29. Anon., review of *My Guru and His Disciple*, *The Economist*, July 12, 1980, 97.

30. Adam Phillips, "Setting the Record Straight," review of *Lost Years: A Memoir, 1945–51*, by Christopher Isherwood, November 9, 2000. https://www.theguardian.com/books/2000/nov/09/londonreviewofbooks.

31. Cited in John Sutherland, "Outsider, Vagabond, and 'Objective Narcissist,'" review of *Isherwood: A Life*, by Peter Parker, *Boston Globe*, January 2, 2005. Sutherland was correcting some of his errors in an earlier review of the UK edition he had published in the *London Review of Books*.

32. Mario Faraone, "Spiritual Searching in Isherwood's Artistic Production," in *The American Isherwood*, ed. James J. Berg and Chris Freeman (Minneapolis: University of Minnesota Press, 2015), 183.

33. See my interview with Bachardy, "Portrait of an Artist as Zen Monk," *White Crane Journal* 71 (Winter 2006–7): 24. https://www.whitecraneinstitute.org/2007/02/wc71_interview_.html.

34. Mark Thompson, *Gay Spirit: Myth and Meaning* (New York: St. Martin's Press, 1987), 48.

35. Richard Rohr, *Falling Upward: A Spirituality for the Two Halves of Life* (San Francisco: Jossey-Bass, 2011), 56.

16. "The Aim of Art Is to Transcend Art"

Writing Spirituality in *My Guru and His Disciple*

"A FORM OF DEVOTION"

In his essay "The Writer and Vedanta" (1961), published two decades after his initiation into this Hinduist spirituality, Christopher Isherwood attempts to articulate a correspondence between the purpose and experience of writing and the propositions and practice of Vedanta, namely, that writing can give access to insights similar to those attained in Vedanta. "Vedanta says that a Reality exists beneath all the outer layers—the external appearances—of this universe," which is Brahman or God, he begins. Awareness of Brahman and recognition of it within the individual as Atman is the "aim of life": "by knowing it within one's self, to be able to know it everywhere . . . , and then to understand thereby that the Atman is Brahman."[1] This "aim of life" within Vedanta is analogous to Isherwood's view of writing:

> The purpose of the art of writing is to understand, to reveal the deeper nature of experience, to make life and its phenomena, and all the human beings and creatures around us more significant. To make our lives fuller of meaning and thereby to render our whole experience moment by moment more significant than it otherwise would be. To open our eyes, to open our ears, and above all to open our hearts to the experience around us. (156)

Vedanta and writing are interwoven in "The Writer and Vedanta" and elsewhere in Isherwood's work, as twin approaches to awareness, to

221

understanding, and to meaning—what lies beneath, or beyond, all appearances. But while Isherwood believes Vedanta is better written about through "direct presentation" (that is, through nonfiction rather than indirectly through fiction), he nevertheless is able only to express figuratively the connection between writing and Vedanta. He gets closer to an explicit correlation between these paired practices when he suggests that "perhaps the practice of the arts may also under certain circumstances claim to be regarded as a form of karma yoga," which in Vedanta "means any way of life, any approach which will lead us toward union with God" (157). Understood in these ways, the art of writing, Isherwood implies, has the potential to become a performative spiritual act. It is, he succinctly asserts, "a form of devotion" (157).

What Isherwood is trying to work out in "The Writer and Vedanta" and elsewhere is a correlation in method, practice, or experience between writing and spirituality. A decade earlier, in his essay "What Vedanta Means to Me" (1951), he had tried to represent directly "some of the reasons why Vedanta appealed" to him, while noting importantly that, where matters of spirituality are concerned, *reasons alone* cannot convert one to its beliefs (*Wishing Tree* 56). After working through some of Vedanta's propositions, he concludes, "I have written all this, and yet I have really said nothing. I have failed to explain what Vedanta means to me. Perhaps that was inevitable" (61). In a longer version of this essay, also called "What Vedanta Means to Me," printed in a 1961 edited collection of the same title and appearing the same year as "The Writer and Vedanta," Isherwood revisits again this inability to express fully what Vedanta means to him: "I have written all this, and yet I have really said nothing. I have failed to explain what Vedanta means to me. I must repeat: reasons are only reasons. They merely form a kind of structure around the more or less indescribable element—our personal experience."[2] Each of these essays points to the limitations of language to represent, mimetically, the spiritual life. Direct representation can inform a text on Vedanta, that is, can provide its context and content, but the ineffable in spiritual experience—"the more or less indescribable element"—needs to be written otherwise, perhaps as analogy, perhaps performatively in an act of devotion. What Isherwood never explicitly or self-consciously articulates, he nevertheless invokes time and again in his writing on Vedanta: the implicit irony that writing opens up access to the spiritual, which is simultaneously always beyond its grasp.

In another attempt to articulate the relationship between writing and spirituality in "The Writer and Vedanta," Isherwood references an analogy advanced by Aldous Huxley regarding transcendence and art. Like Isherwood, Huxley explains art figuratively, here as "a net which is cast out into experience with the object of catching something" (*Wishing Tree* 160). What matters in this image is "not the net itself," Isherwood proposes, "but the holes in the net" (160). Huxley drew attention to these "holes"—pauses in music, breaks in rhythm, space within and between sculptures, gaps and limits in writing—for it is in these absences that access to meaning may emerge. "These apertures, these holes in the net," Isherwood explains, "are really entrances to a world of spiritual knowledge which lies beyond the realm of sense knowledge. So we may say that, where art leaves off, religion begins, and that from this point of view, the aim of art is to transcend art. . . . I think that it is really only in this sense that one can talk about the relation between art and religious experience" (161). Perhaps ironically, it is because of the "absences" in a text—fragments; the unsaid or can't-be-said; ellipses; and failures of language, representation, and generic convention (those outer layers of sense knowledge)—that possibilities exist for other types of "knowing." Bidhan Chandra Roy, in his essay in this collection, explores the "beyond" of language in the phenomenological "experience of God," noting that, in his fiction, Isherwood understood that one must "strip away the illusions of 'surface consciousness' in order to . . . point to, if not define, an alternative experience." Whether in direct or indirect representation, in fiction or nonfiction, *the aim of art is to transcend art*: the purpose of writing for Isherwood is not to communicate, not to represent, but to transcend—to move beyond "external appearances" to reveal "the deeper nature of experience" (see Roy 194; Roy is quoting Isherwood—Eds.).

Of course, Isherwood does attempt to communicate and represent Vedanta. Its philosophies and language influenced his American novels and gave rise to numerous essays, pamphlets, and talks on the subject, a translation of its scripture, and a biography of one of its saints. Over the forty years subsequent to his initiation, he would translate, with his guru Swami Prabhavananda, *Bhagavad Gita: The Song of God* (1944); write essays and pamphlets published by the Vedanta Press; edit the collections *Vedanta for Modern Man* (1945) and *Vedanta for the Western World* (1949); write the biography *Ramakrishna and His Disciples* (1965); fictionalize its practice in many of his characters; record diary entries over several decades that recount many and varied experiences with people, places, texts, and values in the Vedantist tradition; and compose the memoir that attempts to incarnate and to make sense of his journey through all of these undertakings, *My Guru and His Disciple* (1980). Might the purpose and form of this final completed work on Vedanta best exemplify Isherwood's own net, "cast out into experience with the object of catching something"—a glimpse beyond material existence?

"A GLIMPSE"

My Guru and His Disciple is a search for the deeper nature of experience. It is the story of Isherwood's continuous reflection on and reworking of Vedanta's propositions through periods of certainty and uncertainty, of belief in divine presence and skepticism in its absence, questions which remain as vivid for him from 1976 until 1980, the years in which he composed the book, as they were in 1939 and in the intervening decades. It is through writing that he persistently reworks these spiritual themes—the validity, for him, of Vedanta's propositions: particularly, the existence of the divine in Swami, or as he puts it in *An Approach to Vedanta*, "an individual who can give you a dim glimpse of the Atman within him, simply by being what he is."[3] In "Spiritual Searching in Isherwood's Artistic Production," Mario Faraone alights on the difficulties, even in fictional form, of portraying the divine. Faraone does not explore this issue in the context of *My Guru*, but nevertheless he offers a way to consider the relationship between Isherwood's art and spirituality, demonstrating it as "a reciprocal steadier ground for spiritual and professional growth."[4] Faraone writes, for example,

> Meditating and praying may be considered the religious counterparts of devising a novel and writing it: a continuous flow of spiritual and artistic energy that goes to and from Isherwood the Vedantist and Isherwood the artist. (189)

Faraone's claim that meditating and praying are analogous to the act of composing is helpful, as are his broader claims that such practices "progressively influence [Isherwood's] writings and lead him to modify and refine his point of view and, up to a point, to alter and transform his narrative technique" (184–85). Bidhan Chandra Roy's insights provide further significance here: "This is why silence and meditation are central to spiritual practice: God is a phenomenological encounter and, therefore, intellect and abstraction can only take us so far" (Roy 193). Writing, and perhaps more particularly if one prefers, spiritual writing, might be understood, like immersive reading, as a phenomenological experience, a self in flow. In his reflections on how to represent Vedanta and his relation to Swami Prabhavananda, Isherwood finds a hole and thus opens a space for the indescribable.

Within months of Swami Prabhavananda's death, Isherwood begins predrafting in his diary the book that will come to be called *My Guru and His Disciple*, attempting to work out his ideas for the book. It will be "an overview," he begins in September 1976, by which he means, "a sense of how the relationship between these two people, Swami and me, developed and changed. In this way, I shall probably find out a great deal which I don't know, am not aware of, yet. Okay, good, that's how I'll begin."[5] Isherwood does not have the whole of the story figured out yet, but he is open to the journey to awareness and meaning through the writing itself. Huxley's analogy helps to illuminate both the formal shape *My Guru and His Disciple* will take as well as the thematic concerns that get reworked throughout its pages, never quite resolved but openings through which spiritual practice is performed.

My Guru is different in form and content from those texts on Vedanta that precede it. It is a hybrid text composed of "direct presentation," biography, diary, and memoir. Indeed, as he is beginning to write the book, Isherwood notes its difference, in both genre and purpose, and finally decides that the focus of the work should be

> exclusively about Swami. But, as yet, I don't know how to do that. I can't strike the right tone. I am certainly not aiming to write a biography. What I should try for is a highly subjective memoir—always stressing the idea that what I am describing is a personal impression, a strictly limited *glimpse* of a character very different from myself and therefore often quite mysterious to me. Without being fake humble, I should also— even for purely artistic reasons—stress the materialistic, gross, lustful, worldly side of myself—but without making Swami appear merely "better" than me. The real artistic problem is to find a way to do that. (October 14, 1976; *Liberation* 525–26; emphasis added)

As he discerns the genre that might best give form to this guru/disciple relationship, he recognizes the pitfalls of generic convention. To write biography or memoir is not adequate to what he wishes to achieve. Isherwood reflects that the central artistic question here is how to reconcile "external appearances" of self and other, particularly when that other—both Swami and his "self"—remains a mystery to him.

What Isherwood ultimately discovers is that he can only ever offer a "glimpse" of Swami, a partial insight into who he is. Later in the writing of *My Guru*, Isherwood continues on the questions of generic convention:

> While "meditating" this morning, I began to think of that unsolved problem, the postscript to my Swami book. And it came to me that I should point out that this book differs in kind from books on other subjects because there is no failure in the spiritual life. This sounds trite, but I feel there is a very valuable statement to be developed here—namely that one cannot make a statement. I can't say that my life has been a failure, as far as my attempts to follow Prabhavananda go, because every step is an absolute accomplishment. So I have neither succeeded nor failed, and I am always the Atman anyhow. More to be thought about this, I hope. (March 27, 1978; 565)

Isherwood attains to a noteworthy insight about writing spirituality during this meditation: that *My Guru* "fails" to articulate a picture of his spiritual self not because of some failed teleology or resolve but because "one cannot make a statement" about the spiritual life in any case. This point might seem "trite," as he puts it, but it is not. He acknowledges here that the spiritual life cannot be represented, thus the inadequacy, in his estimation, of biography, portrait, or memoir alone. Each step in his attempt to follow his guru is part of a process, not a coherent, resolved narrative. In a shift from the past to the present tense, he realizes, "I am always the Atman"; the spiritual is a "moment by moment" experience, a glimpse of the deeper nature of experience, here rendered through writing.

The sense that *My Guru* will be different in kind from other books is similarly worked out in other passages in his diary and echoed in a radio interview at the time of the book's publication in 1980. Isherwood illustrates that he is well aware of the limitations of generic conventions, particularly of spiritual or conversion narratives: "The very last thing I wanted to write was yet another book in which the author meets somebody, gets saved, now is saved, and is telling people to come and do likewise."[6] If he would not tell a story of failure in *My Guru and His Disciple*, neither would he tell one of accomplishment or "arrival." Arguably, these tropes and structures, with which he was well versed, did not reflect his experiences.

Isherwood's varying intensity of commitment to, and at times disinclination toward, the practice of Vedanta; his fluctuating belief, or surety, in the existence of God; and his simultaneous deeply connected and intimate relationship with, and yet occasional need to distance himself from, his guru, challenge easy definitions of what conversion might have meant for Isherwood. Perhaps not surprisingly, Swami tells Isherwood in that first year, "Maharaj had always been suspicious of sudden hysterical 'conversions.'"[7] In *The Varieties of Religious Experience*, a foundational study for conversion theories over the past century, the philosopher and psychologist William James identifies two narratives of conversion, "sudden conversion" like that of the Apostle Paul, and the "subconscious incubation and maturity of motives deposited by the experiences of life."[8] Conversion-as-turning-point has long been a convention of conversion narratives of the type Isherwood sought to distance himself from. It is a story similar to that told by Saint Augustine at the end of the fourth century in *The Confessions*, held to be the first Western spiritual autobiography, which unfolds its narrative from nonbelief to belief and from physical, material desire to spiritual nourishment. Conversion narratives from the early modern to the modern eras tend to follow a similar generic arc in which the moment of conversion is one of rebirth or renewal as the converted subject becomes integrated into a new community and language.

My Guru and His Disciple rehearses such narrative conventions while simultaneously calling them into question. At the end of a decade of trying to outmaneuver international immigration policies and fascist power and his German lover Heinz's ultimate arrest and conscription into Hitler's army, Isherwood is at the point of what James would identify as crisis, exhaustion and "a temporary apathy" (205). Knowing he could not fight an enemy of which his lover was now a part, Isherwood is at once in a moment of "self-surrender" and at the same time, willfully seeking a new belief system. Shortly after his arrival in the United States, Isherwood's search takes him to California, where British expatriates Gerald Heard and Aldous Huxley introduce him to the philosophies of Vedanta. Though highly skeptical of "the spiritual" as an answer to his crisis and maintaining a metaphorical "suspense account" of Vedanta's values, Isherwood nevertheless realizes he "needed a new kind of support" and so tells himself he'll give its practice "six months of honest effort" (*My Guru* 42, 38, 13). He often wants to measure his progress, to calculate and thus identify some moment of conversion:

> I have no idea "where I am." Have I made progress during these three months, or haven't I? To a certain degree, I do feel yes, I have. Just being with Swami has given me a much clearer idea of what the spiritual life ought to mean. (May 4, 1943; 121)

He also confesses that there were periods when he did not see Swami for months at a time. Through these "confessions," he comes to understand spirituality less as a definable and singular turning point and more as an ongoing lived engagement—with others, with propositions, with his self.

My Guru and His Disciple thus recounts his long transition over the course of forty years, but any notion of a successful resolution is rendered ambiguous, even at the book's close. Isherwood warns that his conversion remains uncertain. He "can't speak with the absolute authority of a knower... about matters [he] only partially understand[s]" (338). At what moment, then, can his conversion be said to have occurred? It is in the moment-to-moment of lived experience and more particularly through the processes of "reading" (of Vedic texts, his life and the world around him) and of writing.

Isherwood certainly had examples of spiritual journeys as a reader of more "formalized" conversion and spiritual narratives such as those of Vivekananda, Augustine, and Thomas Merton, and as told by his personal acquaintances, Heard and Huxley. And, importantly, throughout *My Guru* Isherwood narrates the story of Swami Prabhavananda's own conversion. Prabhavananda was himself a reader of the lives of Ramakrishna, Vivekananda, and Brahmananda (Maharaj) (30). As disciple, Isherwood imitates Swami Prabhavananda, just as Swami followed the lived examples of Maharaj, and Vivekananda followed Ramakrishna, and so on. In his search for faith, Isherwood realizes, "All I could hope for at present was some kind of half answer obtained indirectly through Prabhavananda, by studying his words and actions" (43). Indeed, Swami models imitation for Isherwood: "Instead of claiming the greatness of a spiritual teacher, he was showing us an example of a great disciple—which was what we most needed, being disciples ourselves" (42). When doubt set in, as it often did, Isherwood reminds himself that "by studying [Prabhavananda's] words and actions and trying to get a *glimpse* of what was behind them," perhaps he would come to understand God or Nature or the "Real Self," the Reality beyond all appearances (43; emphasis added). At times, he better understands this Real Self, the Self that is "in all beings," less as a Vedantist than *as a writer* who "taps a great store of universal knowledge" (28).

But Isherwood is both writer and Vedantist. *My Guru's* form results from critical reflection on how best to represent his impression of and relationship with Swami Prabhavananda. The title *My Guru and His Disciple* thus highlights the role of an other in the conversion of the self. This narrative, Isherwood seems to claim, cannot be told through a singular autobiographical voice, the converted self who looks back on and tells the story of an earlier self. Conversion only happens in relation to others, whether human or divine, text or scripture. This understanding of conversion is drawn from Geoffrey Galt Harpham's claim in his essay "Conversion and the Language of Autobiography" that "one is 'converted' when one discovers that one's life can be made to conform to certain culturally validated narrative forms; spiritual 'conversion' might simply be a strong form of reading"—reading the lives, works, experiences, and truths of others.[9] Conversion, then, might best be understood as an interwoven process of reading and of writing. Bruce Hindmarsh similarly contends in "Religious Conversion as Narrative and Autobiography" that "religious converts who narrate their experience generally do so with an appreciation that their own sense of agency is only ever partial and that they have become who they are only because of and through other people, and ultimately, through an agency more divine than human."[10] In undergoing a conversion and, notably, in telling the story of that conversion, we use models in the world around us to think, to learn, to act, and to transform.

Multiple voices thus constitute Isherwood's "self," facilitating its transformation, including the voices of past "Isherwoods" through his diaries. Although biographer Peter Parker is critical of Isherwood's extensive use of passages from his diaries in *My Guru*, as "recycled" material cloyingly re-presented (713), the inclusion of diary writing disrupts the temporality of the book's backward glance and challenges the illusion of a transformed self whose turning point has been "crossed over." Instead, as narrative theorist H. Porter Abbott argues, real-time diary writing conveys "immediacy: that is, the illusion of being there, of no gap in time between the event and the rendering of it."[11] Such immediacy "can convert the narration itself into a kind of action" (Abbott 29). Isherwood's incorporation of his diaries into *My Guru* conveys this sense of timelessness—the actions it narrates of the past are rendered present and seem to be ongoing, thereby drawing attention to the act or process of writing, of composing. Parker's criticism that the diaries are refashioned to be less candid than the originals seems to miss Isherwood's point. The story of the self is not just a reporting of facts but a construction—a work in the making.

In his book *Mr Isherwood Changes Trains*, Victor Marsh writes extensively and eloquently on Isherwood's spirituality and subjectivity, particularly as Vedanta provided Isherwood with a mode of resistance to dominant Western constructions of homosexuality and, more specifically, to a stable notion of "the self." Marsh refers to Isherwood, for instance, as a "disobedient subject of discourses that worked to marginalize him" and who "effectively renarrativize[s] his 'identity' as a work-in-progress."[12] Isherwood resists both inclusion in social institutions and the narrative conventions that support them. As Marsh argues in his essay in this collection, such resistance is illustrated in *My Guru and His Disciple*, in which Isherwood "assertively reconfigures the potential of queer intelligent inquiry into the nature of being in the world" (205). Through rereading and rewriting, Isherwood persistently reflects on Vedanta's propositions: Does it hold homosexuality to be a sin? Need it renounce the body? Can he still write what he wants if he follows its practice?

It might be said that Vedanta, and more particularly, writing about Vedanta facilitates Isherwood's self-reflection throughout the latter half of his life. He never demurs from the most rigorous self-examination, writing often in *My Guru and His Disciple* of feeling, for example, "no affection for anybody," vanity, self-accusation, doubt, sexual desire, occasional impatience with or judgments of others. In other words, he is still struggling with attachments to ego (117). At times these attachments help Isherwood resist religious rules. Often they are presented as struggles in spiritual practice, which persist in the very writing of *My Guru and His Disciple*—his struggles with striking the right tone in the book, with writer's block, with the question of whether it is boring. Marsh refers to this process, using Isherwood's terms, as "the knife in the wound," a form of "self-scrutiny . . . part and parcel of his approach to writing and which was deepened by his spiritual practice" (*Transit* 216). Isherwood's doubts, trials, and struggles more broadly are conventions of the conversion genre, but they also constitute an ongoing discernment of Vedanta's texts and tenets, both in ritual and in written form.

That is to say that Isherwood both narrates and performs conversion, reflecting upon his thoughts and actions and parsing the thought and actions of others. He connects this "attempted moment-to-moment vigilance over one's every thought and action" to the idea of "turning your life into an art form" (*My Guru* 16–17). Indeed, that is the purpose of writing as he articulates it in "The Writer and Vedanta"—"making our lives fuller of meaning and thereby to render our experience moment by moment more significant than it would otherwise be." Writing gives meaning to one's experiences, composing a life that did not exist prior to the act of writing. Harpham's notion of autobiography, writing the story of one's life, is helpful here: autobiography is the conversion of "life into text" (42). Indeed, as Harpham notes, "Language *is* conversion," putting experience into narrative form in a moment-to-moment process of self-making (48). *My Guru and His Disciple* might be read, then, as actualizing Isherwood's transformation in that the act of writing *is* spiritual conversion.

"WHAT MORE COULD I ASK FOR?"

The previous point refers not only to Isherwood's subjectivity—the making of his spiritual experiences—but, also, to the presence and role of Swami in the narrative. Indeed, perhaps the most profound incarnation in *My Guru and His Disciple* is the increasing recognition of the divine in Swami. In a conversation Isherwood records in his diary that took place with Swami in 1956 and is reproduced in *My Guru*, the theme of the incarnation of God appearing in human form is discussed (or, as he puts it in "The Writer and Vedanta," awareness of Brahman within Atman, which is "the aim of life"). Isherwood finds he cannot directly express what this notion makes him feel—"It's quite impossible to convey in words the effect made on you by a situation like this," he remarks (218). The reason for his inability to articulate this "situation" is not due to the proposition of God in human form. Rather, Isherwood's loss of words is due to the presence of Swami in particular, who, through his own words, makes present "a glimpse of *what he is*" (218). The repetition here and in previous citations of Isherwood's use of the word "glimpse" in relation to Swami should not go unremarked. Used here in the noun form, "a glimpse" suggests an inexpressible insight or idea (the divine? God? nature? reality?). Isherwood cannot identify or offer an explicit or direct statement of what this glimpse *is*, suggesting only that it is that indescribable element of experience, what might be called the ineffable.[13]

Isherwood's relationship to Swami exists on two planes simultaneously: "I flatter myself that I can discriminate—bowing down to the Eternal which is sometimes manifest to me in Swami, yet feeling perfectly at ease with him, most of the time, on an ordinary human basis. My religion is almost entirely what I *glimpse* of Swami's spiritual experience" (308–9; emphasis added). Now taking on its verb form, glimpse implies that which Isherwood can perceive in Swami, however partial and undefined that act remains.

Marsh offers this understanding of the guru/disciple relationship in a discussion of "devotion" in *Mr Isherwood Changes Trains*, which may be instructive here:

> Even while the status of human friendship holds, there is another track . . . that allows the personality of the guru to become more and more transparent, as it were, and the deeper identification with the Atman radiates another aspect of Being which the student recognises as a potential within his or her own awareness. (180)

Throughout *My Guru*, though Isherwood often questions divine existence, he also continuously asserts belief in the same. He shares his faith in that beyond-humanness, the Eternal within Swami, because he comes to understand that spiritual knowledge needs both imitation and intuition. When Swami once remarks, for instance, that he "was having such a wonderful time with the Lord" (226), Isherwood thinks:

> It is a measure of my psychological double vision that I can both accept this statement as literally true and marvel that such a statement, made by anybody, could ever be literally true.
>
> I realize, more and more, that Swami is my only link with spiritual life. . . . What more could I ask for? (226)

Another intimate moment with Swami, one of many, comes at the end of 1973, when he helps Swami back to his room by supporting his arm and Isherwood realizes he is holding the hand through which "Brahmananda's blessing was conferred" (319). Struck by the difference between himself and Swami, he notes feeling "inferior" to Swami's divinity: "It was an absurd and embarrassing and beautiful situation to be in" (319). Swami does not "appear merely 'better'" than Isherwood, as he put in his predrafting reflections on how to compose *My Guru*; rather, there is a transcendent quality that exceeds the language that can adequately express it. To write it is, therefore, an act of devotion.

Even as Swami is incarnated in *My Guru*, throughout the book's period of composition Isherwood remarks at times that he cannot feel Swami's "presence." He notes in his diary that others have visions of Swami but he does not: "Does this distress me? No. I keep calling on him" (*Liberation* 543). Again on "July 4. Swami's deathday, his first. . . . Have got to page 157—more than half, surely, of the first draft? I wonder if it is because I am writing this book that I feel so cut off from Swami's presence" (544). Herein lies the irony of writing about the divine, an experience that cannot be caught in the net of direct presentation, an absence beyond the reach of language and reason.

At the end of *My Guru*, Isherwood poses the question he imagines his reader to be asking: "Now that your Swami is dead, what are you left with? I am left with Swami," he answers (335). In 1961, long before Swami's death, Isherwood's belief in Swami's faith helped him to intuit this presence: "I do not believe that the guru can ever abandon his disciples, either voluntarily or involuntarily. I believe that their relationship survives death, accident, betrayal, and every other kind of hazard. No one, of course, can prove me wrong—or right. And I must admit that I have an exceedingly optimistic nature" ("What Vedanta Means to Me" 61). He reiterates this view toward the end of *My Guru*: "The contact I sometimes think I feel isn't with him but with what I believe he has now become, the Guru, a being who exists only to help his disciples" (336). Spiritual awareness becomes present to Isherwood, if only fleetingly, through the person of Swami, and through his writing about Swami: "Such moments reassure me that 'the real situation' does indeed exist and that an acceptance of it is my only safety. I recognize this in a flash of sanity from time to time. Then I lose it again" (336). In this "flash," Isherwood glimpses the Real beyond all appearances.

At the close of *My Guru and His Disciple*, Isherwood reflects on the role that both Vedanta and writing have played in his life. "Meanwhile, my life is still beautiful to me," he begins by way of summation, "because of the enduring fascination of my efforts to describe my life experience in my writing," that is, to turn his life into an art form (337). Unlike in other books of its kind, however, in *My Guru* Isherwood cannot reassure his readers, his "fellow travelers," that "all is ultimately well. . . . I can't reassure them, because I can't speak with the absolute authority of a knower," he admits (337–38). Instead,

> All I can offer them is this book, which I have written about matters I only partially understand, in the hope that it may somehow, to some readers, reveal *glimpses* of inner truth which remain hidden from its author. (338; emphasis added)

If Isherwood's efforts remain inconclusive—of conversion, of resolution, of self-understanding—they nevertheless point beyond "the realm of sense knowledge." It is here, "where art leaves off," that moments of insight might open up, and glimpses of inner truth might be revealed (*Wishing Tree* 160–61). It is in this spirit that he offers *My Guru and His Disciple* to his own readers. What more could we ask for?

NOTES

1. Christopher Isherwood, "The Writer and Vedanta," in *The Wishing Tree: Christopher Isherwood on Mystical Religion,* ed. Robert Adjemian (San Francisco: Harper & Row, 1986), 155.

2. Christopher Isherwood, "What Vedanta Means to Me," in *What Vedanta Means to Me: A Symposium,* ed. John Yale (London: Rider, 1961), 49.

3. Christopher Isherwood, *An Approach to Vedanta* (Los Angeles: Vedanta Press, 1963), 67.

4. Mario Faraone, "Spiritual Searching in Isherwood's Artistic Production," in *The American Isherwood,* ed. James J. Berg and Chris Freeman (Minneapolis: University of Minnesota Press, 2015), 187.

5. Christopher Isherwood, *Liberation: Diaries,* vol. 3, *1970–1983,* ed. Katherine Bucknell (New York: Harper, 2012), 525.

6. Quoted in Peter Parker, *Isherwood: A Life Revealed* (New York: Random House, 2004), 711.

7. Christopher Isherwood, *My Guru and His Disciple* (Minneapolis: University of Minnesota Press, 2001), 62.

8. William James, *The Varieties of Religious Experience: A Study in Human Nature* (1902; repr., New York: Barnes and Noble Classics, 2004), 205.

9. Geoffrey Galt Harpham, "Conversion and the Language of Autobiography," in *Studies in Autobiography*, ed. James Olney (New York: Oxford University Press, 1988), 44.

10. Bruce Hindmarsh, "Religious Conversion as Narrative and Autobiography," in *The Oxford Handbook of Religious Conversion*, ed. Lewis R. Rambo and Charles E. Farhadian (New York: Oxford University Press, 2014), 358.

11. H. Porter Abbott, *Diary Fiction: Writing as Action* (Ithaca, N.Y.: Cornell University Press, 1984), 28, 29.

12. Victor Marsh, *Mr Isherwood Changes Trains* (Melbourne: Clouds of Magellan, 2010), 295, 262.

13. In his essay in this collection, Victor Marsh quotes Samuel Beckett's *Watt*, on the problem of "effing the ineffable" (217)—Eds.

17. A Conversation with Christopher Isherwood, 1979

This interview was conducted by D. J. (Dennis) Bartel on August 26, 1979, at Isherwood's home in Santa Monica on the author's seventy-fifth birthday.

First, there is that voice, unhurried but nervous nonetheless, answering the doorbell. "I'm coming," he calls, as if to add, "don't go." A moment later Isherwood appears below on the walkway. He looks older, even from the back, with his close-cropped hair. When the door opens, I look upon the strained smile of a century. Perhaps that's too portentous, but there he is: Isherwood of Bohemian London, Isherwood of libertine Weimar Germany, of W. H. Auden, Benjamin Britten, Aldous Huxley, and more. The student who scribbled limericks on exams to get kicked out of Cambridge was also the sin-reveler who, between drunken episodes, translated the Gita. Now, with the rest of them gone, even his guru, Prabhavananda, Isherwood remains on the edge of a canyon, with a view of the Pacific, still standing among a small and dwindling handful of acknowledged masters from before and after the Third Reich. His name is in the phone book. He's amazingly busy for a man his age, but he still has the patience to sit for an interview with some kid journalist.

D. J. BARTEL: In the 1930s, you and several others, notably W. H. Auden and Stephen Spender, engaged in various political activities which were considered leftist at the time, yet you say it was impossible for any of you to have joined the Communist Party because you were going through a "Poet's Revolution." Would you explain what that was?

CHRISTOPHER ISHERWOOD: The phrase sounds rather pretentious. I would never describe myself as a poet, in the first place. No, what it really means is that we were too individualistic to fit into this kind of thing. It was all very well to go to Spain, but actually to take part in political activity is something that I'd never done until I got to California. That is, I now engage in very simple civic political activity from time to time. I vote, or I appear here or there, and I speak for the American Civil Liberties Union and also for their gay chapter. That's why I find myself actually far more political now than I was then. In those days it was all mostly enthusiasm that was not really channeled into any particular activity unless, as you say, Auden's going to Spain was a political activity, and so was Stephen's. I suppose by stretching it a very long way you might say that Auden's and my going to China was also a political activity in that a war was going on and we did make what amounted to political speeches. But all this was very superficial. It was much more the kind of thing that any rather adventurous young people might have done for the sake of the adventure.

DJB: You didn't consider *The Berlin Stories* to be, at least, subliminally political?

CI: Oh, certainly. I was raised as an historian and I've always been concerned to give a sense of the goings-on of any particular period that I am writing about. To give a kind of dialectical view of the whole proceedings, in a larger frame of reference. That applies just as much to a book I wrote fairly recently, *Kathleen and Frank,* which is about my mother and father. It is really a history of England from the 1890s to about the end of the First World War. It's so full of social history. I did so much boning up in order to write it. I feel that it is almost more of an historical work than anything else.

DJB: *Mr Norris* began as a much larger book called *The Lost,* which never got written. Were *Sally Bowles* and *Goodbye to Berlin* attempts to complete that book?

CI: Well, I was very much under the spell of Balzac and writing enormous works that would sort of take in the whole of human life. All these characters, all the people I'd known in Berlin, were waiting as though I were a refugee officer in some place like Hong Kong where these people were crowding in. You had to find a place for them, and you look in despair because you cannot imagine how you're going to fit them into the available housing, and this is exactly what I felt like when I was trying to write a novel about my Berlin life. My first real tremendous breakthrough was when I decided that I wouldn't write a novel and attempt to have all the Berlin characters in it together. Now this sounds like an absolutely idiotically simple decision to come to, but it tortured me and finally I thought, well, what do I really know best? What do I know backward, forward, and sideways? And I said to myself, the life of this Mr. Gerald Hamilton, who was called "Mr. Norris." That was something I could really write about. All right, I said to myself, you'll forget about everybody else, and write that. Then I was tortured by what to do with all the rest of the people. How can I arrange them? There ought to be a plot. So I made the most incredibly complicated plot, and I thought I'd get them into it, though of course they wouldn't stay in the plot. Then as it were, another voice from heaven or Mount Sinai or somewhere spoke and said, "Why have a plot?" These are the most dazzling insights—these obvious remarks—when the right person says it at the right time.

I was writing another book at that time, about my experience with the Quakers, and I wanted to put in all the refugees that I'd known when I was working with the Quakers, which was a cast of at least fifty people. Suddenly, one day, one of my friends said, "The refugees are a bore." And this again was like some dazzling insight. All the refugees were thrown out. It turned out to be my worst novel anyway, *The World in the Evening.* But this is typical. You go into these jams, and then suddenly you see how to do it. Right now, I've got exactly the same situation ahead of me. I've got these enormous diaries that I started keeping as soon as I got to this country and I thought now you'd better keep your eyes and ears open. This book that I've just finished, *My Guru and His Disciple,* isn't so bad because it keeps to its point, which is my relations with this monk, Prabhavananda. But now I have a mass of undigested material dealing with working in the movies and knowing so many people in show business and also a considerable number of, as they say, intellectuals, like Bertrand Russell or Gerald Heard or Aldous Huxley and others who have partially appeared in things I have written already. Now there is a really great deal of material that I can't bear to part with and I can't imagine what this book is going to be like. I think it's going to be a total mess. I solved the problem of the book called *Goodbye to Berlin* by saying it isn't a book. It's a lot of bits, and we'll just put the bits together and it'll be just as good as a connected novel because it all takes place in the same area and the reader will make up the joins for himself, and I have indeed found that again and again. Readers have imagined they've read a coherent novel when in fact they've read lots of little fragments about these people. It all adds up because it's got an enclosing historical geographic area that holds it together.

DJB: You said about *Mr Norris Changes Trains* that you made a fundamental mistake, which was that you tried to tell a contrived story. After that novel, you seem to be more interested in what you call "portrait writing" rather than plot and situations. Would you explain the change from what happened after *Mr Norris* and what you consider a portrait novel?

CI: I don't think it should be thought of exactly as a change so much as that I was gradually finding out what it was I wanted to do. After all, the development of many artists, big and small and in all categories really, is that history of finding out what some part of them knows already from the beginning, that is, what they want to do, and what is most suitable to their talents such as they are. This question is just as real if it concerns a quite middle-of-the-road or middle-class, middle-talented writer or a great genius. For everybody, there is always a search before they hit the absolute essence of themselves and feel they can express it.

DJB: Did this lead to more autobiographical writing? You left "William Bradshaw" behind and brought in "Christopher Isherwood" after *Mr Norris.*

CI: At first, I was thinking in terms of fiction, so to speak. It's not that I don't think in terms of fiction now. I rearrange things a bit from an artistic point of view because when you're telling a story, you're telling a story. I don't care whether it's a fish you've really caught in a bay or if it's a fish you in fact didn't catch but pretended you've caught, the same thing applies. You build up to a climax. T. E. Lawrence, Lawrence of Arabia, says somewhere in *Seven Pillars of Wisdom* that his Arab tribesmen, his allies, were marvelous storytellers who would tell the stories about the battles they just fought in, but they turned them immediately into a great epic. It was an art form, in fact, to tell just what had been happening that very week.

DJB: You've been quoted as saying, "With me everything starts with auto-biography." I'd like to understand this better by asking for your response to the observation that, especially the later stories in which "Christopher Isherwood" appears as a character, are not so much about him as they are a chronicle of the events he witnesses, and he witnesses them in a rather detached way. "Christopher Isherwood" may sometimes be engaged in the story, but mostly he's observant.

CI: I think it is very autobiographically true about me personally that, in many situations, I prefer to shut up and listen to somebody, watch somebody else, and enjoy it. This is a personal idiosyncrasy. I don't always want to burst into the conversation and take a leading part in it, although I do quite a bit of that too. In fact, I'm often told that in my old age I interrupt people. But each story was a perfectly sound biographical account. I tended to sit in a corner and watch these people. It's true that at other times I sort of got into the action and took part, but it isn't an entire falsification of my character or my life to say that I was watching these people some of the time and thoroughly enjoying it. To this day Don and I very often say to each other, "Oh yes, I'd very much like to meet her if I could just sit in a corner and watch her." In other words, you don't want to get into a big thing, you don't want to get involved with this particular person. One is usually speaking of some very showy individualistic famous character. Your instinct would be much more, I'm sure, that you would just like to sit there and watch them speaking to other people, watch them making decisions, watch them moving about in the course of their lives. This is what's fascinating. This is not a sign that you are a modest or a retiring person but just that it's another function of pleasure. I never mind waiting for people at the airport because I just adore watching all the people, all the travelers. Sometimes I feel as though I could never tire of it.

DJB: In *Lions and Shadows*, which you intended as an autobiography, there is one crucial omission. Whenever you refer to your mother you do so as "my female relative" or something to that effect. Why?

CI: When you come down to it, I felt that I'd dealt with the familial aspects of my life. As a matter of fact, I hadn't, because I went on to write *Kathleen and Frank*. We all get into difficulties of this kind because life is very untidy. For example, in the book that I've just finished I wanted to stick to a certain character whom the book is about and describe my relations with that character over a period of years; to be specific, from 1939 to 1976, when he died. Now all that time that I was meeting with this character and spending time with him and having a relationship with him, all the rest of my friends, and all the rest of my activities, divided themselves into two parts. One was the people who knew this character and therefore had a place in the story of our relationship, and one was the people and the activities that didn't for one moment impinge on the life of this character, so they're left out of the book. Now this produces peculiar features. There is only one mention in the entire book of Stravinsky, Garbo is mentioned only twice, and so on. Even Huxley doesn't appear nearly as much as he will in the next book because he was partly involved but not totally involved. Sometimes I was away from this person, having all manner of the most fascinating experiences, but they're not mentioned because it's not to my point. In that same way, my mother and my brother were not to my purpose in *Lions and Shadows*.

DJB: Could you tell us about the writing you did with Edward Upward at Cambridge?

CI: I suppose they were what we'd loosely call "surrealism." We did them entirely to amuse each other, and in fact we would aim to write them often late at night and produce them at breakfast. We were both students at the same college and we had rooms—as they say at Cambridge— on the same staircase. And so, we were almost living together. We saw each other constantly, and we talked about nothing except writing and literature. I suppose they had a big basis in Edgar Allan Poe, a sort of macabre thing with the eroticism used really as a kind of shock tactic. In other words, they weren't sensuous, they were—I always hate the word "pornographic"—but they were shocking. They were meant to shock other people. For us they were a big joke, obviously. We laughed till tears ran down our cheeks. We also created a myth about Cambridge itself. This I went into in considerable detail, except that I couldn't put in the pornographic parts in those days, in *Lions and Shadows*. We had a whole myth about the college, the faculty. The whole idea that we were sort of spies and secret people living in a world we totally despised. Therefore, in a way, any kind of contact we had with the other students, the other

undergraduates, was a form of treason to this life that we were living because we had to act like ordinary young men. We got around that by
treating it like playacting. In fact, Upward, who was very athletic, even
got on the college team and did all sorts of things like that and played
poker endlessly because that was the thing to do. Even I played poker
and had a motorcycle, but it was all playacting that referred back to our
stories and what we called Mortmere, an imaginary village where all
these weird, mythological people lived. So it was a way of reflecting these
activities into the distorting mirror of Mortmere and making them seem
absurd. And we had fun.

DJB: Did you save the limericks you used for answers on the exams?

CI: I probably have some of them. They were really very, very unsatisfactory. I'm ashamed of them. Of course, everything had to be done on the
spur of the moment. The great thing to do was to ensure that I not only
failed but that I should be asked to leave the college. That was the object
of the proceedings. And I went straight off into what in my mind was
an earthly paradise. I became the secretary to a string quartet, and entered the whole world of London bohemia. By a string quartet, I mean a
classical string quartet that played Debussy, and Fauré, and the C-sharp-
minor Quartet of Beethoven. The quartet was associated with two really
famous musicians. Pablo Casals used to come and play with them occasionally, and also Alfred Cortot, the pianist. I saw this London world of
studio parties; met and saw in the distance other famous artists, writers,
all sorts of people, and just thought I was the luckiest boy alive, and got
paid one pound a week.

DJB: Stylistically, it appears you have a certain debt to Katherine Mansfield
and also to E. M. Forster. Are there others?

CI: Yes, I would say there's a great debt, which is not apparent in the style so
much, to D. H. Lawrence. What Lawrence said to me in effect was never
mind what that canyon looks like, how does it look to you this morning
when you've got a violent hangover and have just been left by your lover,
when this has happened and that has happened? In other words, it's his
world, a totally subjective approach to what he wrote about, that makes
his writing enormously exciting. Of course, I know that that's only, in a
sense, the negative side of the genius of Lawrence, who I think was a very

great genius. But it's the excitement of the whole thing. It's all through him. Nothing is outside him. So you really narrow your gaze down as though you were under water looking through some kind of goggles and you explore the world of Lawrence. Mansfield influenced me autobiographically, that is to say, the tone of her diaries. She happened to be the first diary writer I encountered who turned me on. Her diaries and her letters. I loved just the tone of her voice. Of course, now I know so many other diarists and letter writers. For example, one of my favorites is Byron, but I'd never read his letters at that time. I do find I can still remember how turned on I was by Mansfield.

Also, Somerset Maugham was a very good friend to me throughout my life. Curiously enough, we were not really very intimately acquainted. But shortly after he met me he started going around behind my back talking about me and saying what a good writer I was. An extraordinary act for Maugham—a man of his age and position. We always remained friends through to the time he died. I suppose I met him first in the thirties and went right on seeing him until the sixties. As for his influence, it exists in the marvelous organization, the economy of the tale-telling, the exactness of the moves on the chessboard. He takes you from position A to position B and so on and moves to checkmate you in the end by utterly overwhelming you with the story. The good ones were unanswerable.

DJB: After Auden and you left Europe, the critical opinion was that the two of you were taking a large chunk of literature with you. Also, there was a good deal of concern that you might not be able to write in America. Whether or not that was a valid concern, the fact is, it took you several years before another novel arrived, even though you were writing other things. There appear to be several reasons, or at least public reasons, for the absence of any fiction. Certainly one of them was your increasing involvement with the teachings of Ramakrishna. Did you find that as a fiction writer you were starting over again because of your move toward Vedanta?

CI: Oh yes, in a way that certainly was a great big distraction from writing. Also, Swami Prabhavananda. It all made a difference to me. Writing was complicated by the fact that I was also a pacifist, a conscientious objector, and therefore, something had to be done about that. What was done was that I got myself involved with the Quakers in a social project in the

East. It was a hostel for refugees from Europe. I spent about a year there. That was another big distraction from writing. Also, Prabhavananda provided me with plenty of chores. They had a magazine I had to edit. Then I brought out a book of selected articles from their magazine. Then he wanted to translate the Gita, so we did that. All this was quite time consuming. Afterward, after I'd written *Prater Violet*, I got into some more work for him. I did a translation of one of Shankara's books and then another one of Patanjali's Yoga Aphorisms with a commentary. After that, finally, I did a popular life of Ramakrishna and his disciples.

For me, it was absolutely necessary, if I was going to live in this country, to become acclimatized before I could write anything meaningful. I wasn't about to come here and make the kind of remarks of a total outsider in the manner of somebody just visiting a country. I didn't realize when I came that it would become my home, in a far more profound sense than anywhere else in my life. We traveled around so much when I was young. I've never lived nearly as long anywhere else as I have in this house. I've lived more than half my life in the United States, and of that life, I spent the great majority of the years almost exclusively in the Los Angeles area and mostly in this very canyon, in which I think I've lived in about twelve different buildings under different circumstances.

DJB: After you had become involved with the teachings of Ramakrishna, how was your fiction affected?

CI: It's very hard for me to answer that question, almost impossible because, you see, the aims of fiction are in a sense within the area that's loosely called "religious." If you write a novel about somebody, I don't care how "evil" that character may be, the very fact that you're writing about him presupposes a sort of pardon, a sort of mercy. You may disapprove intensely of his activities and yet you can't help taking an interest in him. You are forgiving him to a certain extent because you're putting what he's done to one side and saying nevertheless he fascinates me. I want to know him. In that sense you might say that one didn't need Vedanta or anything else. I mean any old novelist does that. If you can't do that, you're just not fit to be a writer of that kind. You could be a polemical writer. You could write terrible renunciations of somebody, but a novelist per se, someone who engages to look into life and report on his findings, is not a naturalist. Or in another sense, he's like a doctor. There's no time for wondering what the moral condition of the patient is.

DJB: Some of the books, then, might be considered pardons of Christopher Isherwood.

CI: Well, yes, a temporary pardon. For instance, the doctor, continuing with this language, pardons a man as long as he's sick. When he's well again, the doctor says, "Now, they're waiting for you outside and they're going to take you out and execute you." Maybe the doctor approves of the execution, but he still works on his patient.

DJB: Your translation of the Gita was by your admission an interpretation. It was not a literal translation. What kind of reception did it get from Hindu groups?

CI: As a matter of fact, some of the greatest Sanskrit scholars in India were sent our translation. Prabhavananda said, "Admittedly, you have to make allowances for the fact that this is written primarily as a literary work, but it always follows the text." And they wrote back and said, "Yes, we have to admit that it is quite accurate." It's just not accurate in the way a literal translation from the Sanskrit would be. Sanskrit is an intensely compressed and telegraphic kind of language, and there's no way of absolutely conveying this unless you translate word for word and then give this sort of scrambled telegram to the reader and put in a paraphrase afterward saying this, in effect, in English means so and so. Then you put in conjunctions and prepositions and everything else, and gradually start changing the thing. I took great liberties, which are admitted to in the beginning. We wrote a perfectly straightforward translation of the thing and it was dull like you can't imagine, and everybody got very discouraged about it. So I thought, well, let's try some experiments. So I just switched into various types of verse. I started off very simply with a kind of heavily stressed, alliterated stuff that sounds rather like early Anglo-Saxon epic poetry. "Krishna the Changeless, horse by chariot, there where the warriors bold for the battle face their foemen between the armies. There let me see them, the men I must fight with, gather together." This kind of thing. Then I thought we'd try some hexameters, so we did another part of it in hexameters. And then I did some sort of dubious things that were vaguely based on my memories of Latin poetry of one kind or another, the different forms used by Horace or Virgil or whomever. But the proof of the whole thing is that it has been a steady success among the various available translations of the Gita, and not just from a literary point of view. An awful lot of people were really turned on by it to a serious interest in Vedanta and the whole Hindu thing. So it was worthwhile. It accomplished its purpose. It was just a deliberate decision to do the one thing rather than the other, because some extremely accurate and good and valuable translations of the Gita exist. There's a very good one by another monk of our order, Swami Vivekananda. He's dead now, but he was the head of one of the Vedanta centers in New York. There, with copious notes and everything, he tells you exactly what these verses mean.

DJB: Have you ever found a conflict between Vedanta and homosexuality?

CI: Oh my goodness. I won't say there was a conflict. There wasn't a true conflict. But a great deal of my new book is about this. I mean, there would be really no ball game if it weren't for my whole personality bumping its individualistic H's [hedonism and homosexuality] against this extraordinary individual and testing him over and over again. That was, of course, my very first concern. I wasn't going to go near this man if he was going to tell me I was a sinner. My God, all I needed to do was go to the nearest Baptist church to be told that, and I'm sorry to say also in many cases to the nearest rabbi because they have been upholding their end of Leviticus with enthusiasm. However, this man provided a distinctly satisfactory answer to my various problems without saying I was pure as the driven snow. Nevertheless, he was extraordinarily broad-minded. As a monk he thought of all sex, from the most legal heterosexual marriage to every other kind of sex, as a diversion from what to him was the one purpose of life, to seek God. Therefore, when you really came down to it, he would have liked every single person he met to become a monk or a nun on the spot, and he quite admitted that this was not practical. And he didn't demand it. He had a large congregation, a household congregation, almost indistinguishable in appearance on Sunday morning from any kind of Christian congregation, except that the Hindus do not demand that ladies wear hats or any kind of head covering in church. But it was very respectable, as they say. It is still to this day, and not freaky at all. We rather kept our Hinduism to ourselves. Many people who came to the lectures simply heard a kind of generalized type of philosophy that was richly illustrated with Christian examples. Prabhavananda, among other things, wrote an entire analysis of the Sermon on the Mount from the point of view of a Hindu. He read a great deal about Jesus, in accordance with one of the basic Vedantic propositions that all religions contain the truth, regardless of how they vary in actual form. He always had an icon of Jesus in a shrine along with the figure of the Buddha and the pictures of Ramakrishna and his main disciples and various other Hindu deities, such as Krishna. He saw no essential difference in any of this. It's just that he had a much more permissive attitude to the *don'ts* and *thou shalt nots* of Christianity. But then so do many Christians. My goodness, if I hadn't become a follower of his, I think I would have ended up as a Quaker. I found their religion magnificent while extremely exhausting because the first thing the Quakers do is give you a job which lasts all day, forever. It's a total commitment.

DJB: There's another conflict that might have come about as a result of Vedanta. One critic says, "Because Vedanta teaches the necessity for detachment from all worldly desires and preoccupations and the elimination of self, it presents a conflict for the novelist who must draw on those very desires." I think this would be especially difficult for a novelist who is writing close to autobiography.

CI: Yes, but you see the critic is not quite watching his language here, because as a matter of fact, art implies detachment. Let's take the crudest example. A graphic artist is drawing a nude. Now, according to his personal predilections, he probably in many cases finds the nude attractive. But he completely sublimates the attraction he feels because he is getting on with the artwork. So as long as he is involved with the artwork, he is in fact doing exactly that. He is rising above the desires. He renounces them.

DJB: Maybe the critic was talking about its being a deterrent to the accumulation of experience that you can then write about.

CI: Well, I never could imagine that anybody could lack experience to write about. I think that is a sort of myth. But that's neither here nor there. It's very nice when you're young to say, "Oh dear, I must get some more experience. If I don't get experience I won't have anything to write about." All you really mean is you want to get more fun. You want to go around saying, "Oh, I must go to Iceland. I must go to Tierra del Fuego, I must do this or that. I must have a lot more affairs with everybody. Because otherwise I won't know about *life*." But of course the actual truth is that a mouse in a prison cell knows about life. What we fundamentally know about is consciousness. Where you see a very good example of that is in some Oriental art where people take one single theme, like the bamboo, and paint it over and over and over again. Never shall I forget going to stay with Georgia O'Keeffe. One evening we spent about an hour and a half looking at these bamboo paintings that she had, and no two were absolutely alike. When I got into the mood, which of course was highly induced by her, I really began to find them interesting. And then I understood how extraordinarily little material you need. The whole point is to get the perception opened wide enough. That's all that matters.

DJB: In your introduction to *Vedanta for Modern Man,* you say that you believe Vedanta is most likely to influence the West through the medium of scientific thought, and eventually it will be relatively widespread. Certainly, it has had a solid and comfortable foundation since Ralph Waldo Emerson backed it in this country. Do you think the proliferation in the U.S. of certain religious groups of Eastern origin is evidence of influence by Vedanta?

CI: I think it was absolutely inevitable that the impingement of the West on the East would produce a countermovement. Indeed, very early in the proceedings, the British, just a very few of them, were taking the trouble to find out about Hinduism and so on. There were some foreigners who went to China and took the trouble to study. They went to Japan. With the interchange in which we kept giving techniques of all kinds to the East, the East was giving forth its goods to us, in a bad sense, and in a good sense. Maybe this interchange has almost stopped now. We're going on in a sort of free fall. I don't know. But certainly, we've gone through that period, there's no question. We've received an enormous amount of stimulation from the East. My goodness, I remember when I first came out here. I was very soon in the position of talking to college groups and meeting lots of students and people. How different things were. I can get up on a platform now and I'll be asked about being gay. I'll be asked about literature, and what I am writing, but it always ends up with religion. There are always people who want to know. I was on the radio on "Stonewall Day" for gay pride. People could call in to the station and talk to me on the air, and in all cases the questions asked were fundamentally religious, and in all the cases I had to say, "This is too complicated, I've only got five minutes. Will you call me at home later?" And they did. You see it's extraordinary. That's something that's really happened since I've lived in this country, this enormous interest in the religious experience. I don't mean that I'm always running up against creeds, particular rituals, or attitudes. On the contrary, I find that it's often not even necessary to discuss any of that, but they really want to know. "Whatever it is you do, does it work for you at all? You're an old man now, you're going to die," as they always say with charming frankness. And I say, "Well, I'll tell you, I'm certainly quite shaken by the winds of life and couldn't hold myself up as a rock, but it does mean something, and furthermore it's the only thing that means something and that's it as far as I'm concerned." The other thing I say is that I believe one can arrive at the truth—by the truth I mean the truth for oneself.

I'm a good Jungian, in all manner of ways. I would never say that I was particularly fated to meet a Hindu. I might have gotten involved with a Catholic priest. The only thing that was profoundly against my feeling was the idea of confessing, because that never was my style. But I can imagine that the individual is so much more important than the group he belongs to. I can imagine a way-out Catholic priest just as, in some respects, you might say that Prabhavananda was a way-out Hindu monk. You have to have somebody who has a great deal of understanding, and you'll find that in every denomination. I had a good deal of experience when I first came out here, meeting all these kinds of people. I got to know lots and lots of Protestant denominations and fundamentalists. One of the people who struck me most was a Seventh-Day Adventist, who, with all due respect, did seem to me to hold beliefs that were incredibly restricted, from my point of view. Nevertheless, this man was so evidently beyond all this, and into a realm of love for his fellow humans, that he was one of the most remarkable people I've met since I've been here. I can't even remember his name anymore. I just met him a couple of times. Such people you meet. You also meet people who have nothing to do with religion, and people who say that they are atheists. That has nothing to do with it either, because all this is just semantics. One of Ramakrishna's chief disciples said that he wished there was a separate religion for every single person living on Earth today. He thought one should be very individualistic about this. This is a very interesting observation. You might say, following the idea of individualism, that my relationship with Prabhavananda as described in *My Guru and His Disciple* is my religion. That is to say, what I was left with as a result of this relationship is all that I have, because it is the only thing predicated entirely on my own observation. At least I know what he said to *me*. At least I know how he strikes *me*. And that is enough. It wasn't for one moment that I thought he was the only person in creation who could have been like that. He was the only person I'd met who was like that, and therefore he was my religion, and very individual as such.

Acknowledgments

A fter more than twenty years of working together on Christopher Isherwood, we have nothing but gratitude. It is a little unusual for scholars in the humanities to collaborate, and both of us have grown so much—personally, intellectually, and professionally—during this time. We have moved cross-country (and across again, in Jim's case); we have gone through many changes in our personal lives, and we have grown to be very close friends. We want to take this opportunity to thank some of the people who have taken this journey with us. No, this is not the end, but it may well close the Isherwood chapter for us.

The University of Minnesota Press, especially Doug Armato, has given Isherwood a wonderful home, and we are honored to be part of the distinguished catalog that Doug and his team have curated. We are especially grateful for the gorgeous cover they made for us.

The Huntington Library in San Marino, California, houses the expansive Isherwood archive, and many of the essays in this collection made use of that primary material. This work continues to deepen and complicate our understanding of Isherwood, and scholars will forever benefit from that treasure trove for generations to come. We especially thank our in-house detective, Sara S. (Sue) Hodson, who processed the collection with acute intelligence and care, and Steve Hindle, the director of research, who facilitated the 2015 symposium on Isherwood that served as the basis for *Isherwood in Transit*. Natalie Russell and Stephanie Arias were helpful in identifying photographs in the archive.

We thank all of our contributors, whose brilliance and insight keep

Isherwood studies growing and changing. Many have been with us since *The Isherwood Century* (2000). Christopher Bram gave us a lovely foreword and was a delight to work with. He read the entire collection before he wrote "A Fan's Note"; he was therefore our first reader, and his encouragement was very meaningful. In the summer of 2015, he joined actor–writer David Drake, scholar Bill Goldstein, and Chris Freeman for an event in New York City hosted by the Bureau of General Services–Queer Division when we were promoting *The American Isherwood*. We had another terrific East Coast event, with Richard Schneider Jr., founder and publisher of *The Gay & Lesbian Review Worldwide*, and writer–historian William Mann. The staff and volunteers at the Provincetown Public Library, especially former director Matthew Clark, and the kind folks at the Provincetown Bookshop were a pleasure to work with.

Our contributor Jaime Harker and the University of Mississippi's Sarah Isom Center for Women and Gender Studies gave Isherwood an audience in the fall of 2018, when Chris gave a talk there. That was the Oxford, Mississippi, version of a talk he gave at Oxford University in England in June 2018.

Our friend Helen Irwin is an avid supporter of our work and helped us proofread, copyedit, and index this book and *The American Isherwood*. Any errors are ours, not hers, to be sure.

The Christopher Isherwood Foundation continues to do important work to support the writer's legacy. Its fellowship program and the annual Isherwood–Bachardy Lecture provide opportunities for scholarly endeavors and intellectual conversation on Isherwood and his circle. The Christopher Isherwood Prize for Autobiographical Prose, which is part of the *Los Angeles Times* Festival of Books, supports the best work of contemporary writers and ensures that Isherwood's name, writing, and legacy will live on. Katherine Bucknell's work continues to illuminate Isherwood, and the foundation is in capable hands with Kate and the Board, including our dear friend Tina Mascara.

Tina and her late partner, Guido Santi, gave the world a gift with their documentary *Chris & Don: A Love Story* (2007). Guido's sudden death in February 2019 was shocking and heartbreaking. We dedicate this book to the two of them for their wonderful film and to honor Guido's memory. Their friendship with Don Bachardy is fully visible in their film, and Don continues to do all he can for Isherwood and for his own legacy.

And now, some individual thanks from each of us.

From Chris: The English department at the University of Southern California has given me a great home, and I'd like to thank David St. John, Peter Mancall, and all my colleagues, especially Dana Johnson, Joe Boone, Larry Green, Richard Fliegel, Janalynn Bliss, and Tita Rosenthal. Tita came to my talk in June 2018 at Oxford, which was so elegantly arranged by Eleri Anona Watson under the auspices of the Oxford Queer Studies Network. That occasion was a lifetime and a career highlight. Séan Richardson provided research help and stimulating conversation. Thanks also to my friends and support network, especially Jane Roberts, Wendy Davis, Lisa Southerland, and to students, who continue to inspire me, in particular, Troy Rayder and Anna McEnroe.

From Jim: Tony Sharpe reached across the Atlantic from Lancaster University to ask us for a contribution to *Auden in Context*, in which a version of our "Fellow Travelers" essay was published. The English department at my alma mater, the University of Minnesota, hosted a lively Isherwood conversation between me and our contributor Lois Cucullu. The fine people at the Borough of Manhattan Community College, Antonio Perez, Karrin E. Wilks, and Erwin J. Wong, hired me and brought me to the intellectual and cultural community of New York, where I work with faculty who inspire me every day. It took Koji Aoshika to make that community personal.

Contributors

D. J. (Dennis) Bartel has written for national publications and publishers such as *Harper's*, Time-Life, Doubleday, and *Stagebill*, and for newspapers and magazines in New York, Los Angeles, Washington, D.C., Paris, and Moscow. He has been a commentator for ABC News and is a renowned classical music radio announcer. He taught writing at The Johns Hopkins University and the University of Pittsburgh.

James J. Berg is associate dean of faculty at the Borough of Manhattan Community College. He was previously dean at College of the Desert and Lake Superior College. He is editor of *Isherwood on Writing* (Minnesota, 2007) and coeditor, with Chris Freeman, of *The American Isherwood* (Minnesota, 2014), *The Isherwood Century*, and *Conversations with Christopher Isherwood*, as well as *Love, West Hollywood*.

Barrie Jean Borich is the author of *Apocalypse, Darling*; the memoir *Body Geographic*, which won a Lambda Literary Award; and her book-length essay *My Lesbian Husband*, which won the Stonewall Book Award. She teaches at DePaul University, where she edits *Slag Glass City*, a journal of the urban essay arts.

Christopher Bram is the author of nine novels, including *Gods and Monsters*. He was a Guggenheim fellow and received the Bill Whitehead Award for Lifetime Achievement. His books include *Eminent Outlaws: The Gay Writers Who Changed America* and *The Art of History: Unlocking the Past in Fiction and Nonfiction*.

Jamie Carr is associate professor of English at Niagara University, where she teaches literary criticism and theory, contemporary Anglophone literature, and nineteenth- and twentieth-century British literature. She is author of *Queer Times: Christopher Isherwood's Modernity* and *Niagaras of Ink: Famous Writers of the Falls*.

Robert L. Caserio is professor of English at Penn State University, University Park. He coedited *The Cambridge History of the English Novel* and edited *The Cambridge Companion to the Twentieth-Century English Novel*. His book *The Novel in England, 1900–1950: History and Theory* received the George and Barbara Perkins Prize, awarded annually by the International Society for the Study of Narrative. He writes about English and American fiction.

Lisa Colletta is professor of English at the American University of Rome. She is the author of *British Novelists in Hollywood, 1935–1965: Travelers, Exiles, and Expats* and *Dark Humor and Social Satire in the Modern British Novel*. She is editor of *Kathleen and Christopher: Christopher Isherwood's Letters to His Mother* (Minnesota, 2005) and coeditor with Maureen O'Connor of *Wild Colonial Girl: Essays on Edna O'Brien*.

Lois Cucullu is professor emerita of English at the University of Minnesota. Her essay in this book is part of a project on Isherwood for which she received a Christopher Isherwood Foundation Fellowship at the Huntington Library. She is the author of *Expert Modernists, Matricide, and Modern Culture: Woolf, Forster, Joyce,* and her essays have been published in *Novel, Signs, differences,* and *Modernism/modernity.*

Chris Freeman teaches English at the University of Southern California. He is the coeditor, with James J. Berg, of *The American Isherwood* (Minnesota, 2014), *The Isherwood Century,* and *Conversations with Christopher Isherwood,* as well as *Love, West Hollywood.*

Jaime Harker is professor of English and the director of the Sarah Isom Center for Women and Gender Studies at the University of Mississippi, where she teaches American literature, LGBTQ literature, and gender studies. She is also the founder of Violet Valley Bookstore, a queer feminist bookstore in Water Valley, Mississippi. She is the author of *America the Middlebrow: Women's Novels, Progressivism, and Middlebrow Authorship between the Wars, Middlebrow Queer: Christopher Isherwood in America* (Minnesota, 2013), and *The Lesbian South.* She is coeditor of *The Oprah Affect, 1960s Gay Pulp Fiction, This Book Is an Action,* and *Faulkner and Print Culture.*

Sara S. Hodson retired in 2017 as curator of literary manuscripts for the Huntington Library. She acquired the Isherwood Papers for the library in 1999 and curated a major exhibition, *Christopher Isherwood: A Writer and His World,* for the centenary of the writer's birth in 2004. She has spoken often on Isherwood and appears in the documentary film *Chris & Don: A Love Story.*

Carola M. Kaplan is professor emerita of English at California State University, Pomona, as well as past president of the Joseph Conrad Society of America and a member of the Institute of Contemporary Psychoanalysis in Los Angeles. She has published two books on modernist literature, *Seeing Double: Revisioning Edwardian and Modernist Literature* and *Conrad in the Twenty-First Century.* She is a research psychoanalyst in private practice in Encino, California.

Calvin W. Keogh is a graduate in English language and literary studies from University College Dublin, the Vrije Universiteit in Amsterdam, and the Katholieke Universiteit in Louvain. His doctoral dissertation, "A Singular Nomad: The Minor Transnationalism of Christopher Isherwood," was defended at the Central European University in Budapest.

Victor Marsh, a research fellow at the University of Queesland, is author of *Mr Isherwood Changes Trains* and editor of *Speak Now,* a collection of essays on same-sex marriage in Australia. He has also written a memoir, *The Boy in the Yellow Dress.* His research has examined spiritual autobiographies by gay men in which identity positioning was relocated through spiritual inquiry.

Wendy Moffat is professor of English at Dickinson College and author of *A Great Unrecorded History: A New Life of E. M. Forster.* She has published on modernism, photography, narrative, and queer biography.

Xenobe Purvis is a graduate of Oxford University, where she read English literature. She is an independent scholar and is working with Katherine Bucknell on a volume of Christopher Isherwood's selected letters. Her published essays reflect her interest in the art and literature of the twentieth century.

Bidhan Chandra Roy is professor of English at California State University, Los Angeles, where he teaches postcolonial literature and twentieth-century British literature. He is the author of *A Passage to Globalism.*

Katharine Stevenson received her PhD in English from the University of Texas at Austin and was a Christopher Isherwood Foundation Fellow at the Huntington Library. She lives in Dallas, Texas.

Edmund White received the PEN/Saul Bellow Award for Career Achievement in American Fiction. He received the National Book Critics Circle Award for his biography of Jean Genet and is the author of a trilogy of autobiographical novels: *A Boy's Own Story, The Beautiful Room Is Empty,* and *The Farewell Symphony.*

Index

Lightning Source UK Ltd.
Milton Keynes UK
UKHW020035030620
364167UK00005B/94